ALL MY YESTERDAYS

ALL MY YESTERDAYS
STEVE HOWE

OMNIBUS PRESS
London / New York / Paris / Sydney / Copenhagen / Berlin / Madrid / Tokyo

Copyright © 2020 Omnibus Press
(A Division of Music Sales Limited)

Cover designed by Paul Tippett
Picture research by the author

ISBN: 978-1-785581-79-3

Steve Howe hereby asserts his right to be identified as the author of this work in accordance with Sections 77 to 78 of the Copyright, Designs and Patents Act 1988.

All rights reserved. No part of this book may be reproduced in any form or by any electronic or mechanical means, including information storage or retrieval systems, without permission in writing from the publisher, except by a reviewer who may quote brief passages.

Every effort has been made to trace the copyright holders of the photographs in this book but one or two were unreachable. We would be grateful if the photographers concerned would contact us.

Printed in the United Kingdom

A catalogue record for this book is available from the British Library.

For Zuni, Diego and Cal

Contents

Introduction		1
Chapter 1	Up Together	3
Chapter 2	Let's Pretend	9
Chapter 3	A Step Closer	24
Chapter 4	Onward	33
Chapter 5	Down By A River	51
Chapter 6	No Disgrace	66
Chapter 7	Butterflies	78
Chapter 8	Big Switch	95
Chapter 9	On And Off	113
Chapter 10	Regroup	117
Chapter 11	The Near Impossible	128
Chapter 12	Launch Pad	146
Chapter 13	Perils Of Empowerment	156
Chapter 14	No Yes	176
Chapter 15	Not Necessarily Acoustic	192
Chapter 16	Twist After Twist, '96	203
Chapter 17	Grand Ambition	216
Chapter 18	Remedy Plus	230
Chapter 19	Finding My Feet	243
Chapter 20	Forty Years On	260

Chapter 21	Merry-Go-Round	276
Chapter 22	Chris Leaves The Stage	288
Coda	Time Is When	298
Discography		310
Acknowledgements		317

Introduction

When I started playing the guitar it seemed like a nice hobby, but it was soon a mad obsession. Eventually it became what it is today, the essence of joy. But it came with a hidden price tag.

While I understand how lucky I've been in most respects, for my loved ones that price has come in the shape of the time I've had to spend away – a lot of time, at that. Zooming off somewhere to play has become a disturbingly regular event, so our time together has always been very precious. We musicians are not alone in this gypsy-like existence but that's of little consequence. It's part of the job description, the touring, personal appearances and on-location studio recording sessions. Rarely are they in London, so travel becomes the norm.

Many things have shaped my career as a guitarist, and there have been many ups and downs in the last fifty-five years or so; plenty of groups, from The Syndicats, The In Crowd, Tomorrow and Bodast in the sixties, Yes in the seventies, Asia, GTR and Anderson Bruford Wakeman Howe in the eighties, then back to Yes and Asia for the nineties. By the year 2000, Yes seemed to be on the rise once more, stopping in 2004, and Asia returned in 2006. In 2008, with Yes reforming again, I was on tour playing in both bands each night for twenty-five shows. In 2012 I departed from Asia to focus more on Yes and to give more time for solo and Trio projects.

I have released solo recordings since 1975, allowing myself more expression than I'd thought possible. From *Beginnings* to *Time*, I've experimented and explored this territory, often alone. In bands, it's all about the compromises and teamwork, but in solo mode it's totally different, especially when I've played with my sons Dylan and the late Virgil, which is a different experience from performing with others.

I've been lucky enough to experience most of the configurations possible of music-making, but the solo guitar is my favourite. Rhino released my double-CD set, *Anthology – A Solo Career Retrospective*, in 2015, followed by volume two, *Groups And Collaborations*, a triple-CD set, in 2017, which demonstrates the length and breadth of my recording output. Putting together these reissues helped me remember what it was I'd been doing all these years in the music business. It all started for me quite tentatively.

CHAPTER 1

Up Together

After a few difficult months discussing exactly how we'd appear together, in April of 2017 the remaining and available *Union* tour 1990 line-up of Yes spoke and performed at our induction into the Rock'n'Roll Hall of Fame. This was no easy feat.

Alan White and I hadn't played with Jon Anderson or Rick Wakeman since 2004, or with Trevor Rabin since March 1992 in Japan at the end of the *Union* tour. Retired Bill Bruford was there, Tony Kaye couldn't travel to New York and Chris Squire had passed away in 2015.

There was a rehearsal the day before and we worked on just two songs. Geddy Lee, the bass player and singer of the Canadian band Rush, wanted to play bass on the first song. I offered to play bass on the second. I felt it would be an appropriate tribute – and golden opportunity – to play exactly what Chris played on the original recording of the second song.

Between the various other inner-circle members the atmosphere was palpably tense. Attempts to pal up were in vain. We kept our distance as we played both songs a few times, trying to get the necessary cues and endings sorted out. Luckily for me, my son Dylan came too, thereby gaining further insight into this strangely dysfunctional outfit. He helped me steer through the extraordinarily weird world of a group that had started in 1968, two years before I joined. I heard some pretty vague talk about the future during the gaps, most of which didn't add up to much in the grand scheme of things.

On the day, the stage was set up as if for a big TV show, with cameras, lights, people talking on headsets, crew wheeling equipment on and off and general pandemonium. Everything was tested – the music and our patience – with our equipment and physical positions noted for spotlights. Various issues raised their ugly heads during the afternoon and manoeuvrings were noted as various managers, publicists and tour managers tested the patience of the Hall of Fame's staff over matters that everyone thought had been agreed beforehand but were now apparently up for debate. So be it. These were power struggles driven by nincompoops without their nine-volt battery inserted!

I was delighted to discover that all wasn't lost, with Dave Natelle mixing the front of house and the broadcast. We were in safe hands as Dave had mixed us and Asia many times, as well as The Rolling Stones and many others. His words of assurance about the clarity of his mix gave me great consolation. This was a slightly coded statement about what would feature in the mix and what might not be so audible. As soon as we could, Dylan and I returned to the hotel for a few hours.

We returned to the dressing rooms marked 'Yes'. Alan, Chris and I had been touring, firstly with Benoît David and Oliver Wakeman, and later with Geoff Downes and Jon Davison, for the last nine years, joined by Billy Sherwood in 2015, and we felt justified to be there as Yes. A separate room was set out for ARW (Anderson, Rabin and Wakeman). Every attempt had been made to avoid unnecessary time with them.

We made our way to the hall, where Dylan and I sat at the Yes table with Alan, Geoff and Billy and Martin Darvill, our manager. After Electric Light Orchestra and Joan Baez had been introduced and performed we were beckoned to the stage. Alex Lifeson, guitarist with Rush, and Geddy talked about our music and introduced us individually. We played 'Roundabout', with Geddy on bass. He certainly did us and himself proud, realising his ambition to play Chris's parts. We had it pretty well down, as at rehearsal we'd discussed keeping some space in the verses and starting the chorus with only my guitar. I moved between my Variax for the acoustic parts and my second-best Gibson ES-175D for the rest of the song ending, like the record, with the acoustic. I sung my usual parts along with Jon, and I seem to remember that Trevor didn't sing many of Chris's parts. I switched to a hired Rickenbacker bass for 'Owner Of A Lonely Heart'. (I now play Rickenbackers exclusively for all my bass parts and this bass was identical to my own.) A sunburst 2001 model, it is, of course, very similar to the model that Chris played.

Once the four-chord intro started, I played the bass exactly as it had been recorded by Chris in 1982. The cabaret ending was a reckless jam and I managed to inject Chuck Berry's 'duck walk' – he'd passed away recently and had received plenty of accolades on the night. The event was live-streamed and the TV broadcast provided a tighter version. Some suggested that we were the best band of the night. It was certainly the weirdest set – only two songs – I'd ever played with Yes, but it seemed to me that some other force was operating, allowing us to get through the performance with the minimum of exposure to each other. We remained two different camps, as we did in our speeches.

Jon Anderson was light-headed and sent his love out many times to Janee and their friends. Alan also spoke for a while. Then it was my turn. I was the only member of Yes to have written anything down in preparation, as the Hall of Fame had asked us all to do.

'I'd like to thank all the fans for believing all these years that we deserved and need to be inducted into this fine Hall of Fame. Fame means different things to different people. Some may long to bask in the glory, others merely accept the notoriety.

'Since the music speaks long after its creation, this serves as a payment of respect for those no longer with us, allowing those remaining to shine a light on all the contributors to the ideas, melodies, lyrics, arrangements and direction of our Yes music. No one can take away the response we've gotten from the audience who obviously have a different ear from the general music lovers, fortunately for us, able to distinguish the textures used, the harmony and discord needed to present music with dynamics of the dramatic, the humble, the soft and loud, and as Bill used to say when asked what Yes music was, would say simply, "Some of it's fast but some of it's slow!"

'I'm completely driven to thank my wonderful wife Jan for being so close to me through the highs and lows whilst stabilising our family, who have all been so inspirational to us both, Dylan and Zoe, Virgil and Zuni, Georgia, Drew and Diego, Steph and Adam.

'Through the last nine years, Alan White, Chris Squire, for his final seven years, along with Geoff Downes, Jon Davison, Billy Sherwood and myself, working together to maintain the standards set by the very idea of Yes, being realised through our recent Album Series tours, we look forward to continuing to unearth more great works of Yes. Thank you!'

My words were warmly received by the 17,000 strong audience. Many friends and fans who saw it online or on TV let me know they liked what I said via emails, messages and in person. I was delighted that people seemed to understand what it was I was driving at.

The tables were soon turned upside down. Instead of keeping with the mood of the occasion, in-house comedian Rick Wakeman embarked on a journey of questionable taste that visited places we cared far less about – crude and banal jokes. The teleprompter flashed 'Get off – time's up' for several minutes to no avail. The final speech was to have been Scotland Squire's moment to talk about her husband Chris, with their daughter Xilan beside her, but had to be cut as a result of the over running. Chris had really cared a lot about this particular award, recognising it as a huge sign of respect from within the industry. As we left the stage I was thinking how infuriatingly naff and childish this experience had been. Scotland asked, 'What happened?', to which I replied that Rick had gone over – way over – not just the time but over the limits.

Afterwards, behind the scenes backstage, we rushed about doing interviews, some with ARW, which were simultaneously disastrous and silly. When we were all asked what we planned for the next year, Yes's fiftieth anniversary, Jon Anderson said, 'We'll all tour together!' To which I immediately replied, 'No way, that has never even been discussed!' Which, of course, it hadn't. Nothing seemed further from reality than these two separate camps working harmoniously together.

The Rock'n'Roll Hall of Fame encourages its reunions with the best of intent, and fans like the concept of bands getting back together or 'filling in the years of not playing together'. But it's not always as simple as that. A case in point is ELO, also inducted that night. Roy Wood was key to their direction but his role that night didn't include playing with his band. Like many, he was sidestepped into a short speech during their presentation. The same was true of Journey's Steve Perry – there on the night but not on stage for the performance.

The reasons are complicated and every case is different. Often, some members have played in a band for years while others have been left behind, sometimes of their own volition, sometimes due to a clash of personalities. Performing much-loved music from a band's prime period can be less of a pleasure and more of a grin-and-bear-it chore.

The following day was 8 April 2017 – my 70th birthday. Before catching the evening plane home to London with Dylan, we had lunch with the rest of the band at our hotel. I was delighted to be presented with a beautiful gift by a dear friend, Charles Scott, who works in film music. It was a replica of my Gibson ES-345 'stereo' guitar. My original was getting very tired from touring and recording, but this 1972 model was in mint condition and all set to go. Now, nothing else could keep me in New York. All I really wanted was to be home with Jan and the family. Dylan and I arrived in London the next morning and we pretended it was still my birthday, spending the day together in gentle celebration of this milestone.

It's been a tremendous journey over these seventy years: joy, happiness, difficulties, sadness, love, loss, ups, downs, creation and destruction, some in full colour, others more black-and-white.

What else would one expect?

CHAPTER 2

Let's Pretend

I held a dream when I was about 10 years old. I would play the guitar and live life as an artist. There would be nothing else for me to do, only to progress on this instrument and excel.

The first tiny steps in the fulfilment of my dream occurred at 34 Loraine Mansions, Widdenham Road, in the north London district of Holloway where I was born, on 8 April 1947. I was the youngest of four children. Cyril, my dad, was a chef, who met Ada, my mum, when they were both working at the Ritz hotel in Piccadilly. I believe she was a maid. During World War II my dad cooked for the army and then at a smart bankers' restaurant in Bishopsgate in the City of London called The Palmerston where he became head chef, choosing the menu each day and supervising each dish. He occasionally brought home very high-quality food, including meat and fish, which set up expectations of decent food for years to come.

Dad was a respected member of the International Academy of Chefs de Cuisine, whose annual UK convention was held at Torquay in Devon. He and Mum were often among the guests and we have a remarkable scrapbook of these events, as Dad won prizes for large flower displays and for creating all sorts of animals and images, often out of sugar. My mum insisted on preparing most of our food, but he cooked at home on Saturdays and also made special dishes like apple or banana fritters. He taught me how to cook omelettes although, if I got up early on a Saturday, I preferred to crumble cheese and throw it in the frying pan. It was much quicker and easier than an omelette! As the cheese melted, I would eat it with a fork. He also showed me how to make pancakes, spinning or flipping them. This was great fun, gauging how high to flick the pancake and trying to catch it.

The Sunday roast was the only meal I couldn't bear and was possibly an indication that I was destined to become a vegetarian. It took a long time to cook, the unpleasant aroma seeped through our flat and I'm fairly sensitive to smells. Even before Sunday lunch was put in front of me, we'd often pop out to a local stall selling mussels and other sea creatures, whose sight and smell was also disgusting.

Dad also had another skill: ice carving. He sculpted a kangaroo for an Australian bank, the creature sitting at the centre of a buffet dinner in the bank's honour at The Palmerston. I believe his ability to create these objects gave me an appreciation of ice carving and, later, fine glasswork. On my travels I've enjoyed looking out for examples of works in glass, and I've now accumulated a substantial collection.

I was a comparatively quiet little boy, content to play with my model cars and trains. I also had army vehicles and soldiers and I would stage battles, firing lit matches from spring-loaded 1/43-scale cannons and tanks. Often, I would play with my brother Philip, who was two and a half years older than me, until we got too argumentative, usually over things like whose army had been wiped out. Our similar ages meant his influence was probably greater than that of our eldest brother John and sister Stella. Philip went on to work in film and television –

filming, editing and directing. He has lived in Sydney, Australia, for many years with Sarah, and has three sons from a previous marriage, Rufus, Paris and Blaise.

My sister Stella was the next eldest. She went on to work as a hairdresser, before raising her sons Adrian and Jason and then managing part of a large department store in London's Brent Cross. She now lives in Spain with her husband Tony. Stella must have put up with a lot from Philip, John and me in Holloway. John was quite the comedian. He'd tease our mum about her food, then pillow-fight with us in a darkened bedroom before dashing back off to the RAF. Once he made the move back to civvy street he worked in the furnishing and textile industry. With his wife Joyce, he has a son and daughter, Christopher and Caroline, who has a daughter called Bethany.

We had no comparison or reference to what other households were like, but there was no reason to complain about much. I loved the summer evenings, knocking a ball up against a wall for hours, the brightness of the sunset and our Friday evening drives across London to Putney to eat fish and chips by the River Thames and then run around Putney Common, where we would be chased by bats as it got dark. At weekends, we would often drive to Richmond or Hampton Court but only once did we visit a farm in the countryside. This made a huge impression – it was like another planet for a boy for whom London was the centre of the universe. It would be about a dozen years before I got the chance to see the beautiful English countryside again, and appreciate it for what it really is.

I was 5 when I first went to school. Mum had to drag me forcibly. I was screaming, not just on that first day but for many days after. School seemed to take away the freedom I had enjoyed and now I was being judged by how well I could store mindless information on a wide range of subjects. Hungerford

School loomed over me like a dark cloud. It seemed so unfair. If you really didn't like something, there ought to be some kind of alternative. In the winter the darkness at going-home time was actually quite frightening. I saw a friend get hit in the dark by a car once, vibrating after it struck him. Luckily, he was only slightly injured. Sometime after that an aggressive kid hit me in my head with a brick, no less. I was taken to hospital and had a stitch. The police dealt with him.

Back on our street at the weekends I'd go out with friends. Where there was no apparent danger, we'd bring stuff to make it more dangerous! We shot burning fire arrows at strategic targets, like a friend's garden or the coal bunker. Chemistry sets were used to fuel rockets, launched from our Meccano sets on metal ramps that we screwed together. Smoke bombs were set off in another friend's basement. Sulphur often burned mysteriously on the steps to the flats. We once entered a disused cinema and played various games amid the dust and dead pigeons. It got kind of scary and I eventually escaped through a door that led nowhere, unless you could scale 10-foot walls topped with broken glass. As this was the only way out, that's what I did. I just went at it, commando style, and straddled the walls with my hands and feet, then leaped down the other side to freedom. I still remember arriving home covered in dust and dirt, trying to hide before could I clean myself up but Mum caught me. 'Are you all right?' was all she said.

Anything that tested nerves and endurance was a high priority. I exorcised my many fears and rid myself of the dark side very early on, through dares and dangers with all the bravado of my foolish youth. Gradually these boyish challenges faded and more promising prospects for my imagination began to appear.

By the time I was 10 years old, I'd started to notice music. It began to motivate my mind and body. I played lively music at high volume on the radiogram in our lounge and there would be debris to mark the occasion. I'd jump and dive from settees to chairs, avoiding touching the floor. I danced and revelled in this strange disconnection with reality. I'd play records of bands performing marches and crooners singing about 'the moon in June' from my parents' record collection, including *South Pacific* and other film music. An enchanted evening became an escape from my ordinary, regimented life. Music was to become second nature to me, and a hard thing to control.

My secondary school was Barnsbury Boys in Islington. I was 11 years old, it was 1958 and the work was quite challenging. The subjects were harder and heavy-handed teachers ruled over us with grim authority. Only woodwork and technical drawing seemed fun, while the rest was a struggle. Many teachers found me placid but, sometimes, I could be opinionated. More usually, and with good reason, I crept around quietly, not creating waves or knowing too much about things. It was a reasonably safe way to avoid getting picked on by other boys and teachers. 'HOWE! STOP STARING OUT THE WINDOW!' sums up my schooldays.

There was a level of brutality at the school that sometimes got out of hand, and that went for both teachers and pupils. When I made a passing complaint during a woodwork lesson, I received a sharp rap over the knuckles with a ruler. On another occasion my whole class were caned because the culprit wouldn't own up to throwing an ink well across the room while the teacher's back was turned. Older pupils once 'turned me over', which involved me being punched and kicked by a group of bigger boys, albeit not too badly, as it turned out.

We were expected to absorb so much information that it became impossible for me to keep up with those more academically minded. French was dropped – I couldn't get it at all – but it was quickly replaced by Spanish, of all languages. This was another failure, as was religious instruction. The teachers we had for physical instruction were brutish and nasty, never missing an excuse to punish us. Running about on the top of the wall bars was anyway far from my favourite pastime. They stood 15 feet in the air away from the wall. Cold showers were compulsory. When a swimming instructor tried to get me into the pool at the Hornsey Road baths he twice pushed me in, and twice I sank to the bottom and only just reached the surface in time to snatch a breath. No more swimming for me for decades. Mr Bayliss, who taught maths, was always equipped with a bunch of rulers for slapping. He also always left for ten minutes for a cigarette – mid-lesson. We could smell it on his return.

I had been asking for a guitar for few years, and what a blessing it was when my prayers were answered in December 1959. Aged 12, I finally went with my dad to choose a guitar. It was a German six-string ('f-hole' or 'cello'), steel-strung, arch-top acoustic guitar costing £14 and was bought from a shop in King's Cross. I was given it on Christmas Day. It had been pretty impossible to miss the rise of rock'n'roll. Perhaps surprisingly, I had already heard some of the most exciting guitarists around before I even owned a guitar. Some would influence my playing years later and probably still do today. A seed had been sown from what I heard on those 78 rpm records in my parents' collection.

Initially, I pretended to play, ignoring the fact that I didn't know how to. Moving on from marches and crooners, I had subconsciously absorbed much of Les Paul's music and his multi-tracked, sometimes speeded-up, guitars with their reverb or echo, without being particularly conscious of it. Also, I'd started noticing the playing of Jimmy Bryant & Speedy West. This guitar and steel duo traded stunning solos on Tennessee 'Ernie' Ford's country/hillbilly recordings like 'Shotgun Boogie'. They certainly both developed the idea of the guitar break way beyond what had been done before. I played these on the piece-of-furniture, radio-and-record-player combined, the family radiogram. Soon, I had my own small record player in my room where I would attempt to play along with The Shadows and Duane Eddy.

I couldn't make sense of any tutor books, but I did like *Dance Band Chords For The Guitar* by Eric Kershaw. This helped me realise different chord inversions and more complex chords, those not often used in rock'n'roll. I would sit in my room at the back of our flat in Loraine Mansions and practise moving from chord to chord, a few scales and then I would try to make things up, imitating the approach used in guitar solos of those days. I was gradually able to conceptualise the entire guitar fingerboard in my head. At any time, I could hear patterns and plan fingering positions for lines or chords. It was like cramming one life alongside another. It felt like I was jumping right in the deep end. Initially, I imagined that a dance-band style of guitar would be a good place to start. I'd often watch guitarists on TV vamping chord progressions along with the big bands, driving the rhythm with the bass and drums on a regular old arch-top guitar like mine. I imagined myself on stage, at the side of a singer awaiting my cue to solo, possibly in a 12-bar break or just a riff or line from the song. Best of all was learning the guitar instrumentals of the day. To learn these was, surely, the ticket to being in a band.

At the same time, I was investigating guitarists, and Chet Atkins soon became my all-time, all-round favourite guitar player. *Teensville*, released in 1960, was the first Atkins album that I bought. His country-picking arrangements were hugely inspirational and I played it and played it on my record player. Although a vocal harmony group appear occasionally – you have been warned – nothing detracts from his outstanding performances. His use of the DeArmond volume and tone pedal, which he took from steel players, was groundbreaking. Mainly, it's his thumb-picking with the melody lines together, often with a chord thrown in too, that is astounding. When he plays single lines he went further still, inventive developments pouring out. Here was a guy who often recorded himself, at home. His sound came both from the way he played gently with his right hand as well as his skill as a producer. He played surprisingly lightly on the strings and moved smoothly and logically with his left hand.

I tried to buy all of his albums but, sadly, only a few were available in the UK. On *Chet Atkins' Workshop* and *Finger Style Guitar*, the sound is incredible. He made those Gretsch guitars sing and swing. Les Paul was also busy building his career at the same time as Chet and I have both their first 10-inch albums. Believe it or not, they are both called *Galloping Guitars*.

Chet's life story is rich in historic achievements. Although an unsung hero for a long time, he was deservingly given many awards for his long service to country music. I got the chance to meet him on a couple of occasions, once at a London concert in the eighties with Doug Turner, an exceptional player in the Chet style (and that's an understatement). After the show, I handed Chet the music for 'Clap'. I would have totally flipped if he had ever played or even recorded it! The last time we met was in the early nineties when we were both playing on a bill with Larry Coryell and Herb Ellis for Gibson guitars in a club after a music trade show in Frankfurt, Germany. (On the last night Larry and I jammed – and what a great player he was too.) Chet and I travelled to the club together each evening and I couldn't resist asking him about how particular recordings were made, but he only remembered some of his guitar, amp and microphone configurations. He had this laidback sense of humour and warmth. I also asked him if he was intending to record again with Les Paul. 'Er, only if he calls me!'

Through his playing, I found where I am most comfortable, not imitating Chet but writing pieces for solo guitar that incorporate some of his country-picking style. He didn't so much invent the style as develop it, often for electric guitar. Merle Travis deserves a mention here as Chet took over where he left off. Scotty Moore, Elvis's original guitarist, brought it closer to rock'n'roll. Chet just happens to be the master-picker, a style also known as thumb-picking, Travis-picking, finger-picking, cross-picking and even claw-picking. Chet's DVDs *Rare Performances By Chet Atkins Volume 1 & 2* are very good retrospectives and all his recordings, with the possible exceptions of *Christmas With Chet Atkins* and *Sing Along With Chet Atkins*, are worthy of attention, especially *Finger Style Guitar, Teensville, Workshop, Down Home* and *The Other Side Of Chet Atkins*.

My daily life was interrupted in 1960 when I was 13 and got whooping cough. I can testify to its unpleasantness, as it lasted over two months and I experienced harsh outbursts of coughing and choking. The treatment was burning coal tar oil in my room at night and I think it made me hallucinate, as my dreams went haywire. I'd previously experienced many vivid dreams, often hovering between sleep and consciousness. Once I was on top of an elephant, crashing through walls somewhere in India, extremely bizarre! Oddly enough, *Teensville* soothed and relaxed me as I went to sleep, distracting me from my strange thoughts.

Back to music, and I began to research guitarists who preceded the rock explosion. Django Reinhardt, injured in a fire in his gypsy caravan, played his Maccaferri guitar with just two fully usable fingers on his left hand, yet his playing was wildly exciting with huge runs up and down the fretboard, many trills and vibratos adding to his often radical ideas. I bought a 10-inch album, its cover featuring just a guitar string and simply entitled *Django*, recorded in 1934 and 1935 and first released in 1957. He and Stéphane Grappelli led the Quintette du Hot Club de France, one of Europe's leading jazz groups.

I heard the sweet sound of Wes Montgomery's Gibson L-5, often enhanced by his use of octave-playing – playing two notes, an octave apart from each other, at the same time. I heard Tal Farlow too and found his playing hypnotic and escapist. He was very much a guitarist's guitarist. I discovered many other great players: hearing exceptional but lesser-known players was really rewarding. Not all great players want to be highly successful; some would rather coast along, earn a decent living and keep out of the limelight. There is a wisdom to this which I admire very much.

The guitar instrumentals in the charts resonated everywhere I went. This was definitely their golden era, with The Ventures, Shadows, Spotniks and Gladiators all enjoying hits. My growing collection of guitar records became harder to house, but somehow I managed to hold on to them and I casually add to the library to this day. Along the way I took in the CD reissue era, boxsets, rare records like 10-inch albums, early singles and even earlier 78 rpm records, particularly of the early banjo and guitar repertoire.

I also knew guitarists personally as I was growing up, including Ray Russell. He is a very well-rounded player who's worked with someone I would have loved to work with myself, the American jazz arranger Gil Evans. Then there was Yosel, who played a Gibson Les Paul Special, a great rock guitar if ever there was one. I used to watch him play at a youth club in Islington and would hang out at his place in Holloway, trying to pick anything up from him that I could. He gave me a bit of an insight into being a rock guitarist, for sure.

In 1962 I left Barnsbury boys' school at the very earliest point one could, aged just 15. My thinking was: 'Get me out of here!' I had no GCE O-levels, failing all seven exams I took (I thought I might have got woodwork, but it was not to be). My brother Philip had excelled in his exams, going on to pass A-levels at grammar school.

I started a three-year apprenticeship as a piano-maker for Barrett Sound, York Way, walking distance from home. It was the only musical job afforded by my school. Day one saw me proving that I could make a dovetail joint out of two bits of wood. I returned home for lunch, seriously worried that the noise of pianos being tuned up from scratch was too much for my hearing! By lunch on the second day I quit: I couldn't take another minute of all that tuning, bashing and scraping. I took some part-time work cleaning expensive houses in north London, then worked for six months at Saville Records, a shop on Holloway Road.

There I was, with a guitar and big lips (people said I looked like I was from India), learning that it was not easy coming to terms with who I was, let alone what I looked like. Believing, as I did, that it was up to me to be as organised as possible in working with others, I began building my own personal ethics and goals about playing music, with the aim of improving my communication skills. I learned as many tunes as possible, expanded my technique by moving about the six strings and seventeen frets and trained my ears to spot the different textures of the guitars I heard on records and the radio. I bought a Guyatone LG50 electric guitar and Guyatone amp from a friend on my street. Soon after I started a group called The Syndicats with bass player Kevin Driscoll, later adding vocalist Tom Ladd and Johnny Melton on drums.

We started out by playing once a week at the Prison Club, where Pentonville prison inmates used to tidy up after the gig. We played in a long, canteen-style room and I remember the sound of my stage amp, a Watkins Dominator that really chucked it out. We also got a residency at the Swan pub on the High Road, Tottenham, where I had some good friends and I would often get a late night/early morning bus back to Holloway after staying up talking and having fun. For a whole year and a half, every night between Thursday and Saturday and on Sunday lunchtime and evening we played a mix of Chuck Berry, pop hits and various obscure tunes. I sang 'Down The Road A Piece', one of the few songs that Berry recorded which he hadn't written himself and which The Rolling Stones recorded for their second LP in 1965.

We tried to stay clear of the drunken fights that were a regular feature of Saturday nights, playing on a small stage with the window behind us to the street where these brawls would erupt. Noisy arguments often turned physical outside on the pavement, often attracting the police who'd pull them apart. We would try to continue playing, our Meazzi PA pumping out the vocals and our amps turned up as loud as we could get away with – you could hear us right down the street.

Playing guitar meant a lot to me: it kept me off the streets and I earned a little money. I definitely wanted to develop my own style and write songs, but in the meantime I suggested adding to our repertoire to broaden the show – little-known tunes like 'Blue Drag' by Django, 'Mama Turn Your Dampers Down' by Blind Boy Fuller and the title track from *Teensville* by Chet Atkins. It was an unusual mix that we added to some hits of the day, including early Beatles songs.

I found it hard to pick out all the right notes in the right order when I was learning songs, and spent many hours slowing down records to grasp the notation. The industry had made the jump from noisy, breakable, large, heavy and dust-ridden Bakelite 78 rpm records to small 45 rpm singles, extended plays (EPs) and 33 rpm long-playing records. The new formats seemed really amazing. If you slowed down an album meant to be played at 33 rpm to 16 rpm, you got all the notes in the same key but simply an octave lower. But Les Paul had sounded great, even on 78s in the late 1940s.

Paul was born on 9 June 1915 in Waukesha, Wisconsin, as Lester William Polsfuss. He had made so many advances – multi-tracked and vari-speeded guitars (and vocals from his wife, Mary Ford) just arrived from outer space. 'Whispering' swung like mad, 'Lover' was strangely bizarre and the incredible arrangements with huge harmony blocks were exciting. They have always stayed in my mind. 'How High The Moon' and 'The World Is Waiting For The Sunrise' are both absolute classics. His earlier records were in a more straightahead jazz vein. With his inventive mind, he redesigned the electric guitar as a solid instrument, though electric lap steel had already established this to a degree. Yet it was the sounds that he extracted from his guitars that initially made him famous. I guess Gibson's later campaign to release the Les Paul model in 1953 didn't hurt. On 'It's Been A Long Time' he plays some of his most subtle and lyrical lines.

A lovable character with a playful streak for changing the rules, Les Paul twice caught me on the hop. I first met him in the late seventies at the time of a Gibson performance, in a hotel at Heathrow Airport. He signed the trust-rod cover of my 'one-of-a-kind, four pickup' Les Paul Custom. Later I was invited to play on stage with Les and his rhythm section. Fine, all started well, we played some 12-bar tunes, then he asked me if I know a certain tune to which I hastily said 'No'. He turned to the band and counted it in. He was playing away quite merrily when he turned to me and indicated for me to take over. I somehow found a few notes that I could build from and switch to a simple octave approach where I could slide onto a better note, when required. Talk about playing by ear!

In the nineties I went to his regular Monday night show at Fat Tuesdays, a club in New York. He came over to me before the show and started chatting. He gave me a Les Paul baseball caps, duly signing it and asked me to play. I strongly tried to discourage him. 'It's my night off, I just came to watch,' I told him, anything I could think of. He sort of agreed, but later in the show he announced to the audience that I was sitting down in the front. I took a bow as he said, 'Come up and play, Steve.' Then the audience joined in, too. I reluctantly took to the stage and chose a guitar from a batch of three or four Les Pauls.

'I'll be at the bar Steve, play a couple of tunes!' said Les.

I'm scuppered, I thought. Then I got to tease Les. I remembered two of his tunes and launched into 'Whispering' and then 'Bye Bye Blues!', both more in a Chet Atkins style. I slid about the strings like Les did, to try and beckon him back to the stage. I insisted we play something like a 12-bar and eased into a version of 'D-Natural Blues' by Wes Montgomery, which was fun and on a level field.

As an inventor, Les's thinking was way ahead of the game. Having eight separate tracks that were properly synchronised created spin-offs like the sort of tape slap-back echo found on most early rock vocals, long spinning delays and tape phasing, as well as the ability to build up the sound, track by track. He used low-impedance pickups, although they never caught on. (Only one model of Les Paul carries those pickups. I used it on 'Cactus Boogie' on *The Steve Howe Album*.) Les recorded two albums with Chet Atkins. They complement one another nicely and there was banter and singing on the records, to boot. Les Paul was the first to realise the immense potential of the tone of the guitar and its reaction to effects and treatment, although it's still his actual notes that are the most fun.

CHAPTER 3

A Step Closer

In 1964, after two years of gigs and many rehearsals, I entered a recording studio for the first time with The Syndicats.

I was 17 and still playing the tiny Guyatone. I also had a Burns Jazz solid electric guitar but stuck with the Antoria guitar on this occasion. We were at RGM Sound, Joe Meek's studio, conveniently located on Holloway Road, only two streets from where I was born and raised. It was Kevin Driscoll's mum who'd brought us to this audition with Meek, one of the UK's top producers. We carried our equipment up three flights of stairs to a room overlooking the buses and trucks going along Holloway Road to Highgate or the other way, to Highbury. The studio walls were covered with egg boxes in an attempt to damp the sound.

We set up and were invited into the control room, where bits of used tape covered the floor – it must have accumulated over weeks, if not months. Meek described to us how he used his two-track recorders and the RCA mixers that hung from the wall. We then recorded Chuck Berry's 'Maybellene', perfecting the backing track at quite a fast tempo, our drummer Johnny Milton thumping his bass drum and the rest of his kit while Kevin knitted tightly with him on his bass guitar. Singer Tom

Ladd overdubbed his vocals in Meek's infamous bathroom, which he reputedly used for all vocals. I overdubbed the solo spot later the same day. The B-side was a song Tom and I had written called 'True To You'. The tempo was slower and the key lower but after recording Joe sped it up until it sounded a bit 'Mickey Mouse' – in other words, cartoon-like. Another trick was to lower the pitch of the tape by a semitone: the vocals could then be speeded up afterwards to assist in reaching very high notes. The single was released in March 1964, ahead of my 17th birthday, an event that warranted a story in the local *Islington Gazette*. We continued to work with Joe, although I had to remind him all too often that I had a girlfriend, as sometimes he'd mention that he 'liked my trousers', among other supposed compliments. It could get a shade uncomfortable at times.

Later in the year I bought the best all-round guitar anyone could hope for. My dad put down £40 as a deposit on a hire purchase agreement over two or three years, which I paid off monthly from gigs, to buy the really fabulous guitar that still gives me immense pleasure today, my Gibson ES-175D. It was 200 guineas which was £210 in 1964 money – over £4,000 today! I ordered it from Selmer's, a big guitar shop on Charing Cross Road in London and had to wait two months to collect the beautiful guitar. I rushed home to plug it into my Fender Tremolux amp. It sounded stunning. The front pickup reminded me of the sound of Kenny Burrell, still one of my favourite jazz players. The back pickup totally rocked. Together they delivered a really big, bold sound, a combination I would use regularly throughout my career.

The ES-175 was first manufactured in 1949 at Gibson's factory in Kalamazoo, Michigan, first with a single, P90 pickup, then in 1953 with a double P90 (hence the 'D' after the

'ES-175'). Later, in 1957, the pickups were changed to revolutionary humbuckers that are still being copied today. Originally, female employees sat winding the pickups at Gibson's plant, chatting about their day, not knowing that a legend was being created. Those pick ups marked 'patent applied for' are still revered today. Even after the patent was granted, the same mark appeared for some time on the pickups. In 1964, the year I bought mine, 349 ES-175s had been made and by the time Gibson stopped providing total output numbers in 1990, around 37,000 had been made. Production continues today, with many variants, including my own SH model between 2003 and 2014, replicating the specifications of my 1964 guitar. I received a percentage of sales and a couple of examples each year. Many jazz guitarists have played my model, including Wes Montgomery, Jim Hall, Joe Pass, Kenny Burrell and Howard Roberts. Other artist versions were developed, approved by Johnny Smith, Barney Kessel, Tal Farlow and Hank Garland, among others, and Billy Bird had the Byrdland. Gibson was endorsed by hundreds of players over the years, but their Les Paul range was destined to become the most popular Gibson model of all time. My original was not perceived as a rock guitar, but I found ways to control the potential feedback using my volume pedal and amplifier equalisation. All it needed was for the bass control on the amp to be increased slightly from zero for feedback to be virtually eliminated: any higher and it became a problem.

The history of the electric guitar can be confusing. As far back as 1924 Gibson's master mandolin and guitar builder, the now revered Lloyd Loar, proposed an amplified guitar via an 'electrostatic system' but Gibson rejected it. Loar released his own model, the Vivi-Tone guitar, in small numbers but to little success. Rickenbacker released their first electric Hawaiian lap steel, endearingly nicknamed the 'frying pan', in 1931, followed by an Electric Spanish guitar in 1934. Other pickups became available from DeArmond and Dobro. By 1936, Walter Fuller had convinced Gibson to 'go electric', which they did with the Gibson ES-150 guitar and an amplifier initially made by Lyon & Healy. The guitar had an electromagnetic pickup that was fabulously exploited by Charlie Christian, the first single-line, electric, jazz guitarist the world ever knew.

Gibson's founder, Orville Gibson, born in 1856 in Chateaugay, New York, brought innovations to all fretted string instruments. He took violin characteristics, like the f-holes and their carved or arched tops, onto the guitars and mandolins he constructed by hand. He oversaw the move to mass production in his Kalamazoo factory to accommodate the demand for banjos, mandolins and guitars. His legacy continued after his death in 1918. By the eighties Nashville was the site of Gibson's main factory while its more customised instruments came from their Memphis location. They once sent me a black 175 SH with gold hardware, for which I was very grateful. No question – Gibson have always been good to me!

I took my new guitar to the next Syndicats session at RGM Sound studio in late 1964. Our second single was called 'Howlin' For My Baby', on which Kevin sung the vocals because Tom Ladd had left the band, and it was released in January 1965. This was a blues song rocked up to give us more of a R&B sound. The group-written B-side was called 'What To Do'. Johnny Melton had also left the band so S. Truelove played drums, and a piano player called Jeff Williams joined us too. Joe Meek was interested in the band but success evaded us, perhaps because Kevin's vocals were slightly punk. 'Howlin' For My Baby' was reviewed by Georgie Fame in *Melody Maker*, when he commented that the guitar break was 'pretty good'. I admit to being quite proud for a minute or two.

Between these recording sessions we continued to gig up and down the country, travelling via the M1 and stopping at the Watford Gap services, where we often mingled with other bands late at night. We reverted to playing fourteen Chuck Berry songs every night – acclaiming ourselves the Chuck Berry Appreciation Society – before settling down to being a blues band. We were actually attacked twice, firstly while driving our yellow Commer van (fortunately without equipment) along Tottenham High Road. We were forced to stop by a car that cut us up. Our windows were smashed in with sticks. Another time we were out of our home territory when some local lads took a dislike to us. They came at us, pushing and punching as we were caught off guard on their turf. It could be rough and dangerous in Tottenham in those days.

The Syndicats managed to get a TV appearance on *The Beat Room*, on the newly launched BBC Two. That night it featured Tom Jones with 'It's Not Unusual' and The Kinks with 'You Really Got Me'. A certain member of the Kinks decided to tell me about his state of mind. He hadn't slept, eaten or changed clothes in a while and was high and had been drinking. Was this normal, I pondered. An emerging band that was messed up? This act of rebellion appeared momentarily appealing but in time I was to discover that too many musicians fell prey to the rock'n'roll lifestyle, living on the edge. I would meet many along the way. A few had great charm and the wit to carry it off, but it's really tragic when their live performances suffer from these excesses.

On the show we played 'Howlin' For My Baby' and 'Hey Bo Diddley', and I have a copy from the BBC that I hope to include in a DVD compilation. It was my first TV appearance and my guitar was looking really clean, as it still does today.

The live side of playing in bands was a serious learning curve for me. To say there were some dodgy people in the music industry would not be disputed. Joe Meek was said never to have paid any of his acts the royalties due to them. This was probably true as EMI kindly gave me The Syndicats' tapes after thirty years for that reason. This allowed me to release them initially as part of *Moth Balls*, a CD of sixties recordings released in 1994, and then two tracks for my *Anthology 2 – Groups and Collaborations* in 2017 on Rhino. EMI released our recordings on Parlophone Records, but they turned down our next attempt at a single, 'Leave My Kitten Alone' (originally recorded by Little Willie John in 1959), possibly due to its screechy and rather sad bluesy sound. The Beatles recorded 'Kitten' at Abbey Road but it remained unreleased until their *Anthology* album in the nineties, and it was also recorded by a group called First Gear, helped on guitar by a session man called Jimmy Page.

John Lamb then became our singer and sung really well on what was to be The Syndicats' third and last single, 'On The Horizon', released in September 1965. This was a great song by Leiber & Stoller that I recently recorded myself. Ray Fenwick played guitar on the B-side. 'On The Horizon' reached No. 17 on the chart produced by Caroline Radio, which broadcast from a boat in international waters in the North Sea. On this song, I used to slight effect a DeArmond volume and tone pedal on my guitar. Just like Chet Atkins, I'd adopted this pedal before getting a much better Fender volume and tone pedal, both precursors to the wah-wah pedal we all know and love.

Unfortunately, we didn't have a stream of gigs lined up and things started falling apart. I left The Syndicats around the time of recording, as Ray Fenwick played guitar on the B-side. He went on to play with the Spencer Davis Group, Tee-Set and The Ian Gillan Band and as second guitar in my Remedy tour band in 2008.

During one of the last sessions, Joe Meek became irritated with how we were playing and after only one run-through said, 'You'd better have this song properly rehearsed by the time I get back or else you're out of here!' He stormed out, returning after about an hour and luckily for us he seemed satisfied with our rehearsing. We saw him get hot under the collar with his receptionist on a few occasions. Nevertheless, Joe knew what he was doing in his studio. His sound owed quite a lot to Phil Spector, but in a Euro pop style, at a time when 'commercial' wasn't a dirty word. 'Telstar' by The Tornadoes became a US No. 1, and his hits with The Honeycombs and John Leyton still sound highly individual. In his earlier days he'd engineered a wonderful Big Bill Broonzy album called *London Sessions*, a credit I only noticed much later on. Broonzy was, and still is, my personal favourite blues guitarist and singer. His writing, singing and playing always sounded world class. 'The Glory Of Love', written by Peter Maurice, still gives me shivers. 'St Louis Blues' and 'Minding My Own Business' are also outstanding.

Electric city blues was becoming more popular, but my roots lay with country blues and its acoustic history. I'd get a sound while sitting on an (unlit) stove, inside an alcove in my parents' kitchen in London that had great ambience, a little like that of Broonzy in the fifties, when he did 'Southern Saga', a talking blues of which I've learned every word. He always played and sang so poignantly. I enjoyed *I Feel So Good*, Bob Riesman's book about Bill.

★ ★ ★

Playing as a 'pickup' musician has always excited me and the first really memorable one-off gig I played blew me away. At that time Chris Farlowe & The Thunderbirds were considered one of the best bands in the R&B/jazz/blues style, and their guitarist was none other than Albert Lee. The Syndicats had opened for them and when Albert first joined the band, I saw them in Watford. Chris had said, 'Steve, you'd better watch us tonight as we've got a new guitarist.' My band members virtually had to hold me upright! That night Albert played a three-pickup, black Les Paul Custom through a Fender Bassman amp. The sound was so awesome, I can still hear it, extremely penetrating and ear-piercing. More than that, it was his musicality that impressed me. He held a plectrum and cross-picked with other fingers, as I'd been doing. Here was a rising star. The band gave him loads of space to stretch out and his solos just soared and seriously rocked on.

Before a later gig in Wolverhampton. Albert was unwell and at the last minute I got a call from Chris Farlowe asking if I was available to stand in. Of course, I jumped at the chance. It was great to be asked and truly amazing to actually stand in the shoes of someone I revered. Also, I was driven to and from London and Wolverhampton in an Aston Martin DB6 convertible, my 175 on the back seat next to me. I was met at the Nag's Head, Holloway, in the afternoon and the Aston Martin raced me up the M1, arriving as the band were setting up.

A list of song titles with their key signatures was handed to me: '"Stormy Monday Blues"/F', etc. After a soundcheck and a run-through of the first song, the audience were let in. A little rushed but by 8 p.m. our set began. I was cued to improvise on top of the band. 'Goodness, who do I have to thank for this?' I thought to myself – it was a complete blast. The different keys, tempos and riffs melted together and I pulled through with flying colours. My love of 12-bar music hasn't since found such a good home! There would be many other enjoyable opportunities to work spontaneously with other players and learn more about the unexpected delights of musical one-night stands.

CHAPTER 4

Onward

My friend Dave ran a guitar store called Lewison Guitars on Charing Cross Road and put in a good word for me when he heard about an opening in a band.

The band was The In Crowd and the singer was Keith West and we got together at an Italian restaurant nearby. They'd recently entered the charts with a cover of an Otis Redding song, 'That's How Strong My Love Is'. Keith had seen me play with The Syndicats at Eel Pie Island and thought I was pretty good. I auditioned for them one afternoon at Club Noreik in Tottenham. Embarrassingly Les Jones, their original guitarist, showed up, too! The rest of the band was John 'Junior' Woods on rhythm guitar and harmonies, Simon 'Boots' Alcott on bass guitar and Ken Lawrence on drums. Soul music was the source of their inspiration. The audition went well and within a few days I was miming with them to their single on a TV show called *Thank Your Lucky Stars*. I learned the rest of their tunes and we started to get quite good. The In Crowd was in the hit parade so I had to get used to the screaming girls and an a increased level of excitement at their shows. It was definitely up a gear from The Syndicats – fun and profitable too.

The group was signed to EMI with producer Roy Pitt. My first recording session with them was at De Lane Lea Studios, Holborn, on a soul song called 'Stop! Wait A Minute', released in September 1965. I remember the sessions quite well. My volume and tone pedal got some use on the B-side, 'You're On Your Own'. Recording with them was a progression in both orderliness and professionalism. It felt controlled but free of the dank backroom vibe of being at RGM. Both songs featured solos from me with a fuzz box that broke up the sound of the guitar – distortion varied by the knobs of the box.

Roy Pitt became a good friend and we often let loose at his house, drinking and smoking, a comparatively light introduction to the wilder side of rock'n'roll. It really became the norm to get quite out of it – or even totally out of it! Music seemed to be enhanced by these substances, and listening to The Everly Brothers' 'Love Is Strange' or Bob Dylan's 'Positively 4th Street' as loud as possible became compelling. Dylan's song was about attitude, about where you stood with someone and how you could be honest, if not a little cruel, about a relationship. Dylan had become the identifiable voice of our conscience. His live version of 'Just Like Tom Thumb's Blues', on the B-side of 'I Want You', was anthemic.

The band might have been united in our love of music but other forces were afoot; no pun intended but one of the big problems was John 'Boots' Alcott. He was smart, slick, perhaps just a little bit shifty, and aristocratic, yet from Kilburn. Always a really fun person to be with, he held his bass head up high, as was the trend, and he was very popular with the girls, always carrying himself in great style. Then, out the blue, he was stitched up for £50 in a Soho club, returned to the place and burned it down. Tragically, someone was killed. We visited him in Pentonville Prison, a hellish place. It was so sad to see him there. Instead of getting a new bass player, Junior, our rhythm guitarist, switched to bass.

Next, our drummer Ken was in the van when he fell off his drum stool and out of our vehicle as it went round a corner, and another change was needed. Pretty Things drummer Twink – born John Alder – joined the band and the group chemistry really started to fire. We played tighter and had a new belief in ourselves. We thought we were the best band around and even began thinking about reinventing ourselves.

We were asked to appear in a film called *Smashing Time*, starring Rita Tushingham, as a group called The Snarks. One scene – shot on a set meant to look like the Post Office Tower in central London – featured a party that ended up with a massive cream-pie fight. I got one very short line, 'Let's do it!' or something like that. Filming took place at studios in South Hampstead, and I remember walking home across Belsize Park Road covered in cream and having to take a bath to wash the stuff out of my hair. By the time this film was released we'd change our name to Tomorrow.

Many in the industry were dabbling with pills, such as 'blues' and 'black bombers', which considerably sped you up, although the first time I swallowed one I became fairly pathetic. After a lunch I swallowed a 'blue', which crept up on me and loosened my tongue as I gulped down bottles of Coca-Cola and smoked cigarettes relentlessly. Not to be recommended. Speed wasn't for me, nor was Romilar, an off-the-shelf cough remedy that, in large doses, spaced you out and changed your reference to how far away objects were. The band adopted a smoking habit: this was calmer and seemed more consistent with making music. One night when we were playing in Brighton there was a drugs raid by the local police. We got a tip-off it was going to happen in our dressing room and quickly put all our smoking materials in a bag that we dangled out of the window. The police came in thinking they'd caught us red-handed and searched the room – but they never looked out the window.

We were free to see the world, as we did when our managers at the Bryan Morrison Agency booked us to play a two-week residency in a newly opened club in Milan in Italy, for what was my first trip outside of the UK. The managers at the agency were Tony Howard and Steve O'Rourke, who dated my sister Stella for a while, looking after us along with Gita Maslen (Rennick), their receptionist. Pink Floyd was their main act, but we always felt a special warmth from the team. When they started getting work for us, Bryan invited us to sign the management and agency agreement and out came a bottle of champagne. We hadn't read the contract, but as musicians do, we threw caution to the wind and just signed it. It would be a fantastic period for the group.

For the Milan trip, we took the ferry and drove through France before having trouble on a Swiss mountain pass that was closed. We arrived in Milan after a two-day journey, when the van's prop-shaft broke near the hotel where we were staying. As if that wasn't bad enough news, the owner of the club decided he didn't like our music and insisted we play regular pop songs rather than our mix of soul and improvisations.

At the end of first week, we were given a hotel bill that was equal to the entire fee we were supposed to earn for two weeks at the club. It was all that butter – butter was really pricey in 1966, and particularly in Italy – and, of course, the wine that had flowed every dinnertime. How we survived I just can't seem to remember, though I do recall that everywhere we went people stared at us and laughed, saying things in Italian and pointed discouragingly. Why, you might ask? Well, we had a fashionable London look, but it was yet to reach Milan: flowery shirts, long hair and stars or tinsel on our faces. It all made us look rather camp as far as they were concerned. We stood out like sore thumbs in very tight pants.

Nevertheless, we goofed about in Milan, taking in the lifestyle and the loud discussions in Duomo Square and riding out the heckling. We got the van fixed and, once the residency was over, drove home. It was around 900 miles each way in a van with all the equipment, a full drum kit, my 175 guitar and Vox AC-50, a bass guitar and bass amp, the four of us with luggage and our roadie. Those definitely were not the good old days.

Arriving home seemed to me to be the right time to break ties with everything I'd left behind, including living at home, my girlfriend and my hard-drinking habit. I left to spend about six months with an American girl who had a comfortable flat in a Belsize Park basement. My brother Philip remained at our mum and dad's place, where I found him in the dark listening to Miles Davis with Gil Evans' arrangement of Rodrigo's 'Concerto de Aranjuez' on their seminal album *Sketches Of Spain*. I loved John Williams and Julian Bream's recordings of the original but here was an example of the morphing of music from one style into another. Adapting other types of music as they had done seemed very interesting.

My playing was getting stronger and the sound I was making sometimes inspired people to say things that went over my head – flattering, but I couldn't seem to absorb it all. It helped to build my confidence but I didn't let it distract me into thinking that the job at hand was done. I'd hardly started scratching the surface of what I hoped was possible. The guitar was guiding me more than I guided it. Echo machines and fuzz boxes, wah-wahs and phasers were the guitar effects of these pioneering days. These gadgets added some extra hiss and general racket to the output of the amp, creating what was called 'frying tonight', the sound of potatoes being dropped in boiling oil to make chips. Echo delay units added to the basic valve sound with tape hiss in these early days. Now, of course, working with effects on guitars has become more and more fascinating with digital modelling and amp simulation.

Listening to the world's best guitarists helped me develop diverse playing styles but I'm not sure where I got the idea of playing two guitars at once, which predates my 'guitar on stands' usage by three or four years. I used to strap a small Gibson Melody Maker guitar (single cutaway and single pickup) over the 175 so it hung at my right side. I'd plug this into my amp's second channel and play sustained spread chords on that while using the 175 for single lines. I utilised this in extended jams as a drone sound a little later. My work with The In Crowd had been exciting but we were soon to go through a major rethink (or was it a D-think, as D became the central key in so many of our experimental, improvised raves).

We were invited to the Hyde Park Hotel to meet the famous Italian director Michelangelo Antonioni, who wanted a band to appear in his soon-to-be-cult movie *Blow-Up*. We met at the hotel and discussed ideas, including the making of a cheap replica guitar similar to mine that I could pretend to break (I'd sooner break a leg than my own precious guitar) – instrument abuse had made some groups quite famous, but it just wasn't my style! We got as far as a day's shooting, after which we were given the bad news that The Yardbirds were going to appear instead of us. Their line-up at that time included Jeff Beck and Jimmy Page and they were certainly more famous than us and it came to pass that, in the finished film, Beck is seen breaking a full-bodied style guitar that was originally constructed to look like mine. Keith had even written a song for the film, logically called 'Blow Up'. We recorded it and played this straight-ahead three-piece rocker to Antonioni, but it wasn't included and now forms part of the less heard In Crowd back catalogue on *Anthology 2 – Groups And Collaborations*.

The In Crowd's gigs included debutante parties arranged, like many of our shows, by Lord Antony Rufus Isaacs, who was a great friend. These debs parties were fun: we'd get fed before being released on stage, often in a marquee around midnight, to rock up proceedings, all great for a laugh. Tony also got us a fashion catwalk show in Knokke Le Zoute on the coast of Belgium (funnily enough, where Yes and I mimed to some *Time And A Word* songs in 1970). The reception we got at the show was pretty dreadful and afterwards we all got fairly sloshed. Stupidly, we threw plates out the window of the fourth-floor apartment they'd provided for us. The Belgian police arrived and took away our passports and we all had to behave ourselves overnight before collecting the documents the next morning.

We opened a show for Cream one night at a club we'd played a few times before called the Birdcage in Portsmouth. We thought it strange that, after their intense show, they came into the dressing room and sat down in silence looking absolutely miserable. We were used to a certain camaraderie between bands and we guessed they must have been fairly out of it as there was no joy or good vibes. I can understand better now the pressures they might have been under, as pushing yourself to the limits at every show along with the tiresome nature of life on the road eventually exhausts everyone. Tensions can run high, particularly if they are fuelled by personal indulgences. Most of us learn all about the dangers in the nick of time, but some don't.

The In Crowd's final recording was 'Why Must They Criticise', released in September 1965. This was a sort of protest song with James Brown's 'I Don't Mind' on the B-side. Protest wasn't strictly our area, although it was heavily influenced by our favourite US band, The Byrds, but that wouldn't be enough to save it. Singles are meant to be commercial, and this seemed to bring about the end of an era.

Keith and I went on to share a hotel room over Blaises, a South Kensington club where we'd been playing a residency. Close to Chelsea, this was a smart place to live, near the Victoria & Albert Museum and Hyde Park. It was at Blaises that Jimi Hendrix first played in the UK and we were there when it happened. He was already leading his trio with Mitch Mitchell and Noel Redding and no one could help but notice how special Jimi was. After his exciting spot, he came and sat down at our table and was a perfect gentleman. We'd often say 'Hello' when we'd share the same bill after that.

The In Crowd played at Blaises twice a week and this was where the nightly ritual really began. We would all share a hubble-bubble pipe filled with tobacco and hashish before clambering on stage. We went on as high as kites but strangely unified, intensely exploring the outer limits of our music. We maintained this throughout the Summer of Love, and far beyond.

We played regularly at the Speakeasy, a club near Oxford Circus that was very popular with bands and singers as a late-night hang. It was a meet/eat/drink sort of place. There were lots of beautiful women, including my future wife Jan, and we'd go there even if we hadn't played. One such night Joni Mitchell, unknown in the UK at the time, gave an impromptu performance. She was captivating, leaving me with a lasting love of her songs, playing and singing. She was terrific then and it was only the beginning. Everyone listened to her beautiful albums, as we still do today. She's a truly great artist.

Keith had some new songs that were really well suited to the band. We seemed to shoot off into a new direction once the door opened. We were in sync with the mood as 1966 turned towards 1967. We rehearsed in a cold, dark basement and began to change direction, stretching out solos, depending on how good it felt. We'd go shorter if for any reason it 'wasn't really happening' and, of course, longer if it all seemed to flow. Most often at our gigs we'd surge to a higher level of interplay than we'd previously managed before. We had discipline and this increased our authority over our shows.

We were morphing into a different band with ideas that fitted the moment. It was the era of flower power, of peace and love. We became Tomorrow, as if the present wasn't soon enough. We were pretty original, visually enhanced by Junior's performance. He danced about madly in skimpy clothing – an only-just-decent loincloth – his face painted. For a while we also featured a dancer called Suzy Creamcheese (aka Suzy Zeiger), an American friend of Frank Zappa, and she could really dance. She and Junior were provocatively acting, their sensuous moves enhanced by the mayhem of pulsating drums and improvised guitar. My extended solos often featured a droning fourth or D string, and I increased the number of individual pole pieces on the pickups of my guitar so that the D string would feedback easily, meaning it was much louder. I darted about over this on the three higher strings above. Although D was often droning, it wasn't necessarily the route note of the mode I was using at the time. The only recording to almost capture the sound of our exploratory moments was 1968's *Tomorrow* album, which includes a studio recording of The Byrds' 'Why'. I also included it on the second volume of my *Anthology*.

At that time it was intoxicating to feel the passion between like-minded people who sought a new kind of freedom, to be 'who they were' or, at least, who they thought they were. Chelsea was the place to be, to walk, shop and eat. It centred around the King's Road, its shops, cafes and our friends' flats. Granny Takes A Trip had the clothes and its own clientele. In fact, I still have the jacket from Granny's that I wore in Tomorrow photos. The choice of highs in the area was limited only by your common sense. LSD was rarely taken and with some caution. Hash and grass were shared as the supply allowed, but speed had become uncool and hard drugs were considered totally destructive, at least among the people we knew. I had seen the horrid effects of those narcotics and I was never going there. I was advised from an early age never to try stuff like that. It was sound advice I got from one who knew.

The pulse we felt in our lives lasted only through the haze of 1967. At that point, fun seemed boundless and telepathic thoughts connected us to people we didn't even know. Peace was the goal, love was the method. One day, we were all in a London taxi going down Kensington High Street, the closed window separating us from the driver, while we shared a smoke when the bell of a police car rang out. They overtook the taxi and stopped right in front. We thought we'd been nabbed, so I threw the white box containing other smokes out the window along with what we were smoking. The police approached the driver, saying that he'd turned right illegally. We jumped out of the cab, claiming that we 'couldn't wait about', before running back down the street to reclaim the box. Only in 1967.

Our music roared in London's most revered venues – UFO on Tottenham Court Road, Middle Earth in Covent Garden and the Roundhouse in Chalk Farm. Tomorrow often opened for Pink Floyd and on one occasion, when we weren't playing together, I was rushed back to UFO after our performance, to stand in for Syd Barrett, who they thought was not going to make the show. I was up for this and was expected to improvise as there was no time to rehearse. Sadly (for me), Syd managed to get to the show at the last minute, although he was a little worse for wear.

We also played loads of one-nighters, package tours and even a seaside weekend residency with Donovan and Tom Jones. I have no idea how package tours held together – we toured with Traffic and Vanilla Fudge, playing with them on the opening night at the Finsbury Park Astoria, which later became the Rainbow. That night Vanilla Fudge had a huge row before going on and quit the tour soon after.

One memorable night was 28 April at the UFO. During one of our improvisations, Junior put down his bass and danced about, a cue for Jimi Hendrix to join us on stage and play Junior's bass. The music ploughed on mysteriously with his contributions. He looked intense, committed to jam along with us. These sorts of solos could go on for ten to fifteen minutes and that night we stretched it out for even longer. If only someone had recorded our set! Our friend Joe Boyd was there and he thought someone was filming but we never found it. Joe was a big fan of Tomorrow and often helped us out on our bumpy road towards near-stardom. We so believed that our music had a rightful place at the very top of the rising bands. The day after our jam with Jimi, on 29 April 1967, we played at the Fourteen-Hour Technicolour Dream concert in Alexandra Palace, north London, along with many of the high-profile psychedelic-era bands. This was a hugely memorable gig in a vast venue that was all kitted out for freakouts and happenings.

We also played on the first John Peel BBC Radio 1 show on 21 September, taped at the corporation's Maida Vale studios.

A new style of radio had evolved, very laidback, which featured longer tracks and live sessions by new bands like us. John was a fan.

I did quite a few sessions for Mark Wirtz, the first producer to book me for an overdub session. When I arrived I was wondering where the other players were but he said, 'Oh, it's just you.' I soon got into the swing of it, playing the guitar parts on what became 'Theme From A Teenage Opera', my guitar double-tracked for the first time. It was a buzz, having the sole attention of the producer and learning about the detail that's given to particular guitar sounds. I still love to listen to that piece.

Mark became Tomorrow's producer, partly because he'd been booking me for sessions – rhythm then lead guitar as he switched me around with Big Jim Sullivan – but also because he asked me if I knew a singer who wrote lyrics. Keith fitted the bill and they worked on the hit single 'Grocer Jack – An Excerpt From A Teenage Opera'. I overdubbed on this track too, playing in a mandolin style with the tape slowed down during the recording. The 'opera' was never completed. The single cost so much EMI shrunk the budget and Mark wasn't able to maintain the level of extravagance. By now he knew half the band, and we wanted to make an album, and Mark got us a deal with EMI.

It has to be said, these sixties deals were rubbish. EMI would never renegotiate. The band still receives only 2 per cent between us. That meant – and still means – 98 per cent of all income is retained by EMI and the four band members receive half a per cent each. How much injustice is needed before justice can be seen to have been done?

When we recorded at Abbey Road Studios, The Beatles – well, Paul and Ringo mainly – would pop their heads into Studio Two and say 'Hello'. This was a buzz and increased our enjoyment of the sessions, in which we were getting quite freaky, trying out ideas that sometimes required the 'men in the white overalls' to come and fix things or bring in the latest gadget. This was similar to the 'bicycle repair men' in Monty Python's world!

Backwards guitar had become the in thing. 'My White Bicycle' was recorded with backward lead guitar and backward hi-hat. The end was reversed at the beginning and the beginning – yes, you guessed – was heard in reverse at the end. An actual on-duty British policeman was invited into the studio – after certain items were concealed – and asked to blow his whistle when Keith sang, 'They'll find some charge, but it's not thieving.' 'Charge' was another name for the smoking stuff. The nice policeman got the idea straight away. He gave it a good blow, making it as authentic as possible. We often played the song at the beginning and end of our live shows and it was released as a single in May 1967, becoming an anthem before the whole album was completed.

Most of the tracks were engineered by none other than Geoff Emerick, who was at the controls on numerous Beatles recordings. We had a limited amount of material and, for better or worse, several strange pop tunes filled the gaps. Our second single, 'Revolution', written by Keith and me, predated The Beatles' song of the same name and is said to have influenced them. The various elements of this track were wonderfully recorded, but they weren't all at the same tempo. Mark tried his best to disguise this by inserting gaps and using echo. We had already recorded a demo – eventually released in 1998 on a partly live CD called *50 Minute Technicolor Dream*. This version had the same intro and ending but was overly affected with phasing. We re-recorded the song itself with all sorts of mood changes, including a string section.

It was great fun playing sitar on 'A Real Live Permanent Dream'. Mostly though, I was playing the 175. My other guitar, the tiny Antoria LG50, covered with multi-coloured cardboard patches, was used for a couple of small overdubs, like on 'Strawberry Fields' for the A to G bends. The arrangement for this song may have been inspired by Vanilla Fudge.

I almost got to play with Ella Fitzgerald. Ian Ralfini, an A&R man we knew, had booked me for the session. I got to Olympic Studios in Barnes in time to pass the great lady in the corridor being assisted out by two large guys. 'She must have had too much of something,' I thought to myself. It would have been great to have played with her. Various musicians appeared, seemingly out of nowhere. Jim Capaldi got on the drums and in the control room was Mick Jagger. That's all I can remember. Something got recorded but I don't think it ever saw the light of day.

I had a bit of too much myself one night, leaving the UFO a bit worse for wear and realising something had been added to my drink. I have vague recollections of being on a bus at Whitestone Pond in Hampstead, then wandering about nearby Hampstead Heath but my memory went blank. I woke up the next morning lying on a bench in front of Kenwood House. This beautiful grand house in its own park was already open to the general public. Falling under the effects of LSD was scary as hell. We had occasionally taken half a tab at a good time and place, but at least when we took it our destiny was in our hands, among friends and somewhere that felt safe. At times, I laughed so much it caused pains in my sides. Music invariably rose very high with the slower passing of time while love seemed telepathic, connecting everyone.

Mark Wirtz wanted to try LSD, which we did one evening at his high-rise flat next to the GPO Tower. *Sgt. Pepper's Lonely Hearts Club Band* – the most important record of 1967 and very relevant to our lives – was on autoplay, good and loud! At first, Mark got into the feeling but then he opened his balcony door and started saying, 'I think I can fly!' Keith and I pulled him back in and shut the door. He calmed down a bit, but we had to keep an eye on him for the next few hours. On another occasion on LSD, I sat in a room and played my guitar – *all night!* People talked and I accompanied them in a somewhat appropriate fashion. Crazy stuff often happened and people got damaged, some only temporarily, while others were not so lucky. It gradually became unfashionable to trip out as, increasingly, people were having to take time out to recover from the effects that took years to disappear.

Tomorrow managed to meet one of our heroes, the great writer and guitarist Frank Zappa. Twink brought him back to his flat in Eden Grove where Keith and I waited patiently. He told me that my guitar solo on 'Claremount Lake', the B-side of 'My White Bicycle', was one of the best he'd heard. I was knocked out, to say the least. We talked about his band and how we loved *Absolutely Free*, the first Mothers Of Invention album, and all his playing and writing. He was very influential and attitudinal. He used the wah-wah cleverly, like a decoy sound that lurked until he stepped on it, when it burst into life – some weird mish-mash of rhythmic wizardry only happened when he performed.

Near the end of the 1967, enjoying the success of a hit record, Keith kindly bought us both a holiday in Jamaica. We flew over in a VC10, sitting in its big armchairs without seatbelts and smoking (not that I miss that last bit these days). We took two Gibson arch-tops to write with. His Cromwell guitar (made by Gibson but released under a different name) made the trip but my Gibson model that was similar, but sold exclusively through the UK's Francis, Day & Hunter shop, didn't survive. BOAC paid for the repairs, eventually.

We didn't write a whole bunch of things while we were there and, instead, lay around in the sun, wondering if there was any way we could stay there permanently. We also asked ourselves, was life real back in London or was 'this' real? We took a taxi to buy the local produce from Montego Bay, then a shantytown with a marketplace and a line of huts that mostly held shoes for sale. The driver gave our money to a guy on one side of the market and we drove to the opposite side, where a package was thrown into the rear seat. We were holding the notorious 'ganja'. Bob Marley would have been proud.

Smoking this stuff left us stunned sometimes and at other times hysterical. I remember one night, on our way to dinner at our hotel, the waiter said to me, 'Would you like to come this way, madam?' with a wry smile on his face. We just cracked up and fell to the ground giggling, uncontrollably. We weren't at all used to smoking pure stuff from a pipe, and this was pretty raw and brutal. Eventually a guy who was decorating the hotel chalets demonstrated the use of newspapers rolled up like cigarette papers. Apparently, this was the local method, but we were only mildly impressed and continued to miss our Rizlas.

It wasn't long before the two weeks were up and we were climbing back on a VC10 to London, having had a different view of things. We sensed the psychedelic party of 1967 was about to fade into the distance. It was January 1968, after all, and we were only vaguely prepared for the year ahead. The mood was going to change. The gigs dwindled, the group divided into two camps, with Junior and Twink thinking this, and Keith and I thinking that. We were heading in different directions.

Keith and I appreciated the kindness of our friends who shared our Cromwell Gardens all-nighter loft, a beautiful top-floor apartment off Cromwell Road. The nights passed in a wonderful haze of music-playing, food and drink, all merrily consumed, and smoking the pleasantries while talk flowed and later slowed as morning began to appear. There was an open door for anyone they knew.

The *Tomorrow* album wasn't released until February 1968, by which time it was too late to make a big impression. In the middle of 1968 we played the Donington Park festival, one of our last live shows together. Keith was rising to fame in the pop world, which had had both good and bad consequences. We would sometimes be billed as 'Tomorrow featuring Keith West' or 'Keith West & Tomorrow'. Yet his spirit remained very much with the band, as he was sacrificing his solo career by staying with us. He didn't want to be just a pop star but rather a vocalist with a band. In Ireland they expected the Keith West & Tomorrow style of performance and the shows got a little crazy. They wanted the kind of song for which he was now famous, not some out-there psychedelic rock and they threw coins at us. We played a guitar trio arrangement of 'Grocer Jack' that they were less than happy with. No return booking there.

Tomorrow had enormous potential but it now seemed a band of individual talents rather than collective strength. Mark Wirtz had been producing what were supposed to be further Tomorrow 'solo' releases to balance Keith's success with 'Grocer Jack'. I recorded a tune called 'Moth Balls' that never came out. Junior and Twink became The Aquarian Age and released a song, also produced by Mark, called 'Ten Thousand

Words In A Cardboard Box'. Meanwhile, Keith and Mark released their follow-up single to 'Grocer Jack' called 'Sam', which didn't fare so well.

CHAPTER 5

Down By A River

Keith and I moved to the Highgate and Muswell Hill borders, where my brother Philip had some space in the top two floors of a house overlooking Alexandra Palace.

It was here, in an attic room, that I listened to a lot more classical music. It became like a lifeline of head-clearing sounds, often with all the absolute beauty of a full orchestra. Playing music by Vivaldi, Mozart, Villa-Lobos and Bach seemed to revitalise my senses. I thought then that we should never underestimate the power of the performers who brought these writers' works back to life, players like Ashkenazy, J.-P. Rampal, André Previn and John Williams. I sensed also the unquestionable level of genius of many great composers, inventing and orchestrating their works directly on the written stave. They could hear the intricate harmonic modulations, from the highest to the lowest, in their head. From Vivaldi's flute concertos played by J.-P. Rampal to Rodrigo's *Concierto de Aranjuez* played by John Williams, this music had such drama and tension, such subtle release and mellowness, that captivated me, as it still does today. This great musical heritage is left for the hands of dedicated musicians, who reinterpret and redefine the lifeforce within the written dots on the page, bringing it into the moment with their understanding.

As you look further back in time to, say, the Middle Ages, you'll find that music has always represented the mood and sensibilities of its era. Julian Bream, for example, not only played the great twentieth-century guitar music but reintroduced the lute and the music and songs of sixteenth-century composer John Dowland into the concert repertoire. His playing was full of emotion and expression; he truly felt every note he played. *A Life In Music* is a wonderful DVD documentary, where you learn that even Julian played some jazz. In the seventies, Jan and I attended many of Julian's performances in London, and eventually John Williams introduced us after one of the concerts they played as a duo. (Segovia said that the only thing better than a guitar was two guitars!) Julian looked ready to leave his dressing room and seemed to us rather like Zorro, with a wide-brimmed hat and flowing overcoat. Fortunately, he agreed to visit John's flat in Hampstead where I got a chance to talk with him. He asked if I was 'the guitarist with three trucks of equipment'. I had to admit that I was indeed 'that' guitarist.

Around October 1968, Keith began recording solo tracks for EMI on which I played. Some had Ronnie Wood on bass guitar and all featured Ansley Dunbar on drums. On 'On A Saturday' I played Spanish guitar and on the B-side, 'The Kid Was A Killer', I played bass and electric guitar, also playing on his next single, 'She'. Mark continued to have all sorts of sessions for me, a few tracks with Caroline Munro and many German pop covers, all of which I've never heard again.

Sessions were OK – they could be fun. I would meet up with lots of people who had no real responsibilities for each other and three hours later I'd leave, off to another. It was a kind of treadmill. Perhaps that's why I never thought of sessions as any kind of career move. I just played and then got paid (if I was lucky and had a fixer to book the sessions) but I had no royalties, relying on income collected by PPL (Phonographic Performance Limited). If a track sold in large numbers and/or was played on the TV or radio I'd get a small repeat fee via PPL. Bands were what I knew best and I decided that this was where I was going to focus.

For the meantime, I continued doing with other sessions, which somehow led me to Deep Purple's management. They were looking for a guitarist to complete the line-up of a new band they were trying to put together. I met up with Dave Curtis, a singer, writer and bass player and his drummer friend Bobby Woodman (Clarke), who had previously played for Johnny Hallyday. We started out as Canto and recorded a few demos, including 'The Spanish Song', which was released on *Anthology 2*. With the inclusion of a young lad called Clive Skinner (Maldoon), we soon became Bodast – *Bobby-Dave-Steve* – not the best method to settle on a group name, particularly as there was no reference to Clive.

We lived in a rented house in West Finchley on a small weekly salary, writing our songs and hoping to get gigs. I have never or since been supported in this way. We were tied up in terms of management and publishing and this meant our weekly wage was like an advance which could be recouped if and when income came in. We wrote and rehearsed a fair bit around the time The Beatles' *White Album* was released to much hurrah. Things were moving at a slow pace, but at least I was still living my dream and was free to write and play whatever I wanted. We sounded pretty good, too.

Friday evenings saw the arrival of a friend with an interesting briefcase. Click, click went the latches and in front of us would be a choice array of Moroccan, Afghanistani and Indian hashish plus kief and Thai sticks or African grass. Hash was about £8 an ounce. So many respectable people enjoyed these mellow substances. It was obviously already pervasive, so much so that even the police force enjoyed it. But old-fashioned UK culture fought anyway, not realising they could never control it. It has remained a universal pleasure, like drinking wine or beer, but it's only more recently that we've begun to see it legalised anywhere in the world. Holland was first. Many of us enjoy visiting their coffee shops. Now, of course, the US has opened its floodgates, state by state, with different takes and different laws. I'm not interested in grass any more, I've always been more European in my tastes.

Music and lifestyle and love collided with Bodast. We only played a handful of shows, one of which was on 4 July 1969, at the Royal Albert Hall pop proms, the only pop music proms ever, as far as I am aware. The Who played the first night and Chuck Berry played the second, backed by Bodast – minus myself. I only found out during the rehearsal that afternoon. We had already soundchecked when Chuck arrived. He came on stage and pointed at me: 'We don't need you.' Presumably I interfered somehow with his plans. Unperturbed, I later took my 175 backstage and asked him what he thought of it. He played and said, 'Yeah! This is a damn good guitar.' I've only allowed one other guitarist to play my very best guitar, the impeccable Martin Taylor, and that was when we recorded *Masterpiece Guitars* in 1998.

Chuck Berry generally played the Gibson slimline range of semi-acoustics, like the ES-340 T and later the ES-345 Stereo or ES-355. He would hire two Fender Showman or Fender Twin amplifiers, playing through both on stage. I'd listened to him so much in my early days. He was the first singer, player and writer to have his own hits in the fifties. Besides his recordings, he headlined the first package show I ever saw. Carl Perkins and The Animals were also on the bill at the Lewisham theatre in London. (In 1980, the *Drama* line-up of Yes would also play there.)

The year 1969 ushered in a totally new phase of my life. My first wife, Pat Stebbings, gave birth to our son Dylan and the idea of family became my whole focus. I could no longer see things selfishly or in the short term. Providing for them became my motivation. Although our marriage wasn't to last, Dylan received all the love and attention possible. In 1971, it would be my responsibility to raise him. Not many husbands get this opportunity. I wouldn't have been able to succeed with this had it not been for Jan Osborne, whom I married later in 1975, and she made this intricate transition work. Love is so many different things all happening at once. It often shifts from one perspective to another and the changes always take some negotiating because there's so much to learn about raising children. I can clearly remember a red pedal-car that we gave Dylan on his 2nd birthday in 1971 when he returned from Malta with Jan after a holiday with her family. This thrilled him so much; he went riding off around the courtyard of the flats we had moved to. Jan later gave birth to three of our children – Virgil in 1975 (who tragically passed away in 2017), Georgia in 1982 and Stephanie in 1986. From 1971 onwards, Jan was the most important person in the world to me.

Bodast were still living rather hand-to-mouth, although we recorded an album at Trident Studios with engineer Ken Scott and producer Keith West for a label called Tetragrammaton. Unfortunately, they closed their UK setup and the record was never released. The feeling of rejection and the problems that pursued us undermined the whole operation. The recordings would lie dormant for eight years until our wonderful vocalist,

Clive Skinner, who was also a fine writer, fell victim to a sleeping tablet. He had forgotten he'd taken it and drank alcohol, although perhaps the mix was made also because he felt neglected and under-appreciated. Hearing of his death while on tour in the US during 1978, I felt motivated to remix the recordings in stereo and I asked Gary Lanham to engineer. We had a budget for one day and completed all eight tracks. Cherry Red released the results later in 1978 on vinyl, calling it *The Lost Bodast Tapes*. Later the recordings were released on CD including the stereo and the original mono mixes. Finally, in 2017, a remastered version was released called *Towards Utopia*, the best version.

I'd thought of all the struggles in previous bands as my apprenticeship in the music business but it was now becoming clear that our livelihoods depended on a strange psychological balance. Grasping the situation at hand meant that any musical weight you brought in allowed you a level of undefined control. Many other things contributed to the balance but control was fundamental. Confidence didn't have to be arrogance. I learned to take musical criticism and be able to sympathetically criticise other people's ideas, generally for the betterment of the band. I had become used to the mutual dependence that came with living together, in what was a really a commune. Yet we left Finchley under a cloud, when Deep Purple's management decided to fire us after a naff engineer at Kingsway Studios alleged that he'd seen us taking heroin. OMG, no way! We assured them this wasn't true but they fired us anyway, right before Christmas.

We moved to a house in Lots Road, Fulham. It had been previously occupied by the group Family, who had painted the interior walls completely black, and it is here that I had another extreme learning curve. A fellow resident was that space cadet of an early rock singer, Vince Taylor. He rarely ventured out of his room, usually only into the kitchen. We were never sure what he did the rest of the time! People came and went, moved in, then out, stopped overnight and then returned with newly born children! It was gritty and a real down-to-earth existence. There were so many bizarre happenings, as people would freak out and run amok in a drug- or drink-induced state. We ate an awful lot of rice, onions and tuna fish. It was our staple diet.

Believing that our album recordings had been canned for good, I later used my parts from a song called 'The Ghost Of Nether Street' for Yes's 'Starship Trooper'. It reappeared as 'Würm'. I kept the chords – G, E flat and C – with modified bass routes and the opening theme of my guitar break after Yes had built the structure up and up. Riffs in 'Southside Of The Sky' came from 'Tired Towers', 'Close To The Edge' has a part from 'Black Leather Gloves' and the verses of 'One Step Closer' by Asia are based on the end section of 'Come Over Stranger'. My structures and melodies showed themselves able to work in different stylistic frameworks.

I quit Bodast, but before I did there was another big letdown. We were spotted by an American production company who thought we were perfect for a movie capturing the rise to fame of an unknown band. They could see we were struggling but they believed we would make it, big time, and planned to film the band in 35 mm. They said they would get back to us with a deal (i.e. money) within three weeks. Nothing happened and they blanked our attempts to get in touch.

I decided enough was enough. After all, earlier that year I'd walked away from positions with other working bands that had gigs, including The Nice featuring Keith Emerson, a must-see band. Keith's playing was steering them towards notoriety. After Davy O'List left, they were looking for a guitarist. The afternoon I spent playing with them remains fresh in my mind. We tried some of their tunes while Keith and I talked about what we could do together since we both loved the music of Antonio Vivaldi – I later wrote 'The Nature Of The Sea' for my first solo album, drawing from Vivaldi's *La Tempesta di Mare* flute concerto. It seemed as if we were destined to play together, I agreed to join and we subsequently went to a pub and met their manager. He took money out of his back pocket which he distributed while we were at the bar. It seemed a bit unprofessional.

I got back to the house in Nether Street, Finchley, and explained to the guys that I was going to leave. They were very unhappy. The band would fold, we would lose our accommodation and our wages and be out in the street. By the next morning I had reversed my decision, mainly as I didn't want to leave the rest of Bodast in the lurch and I was concerned about the style of The Nice's management. This was not the way to make good career decisions, as you must always look beyond the effects of merely moving on.

I also auditioned for Atomic Rooster. The music didn't jell and I wasn't that keen. The extraordinary thing is that Carl Palmer was the drummer but, by the time we played together in Asia, he said he couldn't remember this audition. I also had a call about a gig with Jethro Tull after Mick Abrahams left them, but it was stressed, 'No writing is required.' They just wanted a guitarist and that sounded alarm bells. I needed an opening with a new band – I wanted to have an effect on creating the identity of a sound.

Having soldiered on through some very bleak times for little return, I needed to get the word out that I was looking for a new guitar-playing position. In late 1969 I got a call from Jim Morris, who was married to and managed singer P. P. Arnold, asking if I would play with Pat along with Ashton, Gardner & Dyke, a really good, organ-based trio. They were opening for Delaney & Bonnie with Eric Clapton on a month-long European tour. Of course, I was delighted by the idea, something of a warm-up for the time when Yes would open for Iron Butterfly in 1971. This tour was a major step forwards and it was a seriously good buzz.

We rehearsed for a while with Pat and then eventually we visited the Lyceum theatre in London, where Delaney & Bonnie with Eric C. were doing final rehearsals. When Delaney & Bonnie kicked into a song we were all blown away. The huge stomping sound from this line-up could never be reproduced: it was awesome and exciting and nicely captured on record by Jimmy Miller. That provided a beautiful memory of the tour. I know every note of every song on the live album.

We started the tour on a bus heading for George Harrison's home to pick him up. He played on the tour for the first week, along with Dave Mason, who stayed throughout. Every night, they rocked the venues. At the Fairfield Hall in Croydon, the DJ couldn't make it to introduce the show and I stepped in. The walk-in music ended and it was up to me to announce who was going to play and when. It was kind of scary but a good confidence-builder.

I very much regret not taking up the invitation to join Delaney & Bonnie and Eric on stage. I was a touch shy and felt that, with Eric, Delaney, George and Dave playing, there would be too many guitarists. It was a missed opportunity. I remember Eric one day saying to me on the tour bus that, although we were both born under the Aries birth signs, we were nonetheless 'very different' Arians.

I saw so much to admire in Eric on that tour alone, never mind everything he's done for music and the betterment of others since. He's always been generous and considerate. I visited his apartment in central London before the tour and he asked me if I knew how to play Mason Williams' 'Classical Gas'. I played it and he was pleasantly amused. Another time he had Albert Lee playing in his band when we happened to be staying at the same hotel in Chicago. I visited Eric's room for half an hour along with Albert. We did a little tentative jamming before deciding we were all quite tired so we wrapped up with a quick game of pool on the hotel's table.

The Delaney & Bonnie tour took in Scandinavia and went all over Europe. It was an all-round fabulous experience, listening nightly to their riveting music. I had already written 'Clap' and I'm sure one night I played it during Pat's set. The tour nicely occupied all of December and was my first close encounter with a big-time music experience. How else would I have heard George Harrison strumming his acoustic guitar and singing 'Here Comes The Sun' in a dressing room? It was unforgettable. Also, I heard George give an interview in a Manchester hotel lobby. He ran amok with his wit – he was so funny, an absolute charmer. He and I talked guitars many times. He had a custom guitar by Gibson that he felt hadn't come out completely right – they had reinterpreted his order. Custom Gibson guitars of any kind were something quite rare at this time. Britain was starved of high-end models for a long time and we had to rely on European manufacturers until the more desirable makes started coming in.

One of the UK's first sightings of a Fender Stratocaster was on the cover of *The 'Chirping' Crickets*, where Buddy Holly clasps an example of what is arguably the most played and recognisable guitar in the world. So much drooling went on over that sleeve, on which another Cricket held a Gibson ES-225T model. Our excitement was born out of the hunger to see and play these US rock guitars that would become classics. I'd collected guitar brochures simply to examine the shapes and colours, only imagining the exquisite sounds that might come from them, especially when wired through a Watkins Copicat echo chamber, blaring out of a Vox amp.

As the sixties progressed I'd watch players switch guitars for different songs, often between a Fender Telecaster and a Gibson ES-335. Their timbres differ considerably, driving the music in different directions. The thin, icy tone of a Telecaster's cutting treble twang contrasted with the thicker, deeper 'gonk' of a 335. Their construction makes them feel distinctly individual, too. Their lure hangs from the strap as you become a proficient guitarist. I often say that it is only when I actually walk on stage that I fully realise that I *am* a guitarist.

When I'm about to play on stage, nothing else should interfere: it's pure music time – leave the baggage and everything else backstage. On 1957's *Sing A Song Of Basie* the vocal trio of Lambert, Hendricks & Ross sing a collection of lyrics written by Jon Hendricks to a dozen Count Basie tunes, one of which is Basie's 'Blues Backstage'. This often goes round in my head. It's about a guy whose 'girl just quit with him' right before a performance. The show must go on, but underneath he's frowning, hiding his feelings. It can take some doing when you're not feeling good but you have to perform (been there, done it – all too often). It was my sister Stella who got me into this record. It's filled with dynamic energy and swings like the clappers, as they wisely used Basie's rhythm section of Nat Piece on piano, Freddie Greene on guitar and Eddie Jones on drums. Another great song from this collection is 'Pony Ride', which ends with a vocal breakdown where they scat, 'Get a record that'll play a week… Good bebop good be… What a wonderful pony ride.' They created multi-tracked harmonies beyond what Mary Ford had recorded with Les Paul.

It has to be said that the voice is the greatest instrument we have. Everyone has an opinion about it, but its supremacy is obvious. We first hear sounds – including talking and singing – when we're in the womb. As a newborn baby, way before seeing anything, sounds connect us to the world. Sounds totally connect us to language as all speech has pitch (this is particularly true the further east you go in the world). If you listen to a spoken phrase over and over it becomes more obvious. There are ascending statements crossing over descending statements. Subconsciously, this is how we detect the mood of the person speaking. Accents are a beautiful variation within language. In the UK, our ears are geared to detect someone's hometown from their local accent. This is the same the world over. We are able to recognise our own national and local accents. Similarly, we can tell where someone is from by their accent, even if we can't understand a word they say.

I hope your linguistic powers are better than mine. I'm a monoglot, having failed to grasp any foreign language. But singing is a joy everyone should or could experience. I learned a fair bit about singing during gigs and studio recordings of the seventies, as I had done little public singing before that. In fact, it wasn't until 1993 that I actually took a singing lesson, from Tona DeBrett, who taught many great singers from her north London home. This was to prepare myself for the vocals on my fourth solo album, *The Grand Scheme Of Things*. With Yes I've mainly sung the 'low parts' – they're the only parts I know! – as I have a deep voice. This worked well in support of Jon and Chris, who both sang high, giving us a very distinctive sound.

In the late sixties, writing and recording guitar ideas and songs on different tape systems was a learning process in itself. My

Down By A River

brother John had an early home-recording machine, a Grundig mono recorder that was regularly set up to record the BBC's *Saturday Club* radio pop show. John recorded The Shadows playing 'Apache' live in the studio before I bought the single and I remember how alive it sounded compared to the tame release.

When I started recording guitar ideas at home, I tried to use a German Telefunken two-track tape machine that was quite complex due to its complicated tape path between the spools. The text on the buttons was in German, which didn't make it easier. Cassette players became available later on and these were quickly followed by cassette-based recording decks. Finally, they released portable, battery-operated machines with built-in monophonic microphones. I had one with a vari-speed. This was useful as cassette machines never ran at exactly the right speed, and with this model I could adjust playback to bring it back to concert pitch. Long before digital tuners we used a tuning fork as a pitch reference (or a piano, if it had been tuned, or an organ).

With these machines I could capture an idea, rethink it and rearrange it later, as I saw fit. Since I didn't read or write music down in any conventional method, this is how I wrote music. I still have an enormous collection of writing cassettes from home and from tours. Writing with other people fills many sides of these tapes. They're usually labelled with a town or city name, often with audio of me writing with Jon Anderson or plucking away alone in some hotel room. Later mini-cassettes came out and *way* too much could be stored on these tiniest of tapes. It was extremely hard to correlate what was on them. They played backwards, too!

For many years I've compiled my own ideas, creating a library from which I can extract and use music when it's needed. Back then, everything was so extremely low-tech that there was no real reference for it. Things could only get better. There's much one could say about the history and development of sound recording. *The Guinness Book Of Recorded Sound* covers early periods very well, as does *Perfecting Sound Forever* by Greg Milner, one of the many interesting newer books about recording and releasing music. Analogue ruled, with its glowing valves and solder connections, cables everywhere leading to and fro, transformers and many other bulky boxes that each did just one single audio job. These were the days of inherent distortion and hum, yet so many great recordings were made with only a few tracks and a few editing tricks up the recording engineer's sleeve.

Physically cutting tape between takes, movements, or even cutting between a different day's work, formed a fine old tradition. The engineer used to need loads of razor blades, Sellotape, cutting blocks and chinagraph pencils. One small mistake could have catastrophic consequences. Today, digital editing is employed for just about everything we hear. Now we achieve and prefer everything in time, in tune and we are able to switch everything around at a whim, after the main event. It's called post-production. Thank goodness we can now reorganise anything about our music. The Pro Tools recording system has become the music business industrial standard, aided by thousands of plug-ins, one of which can pitch and time change to extremely minute degrees, sort out words to align in-sync and has every possible mixing option imaginable. If you can imagine something, it can be done. (You might go round in circles at the same time...)

By this point I had six good years of gigging around venues in the UK and Europe, quite a lot of session work and one released (two recorded) albums behind me, and I was ready to take serious steps towards becoming a noteworthy guitarist. Building on being me, myself (and I), I hoped and believed that something would happen, as throughout my career there's been a strange pattern where I would only be out of one band for about two months before being in another. Something would come my way so I could be off playing again.

CHAPTER 6

No Disgrace

One day in early January 1970 I climbed a steep staircase to answer the payphone that hung on the wall of the first-floor landing at our mostly redecorated house in Fulham. It was Chris Squire of Yes and I agreed to meet them for an audition in a few days.

Jon Anderson had seen me playing at the Speakeasy with Bodast and Chris knew me from shows with Tomorrow. The offer sounded promising – they had a manager, a record deal, gigs, an advance for new equipment and a retainer of £25 per week. Yes had recorded two albums: *Yes*, and the soon-to-be-released *Time And A Word*. Both featured Jon Anderson, Chris Squire, Tony Kaye, Bill Bruford and guitarist Peter Banks.

I took my 175 and a few pedals to the cramped basement of their manager's house in Barnes, south-west London, where I met the band and we played a few songs. We played songs like 'Everydays' and 'Then'. The abundance of talent in the band was enormous, but it was Bill Bruford's drums that riveted me to the ground. We all seemed to get on quite well and later I went with Jon to his flat in South Kensington. We swapped ideas about ReVox recordings and cats. Yes had liked what I played and offered me the gig. I accepted. The chemistry had such strong potential and we all had an abundance of high ideals.

Soon enough there were gigs to play. My first performance with Yes was on 17 July 1970, at London's Lyceum Ballroom. I'd learned much of the *Time And A Word* album and parts of *Yes*. I wasn't too sure how well I'd played on the night but bootleg recordings make it sound like I was having fun. I didn't stick rigidly to Peter's parts but usually played his main melodic lines. He was an interesting guitarist to have to follow. He, too, adopted different guitar styles and had already set a scene I could relate to. He was a sweet guy and came to many of our early gigs. I can't think of many other ex-band members doing that – I mean, right after they've left the band. This was a whole new beginning for my love of doing live gigs, and I went for it, big time, with all my energy. Tomorrow was the last group I remembered feeling this good about. As the belief built within the audiences and the critics began to take note, it was apparent we were hot. A new album could establish that this new line-up was capable of even greater things in the studio.

The sleeve of *Time And A Word* had been rejected by the US market, where it was considered too sexist, and a brand-new picture of the current line-up was used on the cover instead. For this reason, many people in the US thought I was the original Yes guitarist. I took issue with Atlantic Records about this and, eventually, the UK image was adopted for the States. It doesn't really surprise me there's so much confusion over who was in the band at any given time, not just with albums, as this would keep happening when other members left or returned. We'd often show up for a show and see an out-of-date photo of the band with a wrong ex-member included: Tony after Rick joined, Bill after Alan joined and Patrick after Rick re-joined. It went on for years.

Plans to rehearse an album in the countryside to escape the big city were advanced by a call to a young promoter in Devon. He found us Church Hill house in the small village of Churchill, Barnstable, where we stayed for two weeks, setting about creating the embryos of 'Perpetual Change' and 'Yours Is No Disgrace'. We soon felt restricted. It wasn't nice enough and evening sessions had to end too early for our liking. The promoter placed an advert in the local paper, 'Band looking for rehearsal space and boarding', leading us to an old farmhouse where we stayed for two months, finishing off writing and rehearsing most of *The Yes Album*. This new rehearsal space turned out to be quite special.

A mile-long drive down a single-track country lane led to the old, thatch-roofed farmhouse. It was completely in the middle of nowhere, absolutely no neighbours. I banged my head on the low door going in. I'd never been anywhere like this before in my life. It had character and a certain strange charm. All the ceilings were low with nooks and crannies in every corner. In the Domesday Book, of all things, it lists a dwelling on this piece of land and parts of the current house dated back over three hundred years. Ten years later, Jan and I bought the place. It's become my workstation, studio, equipment store and an occasional family retreat. Yes added something to the history of this building but, like many old farmhouses, it needed people to care for it. Jan and I seemed to be those people and our renovations would see it into the next millennium.

We were able to play any time we wanted. The place was a Devon longhouse and at that point owned by the Dartnall family, who slept some distance from our evening and late-night practice sessions. The next day they'd be up early in the morning to feed their animals on their hundred-acre farm. The band could all focus on the work at hand as nobody had to travel to play. We were highly industrious and even after dinner we'd often get quite a lot done, from considering song fragments to learning each other's riffs and trying out words and finding different rhythms to complement melody lines. This resulted in some of the best examples of our arrangement skills.

Jon might say, 'Let's go down', Chris might add, 'But after, let's go up again', then Bill might add, 'But in double time', and we'd try out all these ideas and agree on which was best. That sounds a lot easier than it was to accomplish in practice, of course. Often, I would try to record us playing an arrangement on a reel-to-reel machine or cassette for our reference, as only too often the very next day we'd forgotten what we'd done or couldn't agree on how we'd left a song the day before.

Chord structure charts helped but we didn't notate much, just the outline in chord symbols. I could understand mine, but no one else could. Often charts were made as the song was being constructed, before it had a title. Later we might change the key or write a new beginning. Connecting an untitled chart to a particular song was often difficult. I've got plenty of early notebooks in which each page is a mishmash of chord patterns and arrangement notes. I can tie some of these to a particular song, while others have scribbled working titles that are really as good as anonymous. However, I do have many titled chord charts that come in handy after not playing a song for thirty years or so. Most of the arrangements are stored in my head, somewhere, somehow…

Before rehearsals started on sunny days, I would wander about in the fields playing my Martin guitar, sometimes recording ideas on cassette. I composed a lot of pieces that would later infiltrate the band's music. When I played the band my first country-picking guitar instrumental, 'Clap', they said that it ought to be on the new record. This was an important moment for me. I was delighted they felt it could fit alongside the pieces we were writing together. A solo spot was a golden opportunity to introduce myself. Bill and I came up with the title, but then Jon announced it on the live recording as 'The Clap' which, unfortunately, stuck for quite a while.

We carried on putting together songs, like 'Your Move' and 'I've Seen All Good People' and continued to develop 'Yours Is No Disgrace' and 'Perpetual Change'. I recall that 'Starship Trooper' and 'A Venture' were written exclusively in the studio. 'Starship' would become one of our most popular live songs. It's really three different segments yet it comes across as one whole song. We just couldn't say enough in three minutes and twenty seconds. We needed eight to ten minutes to explore our material, develop its ideas and transcend the formula of a typical song. We imagined the lyrics might lure the listener into a dreamlike state with surreal combinations of finely articulated music twisting their expectations.

After a few weeks of working like this, the manager showed up with bad news. He was leaving and taking some of the money from the pot that was apparently due to him. This was the end of the £25 a week that was anyway barely enough to keep us alive. Now there was only the gig money to support us. Times were hard once more, but there was one eventual win. The manager had planned to hold on to his share of the publishing, acquired through also being the publisher. To take commission on the writer's share and own part of the publisher's share was considered unconstitutional and illegal and this was later terminated. After all, it was simply 5 per cent for nothing!

One evening in June, near the end of our stay, after Jon, Bill and Chris had all gone to bed, Tony Kaye and I looked at the embers in the fireplace and, for some crazy reason, took half a tab of LSD each. This would be the very last time I'd go through this experience, possibly because it was the best time. The effects began to take hold and we went into the rehearsal room, a small parlour next to the main lounge. Our equipment sat there humming away. We noticed that the Leslie cabinet connected to the Hammond organ was really whirling. Tony played the chord of F major and, ten minutes later, we were both still amazed at what we could hear – shifting harmonics, unimaginable overtones and total musical fulfilment! Later, just before morning, we left the house to explore the outside world, the world of nature. We were deep in the remote English countryside. Tony and I climbed aboard our Rover three-litre car and very slowly drove about the local neighbourhood, along single-track roads. We passed pink cottages with wall flowers all over them, and a man walked by, looking ghostly as he waved to us. On our return to the farm we couldn't help but notice that the chickens looked so 'nice'. We lay on the ground next to the birds, to see the patterns of their feathers were the same as the patterns in the pores of our skin. We laughed with amazement till Mr Dartnall came out and asked, 'What are you doing?' We sort of fobbed him off as if it wasn't unusual to be out at 5.30 a.m., crawling on our hands and knees on the hard cobblestones admiring his chickens. It was a long, fun night.

Atlantic Records, fortunately, came through with a deal for the third album, the last they were contractually committed to release. Although I didn't know it then, it was said that if this album wasn't successful they would drop us from their roster. It could be curtains for Yes if this new record didn't chart and sell loads of copies. With a new deal, we were finally ready to book some studio time

Eddie Offord was invited to engineer, as he'd done with *Time And A Word* (with Tony Coltan producing) and also to co-produce with us. He was gaining a reputation as a hot young engineer and the team-up was a good opportunity for both sides. It would reap benefits for many years to come. He knew instinctively how to balance us while we played different lines across one another, a style that made the levels and positioning of each part extremely critical. His unique audio style came to the fore. He was comparatively innocent of the madness of the music business and its temptations, making him a bit of a back-room boy who just loved the technical side of recording and compensating considerably for the fact that we knew very little about it. He gained our confidence, helping to select which takes were good enough. He was our sixth member, an extra pair of ears that we particularly needed when we were out in the studio hammering away.

We were at home in Advision Studios. Eddie was the main resident engineer at this well-equipped complex of two studios – one large, one small, each with its own control room, as is well documented in *The Great British Recording Studios* by Howard Massey. So it was that in the middle of 1970 we knuckled down to our own 'adventure in modern recording'.

We were serious about our commitment to some kind of higher music. I thought it was a continuation of psychedelic rock but it later became dubbed 'progressive rock', or 'prog rock' for short. Others thought of it as orchestral or symphonic rock. I preferred my idea of calling it soft rock, but this never caught on. The backing tracks were masterpieces in their own right, our road maps to fantastic parts we hoped to overlay. They were meticulously inspected and improved upon whenever possible.

The Yes Album utilised all the technology available to us at the time. We were on an enormous learning curve, driven by the desire for recognition and success. Having being one of the first studios in London to upgrade from eight-track, Advision had sixteen-track multi-track machines early on. Often, we'd record backing tracks with just guitar, bass and drums, plus a guide vocal if it was a song segment. We overdubbed keyboard parts later. Only occasionally, when recording a keyboard lead structure, I'd sit it out and leave it to Tony or, later on, Rick, Patrick, Igor or Geoff.

On 'Your Move' we started with me playing my Portuguese twelve-string guitar against a bass and drum loop, repeating a 'dub-dub' phrase until the start of the second half of the song. I mapped it on out on tape according to the agreed arrangement – intro, verse, chorus, etc. Later, we recorded the recorder parts I'd thought up, starting just before verse two. This was played by Colin Goldring. (On my 2001 acoustic solo album *Natural Timbre* I re-recorded 'Your Move' as an instrumental with the recorder part played by Andrew Jackman.)

We would add three-part harmonies, solos and dreamy embellishments, making for those 'Yes moments'. Most of the band liked to stay in the control room throughout the overdub sessions to hear and comment on the new ideas. It really was a collaborative band, but it didn't all happen without some difficulties. I wasn't entirely ready for the baggage that came with two highly competitive musicians who, since the beginning, had fought over its direction and for its control. Perhaps I'd been born to sit between these two battling factions. I could only come up with worthwhile compromises by having an intelligent opinion with complete indifference to who won – neither could lose out the whole time. I was the new guy on the block who didn't know the depths to which this rivalry could take us. The tension between them would continue in perpetuity.

Conflict halts the flow of a band as the creative fuel of collaboration struggles to find balance. We all tried ideas that met with someone's resistance but it was also important to realise that to insist on your own ideas too much would make you appear inflexible. Vast improvements could be made in the studio to revitalise songs as we attempted perfectionism. Each song needed to be different, colourful and emotional.

Tony Kaye was positioned perfectly on the Hammond organ and piano, giving me a big and exciting window to play through. There was not a moment where I was uncomfortable with anything I played. It appeared to me that soft rock perfectly fitted this record. It's fun listening now to the clarity and mellowness of the triplet lines I play over the theme in 'Yours Is No Disgrace'. My 175 is so adaptable. I play it virtually throughout, except for the acoustics and the 1967 Antoria LG50 electric guitar that appears at the end of 'Perpetual Change'. This has more of a Fender sound. With hardly any choice of guitars, I stayed focused on getting more from less.

'Perpetual Change' includes many contrasting structures. It's broad, with dynamics highlighted at every turn and the route the counter-riff section (two line-ups of Yes simultaneously) takes to the final chorus is very complex, yet mathematically logical. We'd often talk about how two independent musical ideas could start together, be in different time signatures, cross over each other, but then conclude their cycles on the same beat as the other. We'd sometimes hear different harmonies, one note in a passing chord or scale might be played or sung a semitone up or down, then the questions went the rounds: 'How does that sound to you?' 'Was it better with an E flat or a D?' Sometimes it could be resolved by a majority vote or even one person's insistence that they were right. The ear is an unusual organ and, as with our other senses, we have our own taste or opinions, as the ear seems to be incredibly refined and different in every individual.

On 'Yours Is No Disgrace', the guitar solo was really exploratory. The band have stops while I play down low with a wah-wah pedal, then several other sections develop. A couple of moving chord parts alternate with slide-ups between the guitar and organ and a sustained, muted, melodic guitar part comes in with dreamy echo and delays that wind up and down gently before it's superseded by a dry and close-up jazzier-style section, ending with a rising/falling/rising chord progression. Quite a mix of divergent ideas. After I'd recorded the solo, Bill said, 'I wish I'd known what you were going to play on top.' The truth is, I didn't entirely know myself!

I will never forget recording 'Clap' at the Lyceum Ballroom in the Strand. Hearing the recording today brings back into sharp focus the way I felt playing it on stage that night. It was pretty intense and stimulating, with all the vitality of a newly found freedom. It was recorded on a ReVox two-track-simple machines but they had great Swiss quality, built to travel and built to last.

The responsibility for the final mixing sessions of *The Yes Album* lay mainly on Eddie Offord's shoulders but was shared by Jon, Chris, Tony and me. Eddie sat dead centre, overseeing the drums and the overall mix, with me on the guitar faders, Chris on the bass, Jon on vocals and Tony on the keyboard. If any member couldn't be there, Eddie took care of their levels, but we all wanted a great mix and rarely left our perch. Listening 'in solo', which commonly meant that you'd hear something 'on its own', came to have a sarcastic use – your track was 'so low' in the mix that you couldn't hear it. The slightest change in one fader would bring about fader movements from other members.

Eddie had the final say on the overall mixing from his supposedly less biased position. He didn't play an instrument and didn't have any particular axe to grind. He would orchestrate the balance beautifully, helping us to achieve the sounds we had in our heads.

We found a new manager, Brian Lane, after Bill, Chris and I had been booked for a session at Advision to play for a young singer managed by Lane, who took a shine to us. He was to endure through many periods of Yes. Working at Hemdale movie production company just as their fortune took a big surge upwards, his style was to run his business without others knowing too much about it, almost from his back pocket. He arrived at the right time. We needed someone to sell our show to the whole wide world. 'A-deal-a-day Lane' became a nickname we'd laugh about, checking in with him to see if he'd done his deal of the day. (Brian once negotiated a deal for me with Martin Guitars that meant I was to receive any number of guitar strings for free, for ever. I let them off the hook on that!) Touring would increase his desire for us to make money and, although not everything was strictly above board, he made the wheels turn in such a way that we got the action and results we wanted – an album at UK No. 1 and US No. 30. Gigs were plentiful in the UK and Europe. We had the music; he had the mouth.

Yes continued to travel about the UK in a green Rover two-litre car. It endured many an adventure. Late one night we were returning from a gig in Plymouth when Chris drove at the same time as he was talking to Tony sitting next to him. Seeing, as Chris hadn't, that we were approaching an oncoming car, in their lane, I yelled, 'Look out, Chris!' Both cars veered to avoid a head-on collision but there was still a hell of a bang as the cars met side-on. We were taken to hospital. Tony came off worst, with a broken ankle. We were released later that night. When we posed for the album photo, Tony had his foot in a cast.

Another time, Chris got out of a car on a hill, leaving both our families inside and the gear in neutral, but forgot about the handbrake. Somehow he struggled back just in time to brake before a T-junction.

To this day, I prefer driving myself or at least being sure I have an attentive driver. I still tend to keep a close eye on what's happening around me. After these early experiences, I know how dangerous roads can be.

CHAPTER 7

Butterflies

On 3 January 1971, we began a big tour, opening for Iron Butterfly in England and Europe.

We learned so much, like the importance of having a soundcheck every day. It paid huge dividends. Our expectations about the quality of live sound increased after we noted that Iron Butterfly brought their own American PA system to Europe. We bought it from them for the considerable sum of £5,000, loaned by Hemdale. This system had Ampex mixers, two W-bins, and mid-range and high-frequency horns that projected the band's sound better than anything else around at the time.

We had a lot of laughs with the guys in Iron Butterfly. There was rarely a dull moment. Amsterdam was memorable for them as Americans: they hadn't ever visited this city of freedom, where getting high was legal. The coffee shops were frequented, though everything had to be disposed of before leaving Holland and the back of the bus got very smoky as the guys savoured the last of their stash.

The Albert Hall gig on 13 January goes down in my memory as a crystalline show at which we were at home and on form. Music journalists – *Melody Maker*'s Chris Welch in particular –

were writing really nice things about us. We sometimes stole the show from Iron Butterfly but they weren't under any pressure and continued to deliver their great performance. We jammed together on 25 January in Copenhagen and the European leg lasted until 2 February, when we played in Paris. The number of gigs we did back then was remarkable.

We were now combining material from *The Yes Album* and *Time And A Word* on stage, creating a neat set list that included 'The Bass Odyssey', which became an extremely rare bootlegged recording. This was a duelling bass extravaganza between Chris and me. In one section we harmonised a tune I had picked up from the great jazz guitarist Jim Hall, in a recording by the Chico Hamilton Trio called 'Blues On The Rocks', written by the bass player George Duvivier. Other parts were similar to later riffs used in 'Sound Chaser'. The song 'A Venture' was another such vehicle in this unmastered work. I played Chris's Fender Telecaster bass as it was better than my own Vox bass. Since we both had Fender Dual Showman amps (Chris had two), which have two 15-inch speakers, the bass didn't tear my speakers apart. We had extension cabinets that fanned out over the back line so we could hear each other with the actual sound we produced. This was most certainly the best system we ever used, and I wish it was still implemented today. It gave a true stage balance, enabling us to create more real light and shade.

This concept was replaced by 'monitoring', a separate system that sends each player whatever they want to hear to their own personal speaker cabinet, usually on the floor in front of them, a mix controlled and balanced by the monitor engineer. We were sceptical at first, as tones could change from the original source, particularly when a stereo signal was sent to a mono cabinet. We had relied on the ability to hear each other's actual dynamics and volume levels, controlled by ourselves and we came to rely immensely on a skilled monitor mixer, a distinct role from that of front-of-house (FOH) engineer. I have always got on well with engineers – they're good people to have on your side. There are stories about Eddie Offord, who became our most flamboyant and famous FOH engineer. We were looking for people with a high sense of professionalism and expertise. We needed to be at the leading edge of technology to pull together the best possible show.

Our more general goal for the band itself was breaking the US market, where Atlantic Records hoped to sell high-quality product. *The Yes Album* opened up the market with Yes's first chart entry in the US at No. 30. Premier Talent, a big booking agency with a roster of hugely successful acts, remained our agents for the US until 1980's *Drama*. Their Barbara Skydel stuck with us throughout. Our first North American tour, supporting Jethro Tull, started on 24 June 1971, in Edmonton, Canada.

We spent the week before getting acclimatised to the time change in New York, a very scary place at the time. This was a different world and not all was to the good. We stayed near a busy fire station with sirens ringing out day and night. The people in the street below seemed either homeless or unemployable. From that base we promoted the album with interviews, before meeting Atlantic co-founder Ahmet Ertegun and other record company executives and then heading on to Canada.

Waiting in the dressing room just before our first set, there was something missing... nothing to smoke. Someone was supposed to be looking into it, and in the nick of time a familiar substance arrived and things got off to a good, high start. Canada had strong European ties and I've always felt more at home there. How we managed to get to Vancouver to play the second show the very next day, I'm not quite sure, but we managed it in time. We then toured down from Washington State to Los Angeles in California, followed by cities in the Midwest and Texas, before reaching the north-east corner and a slew of cities like Detroit, Philadelphia and New York, ending on 24 July in New Haven, Connecticut. Lo and behold, only six days later Yes were playing at the Crystal Palace Garden Party in London with Elton John. This was to be our last gig with Tony Kaye.

A writing and rehearsal period ensued in a ballet school in Mayfair, London, when it became apparent that Tony wasn't going to become the multi-keyboard player we felt he ought to be. I can say without any doubt that there were absolutely no personal issues going on that determined Tony's departure. He was a good team player and his performances were always exciting, but a change was inevitable and we started talking about what sort of guy we were looking for. Whoever it was had to be already heading in the direction of what we were looking for – someone with an ear for expanded sound textures, virtuosity and good equipment.

In August we went to see The Strawbs to watch their keyboard player Rick Wakeman in action. We all liked his style and asked him to our rehearsal room. This run-through went well; he had all the angles covered, producing a much wider sound palette with organ, piano, harpsichord and his use of early synths. Each came across through his fine technique. He appeared to have the same standards and capabilities as us and could move things up a gear or two.

While on tour in Scotland, Jon Anderson and I had already started putting songs together in our hotel rooms. Our first co-written song was, in fact, 'Roundabout', one of our most successful songs, nicely setting the bar for the next album. At the rehearsal room in Mayfair songs like 'Heart Of The Sunrise' evolved. These two became the bookends to Bill's idea for the title and solo tracks on *Fragile*, my second album with Yes. There would be five solo tracks each led by one member of the band, complemented by four, larger, group works.

There was a bit of stop-start because of initial uncertainties and session dates on Rick's part, but rehearsals got under way. Some fairly complex arrangements unfolded, with long debates about what and how to play the abundance of different ideas involving the five of us. Structure was the main element to begin with, as the detail could come later in the studio, providing we had a good, tight skeleton to work on. The architecture was devised by teamwork, but the overdubs were more individual adventures, focusing on high levels of coloration. Recording took place again at Advision London from 11 August, on and off, until 5 September. If *The Yes Album* had opened the door to transatlantic success, then we needed to push it even wider to win over the USA.

I enjoyed playing my ES-175D, but started on a quest to experiment with different guitars on each album. I was searching for my own sound, as if I didn't already have one. I wanted to collect other beautiful guitars and play them in the studio and on stage. No sooner had I decided on this than I got a call about a deluxe Gibson for sale at Pye Studios, Marble Arch. Tim Renwick played with Quiver and would later work with Pink Floyd and Eric Clapton, among others. He opened a case and – bang – there it was, a 1959 blonde Gibson ES-5 Switchmaster. Dreams are made of guitars like this! In fact, I'd seen Carl Perkins play a similar model but with what's called black P-90 pickups. Tim's version had three humbuckers. Only three commercially released Gibson models have three pickups –

the ES-5s from 1955, the Les Paul Custom from 1957 and the deluxe Firebird model. The ES-5 has large, pearl fingerboard inlays, a four-position pickup selector switch enabling all variations of the three pickups, three volume and three tone controls, a wonderful blond body and a beautiful double-eight tailpiece. It sounded great and felt very nice to play. I bought it on the spot and took it to rehearsals and later to the studio where it became the featured guitar on the album (excepting 'Heart Of The Sunrise', on which I played my old favourite ES-175D).

'Southside Of The Sky' and 'Long Distance Runaround' were mainly written in the studio, making, along with 'Roundabout' and 'Heart Of The Sunrise', five individual tracks. Bill's piece, 'Five Per Cent For Nothing', was built from his drum part, and we each played a part in sync with only one of his drums, making it highly syncopated and very unusual. Only when Yes developed the Album Series Live in 2012, when we played the whole of the *Fragile* album with Chris Squire on bass, did we ever perform 'Five Per Cent For Nothing' live on stage. It's a decidedly tricky piece. The secret is to finish together – this is most crucial.

Rick arranged some Brahms, hence 'Cans And Brahms' and Jon cut 'We Have Heaven'. 'Mood For A Day' was another guitar solo by me, but this time on classical guitar (I now play this in a much more gentle style) and Chris recorded 'The Fish', a bass extravaganza with singing, to boot. Bill hoped we'd all lead the band with a tune of our own but, as Rick and I played solos and Jon built up his track, it left Bill to play on 'The Fish' as the only other example of his idea.

It was noticeable that Eddie Offord had upped his game, giving us a really solid band sound, tight as a duck's arse. The studio had what are now called classic microphones, such as

Neumann U 87s, U 67s and U 64s. The AKG C28 was often used on my guitars. The EMT 140 reverb plate was all over our mixes, featured mainly on certain vocals or instruments. Back in the early seventies, reverb and echo repeats were used sparingly, but actually to great effect. I enjoyed working closely with Eddie, watching how he did things. Also, he was on a health kick and soon we were all considering turning to vegetarian food, which was lighter on the stomach. I committed to be a vegetarian in a New York hotel on 9 February 1972 at lunch. 'No, that's it for me,' I said. 'No more meat or fish.' I have never regretted the decision or missed anything that I ate before.

In later years Jan and I would also come to realise that we were too reliant on dairy produce, creating imbalances in our bodies. Macrobiotics then came to the rescue. Macrobiotics is based on Japanese 'peasant foods' and was revived by George Ohsawa and then Michio Kushi. You'd have brown rice, raw, pickled and cooked veg, seaweed, savoury tofu, tempeh or seitan from soya beans and salads, all on one plate. Alongside the dietary balance was a wonderful guidance system for a better understanding of life. Ohsawa and Kushi wrote several books each about the broader topics of macrobiotics.

Today, if I used the term 'interconnected' you'd immediately think of the internet and social media, but nature also has an interconnected landscape. Taoist ideas with Japanese interpretations re-emerged into macrobiotics. The principle of yin and yang, the Twelve Theorems of the Unifying Principles and the Seven Unique Principles were ways to sustain and succeed through a better understanding of nature's connectivity, including food and how this might affect your thoughts,

Jan and I have continued to this day to combine this style of eating with general vegetarian foods, including dairy. Jan took cooking lessons at the East West Centre in Old Street, London, which had a store, restaurant, treatment and consulting rooms that offered various natural treatments and educational classes. Their food tasted delicious and was structured round a balance of natural ingredients, providing an all-round nutritious healthy diet. Michio Kushi's wife, Adeline, taught Jan at at the centre.

Instead of using pharmaceutical drugs to get well, a range of natural remedies from herbal to homeopathic medicines, and treatments like shiatsu and reflexology, could cure us instead. Exercises like yoga and relaxation through meditation helped. Natural healing is such a broad realm that I could hardly do justice to it with just a few sentences. For instance, I went to a class about psychosynthesis, then read a book about it and found it completely fascinating. You have to do the work and dig through the available information that, at first, appears to be taking you to uncharted waters until you are reminded that the Chinese discovered the body's 'meridian system' a thousand years ago. Do the homework – after all, we live on planet Earth with other species who all have as much right to be here as us. If they dwindle, we'll all dwindle. It's almost too late to mention this: we need to get very ecological right away, as Timothy Morton suggests in his book *Being Ecological*.

With the mixed tracks ready for the next stage, Eddie took them away to cut the master to disc. This required considerable expertise, particularly in regard to the bass frequencies, although the highs also needed controlling to achieve a loud but good-sounding finished pressing. One consideration was that the quality of the sound could diminish as the needle got closer to the more central, and smaller, grooves. Mastering is the final chance to smooth things out. It's good to see the revival of vinyl records, the increased production of record players and with it mastering has come back into focus. Back then, we would receive copies of the test pressings and, after taking comments, Eddie would either move on and deliver the final version to the label or sometimes he would go back to modify the cut.

The band's backbone for many years was Mickey Tait. Hailing from Melbourne, Australia, he was first and foremost our tour manager but ended up doing just about everything. He built an array of Marshall amps and quad speakers for an experimental PA we used before purchasing Iron Butterfly's. Mickey has a Rolls-Royce now, which is a far cry from the truck we first rented in Boston together. On that first tour our equipment had, surprisingly, travelled as excess baggage. We had watched as baggage handlers threw the cases with their delicate contents onto conveyor belts, sending them up into the plane's hold. Mickey would eventually focus on lighting and staging, setting up his own company, Tait Towers, in Lititz, Pennsylvania. This expanded very successfully into a huge staging and set-building business used by all the biggest international acts.

It was Mickey who would go on to design our round stages. He was always an optimistic person, with a serious but inventive mind. Everything was always possible to his way of thinking and he never built things that didn't work. Simplicity was always in his designs. Perhaps he was an expert on the importance of the unimportant. He used unusual words and catchphrases in everyday conversations. He'd tell you the time, announcing that it was '10 a.m. Buliva time', or there was his use of the word 'biffy'. I'll let you use your imagination there. He smoked cigarettes at the time and swore by 'Kent menthols'. On his self-built lighting console, he had a pair of ashtrays, one each side, which he referred to as his 'stereo ashtrays'.

Staging can be too cumbersome to keep after a tour and, in a quest to make his mark more permanently on the planet,

Mickey decided to build a castle in Lititz. There aren't too many castles in Pennsylvania that are based on a French chateau. Having the pleasure of staying there a few times over the years, I can say that it's a real show-stopper.

Fragile came out in September 1971. Following more UK and European dates, we crossed the Atlantic for our second US tour, starting on 2 November on the West Coast in Oakland, California, where things were nicely different. There was a lot more looning about and getting high as a kite in the heat of the sun, amid the waving palm trees. It was much more laidback than the East Coast. The really good news was that the edited single version of 'Roundabout' and *Fragile* were leaping up the charts, the album reaching US No. 4. The longer, unedited version of 'Roundabout' was played across radio stations. DJs got behind us, Ed Sharkey in particular. His radio shows came out of Philadelphia and he played complete tracks and even whole albums at times. Other fanatics like Lee Abrahams did as much as they could to show their listeners their appreciation for what we were doing.

Meanwhile, the response to our concerts at the Spectrum in Philadelphia demonstrated a level of intensity that seemed to indicate that these were our most appreciative audiences. Ohio was the first state we broke and that was where we began to do headlining shows. We knew that if we did well in New York our career in the US would take off. Fortunately for us, the whole of America's north-east corner took to us instantaneously. This tour went coast to coast, finishing down south in New Orleans on 18 December.

It was always great to get back home after any tour. It was new to us, being away from loved ones for so long. Jan and I tried to speak on the phone every day and it was considerably harder back then – no Skype or Facetime. Getting a decent line was purely luck and the cost per minute was extortionate, albeit worth every penny. Concerts in the new year were, at least, in the UK – at first anyway. No sooner had these ended than we were back in the US at the Memorial Hall, Plattsburgh, New York, on 14 February. This was a tour that finished on 27 March in Boston, supported by none other than King Crimson. This would be Bill's last live gig with Yes in the seventies.

Gibson guitars asked me to advertise their strings. As I did genuinely use their strings – in fact, I changed my strings every night – and as they offered me any guitar of my choice, I agreed. No surprise there. The guitar I chose, which would become the featured guitar on Yes's next record, was part of the 335 range of semi-acoustic electrics, an ES-345 stereo. Each of the two pickups fed into different amplifiers and speakers, one left, one right. I controlled the pickups independently through two volume pedals going to two amps and could vary the effects on either side of the signal, allowing for lots of tonal variations.

You stood directly between the two amps to find the magic sweet spot, where each pickup complemented the other. You had to follow rules to avoid phase cancellation – when half the sound disappears and, instead of a sweet spot, you got an unusual ethereal impression of the position of the stereo image that appears to be coming from one particular place but then cancels out when you moved off the centre. One reason for this is a single sound being picked up by the two guitar pickups when one of the cables has its positive and negative the wrong way around. You may have found exactly the same thing with home audio systems: cabling must be consistent.

These ES-345 stereo guitars were slim, making access to the higher frets much easier than with full-bodied models. Its smooth fingerboard helped me move about and, beside the three-position pickup switch, the model had a five-way toggle

1951: Aged 4 in the middle between Mum, Philip, Dad and Stella.

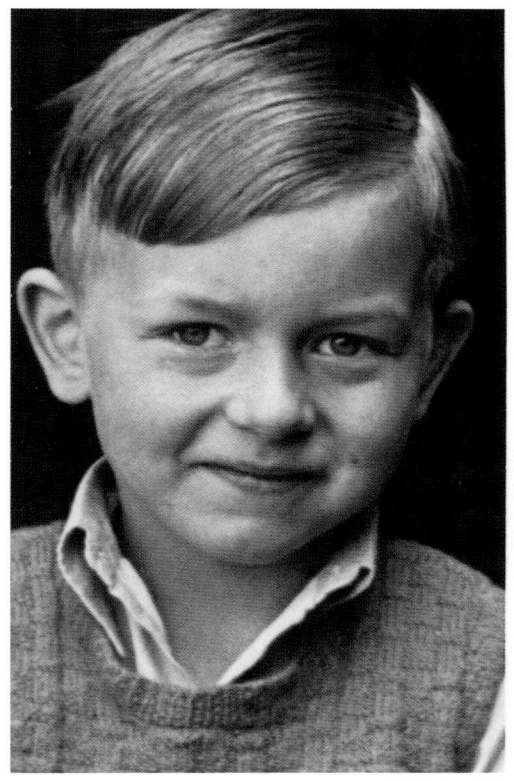

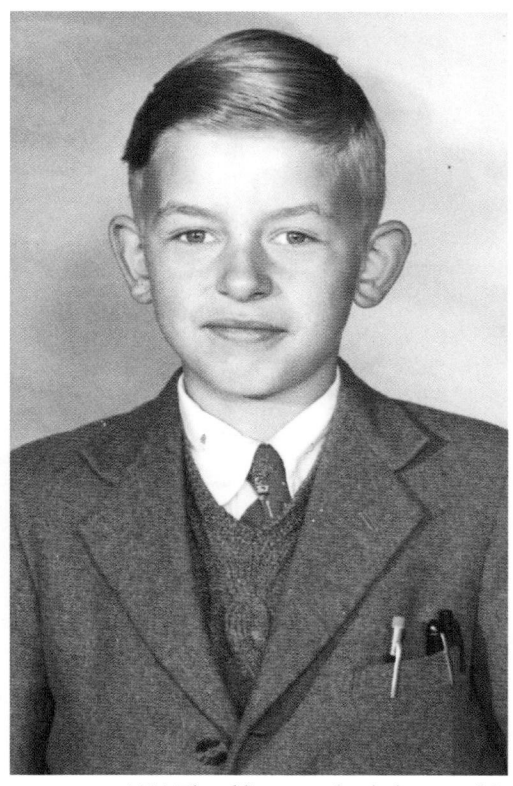

1952: Aged 5.　　　　1956: The obligatory school photo aged 9.

1967: Keeping warm with my Tomorrow bandmates. Junior Wood, Twink, me and Keith West.

1967: And exploring somebody's garden.

1970: A garden writing and rehearsal session for *The Yes Album* in Devon.

1971: Me, Tony Kaye, Chris Squire, Jon Anderson and Bill Bruford. *Barrie Wentzell*

1971: *The Yes Album* tour. My first tour with the band. *Barrie Wentzell*

1972: Yes in the studio with Eddie Offord, top right. *Barrie Wentzell*

1972: Sharing the mic with Jon Anderson on the *Close To The Edge* tour at Gaelic Park, New York City.

1976: Mirror, mirror on the wall… Chris Squire and me at the Plaza Hotel in New York City. *Len DeLessio/Getty*

1977: Hanging out in London with Les Paul, the legendary guitarist, songwriter, luthier, and pioneer of solid-body electric guitar.

1978: Yes live at Madison Square Garden on the *Tormato* tour. *Michael Putland/Getty*

1978: Howe HQ. My home studio.

1979: In Abbey Road's Studio 3 recording 'Double Rondo' and Vivaldi's 2nd movement Lute concerto for *The Steve Howe Album*. *Miki Slingsby*

Early 1980s: I dread to think how much I've spent on strings over the years! *Victor Watts/Alamy*

switch that selected different tones, making the choice of sound mine. My model has a couple of other slight modifications: I asked Gibson to make a custom, ES-5 double-eight tailpiece but with 'ES-345' engraved on it. The 'ES' (for 'Electric Spanish') series was begun in 1936. The late fifties ES-335 models are highly sought after today and can often command a $50,000 price tag.

Not long after the tour finished, in late May 1972, I played a Lincolnshire festival with Maggie Bell & Stone The Crows. Their 27-year-old guitarist, Leslie 'Les' Harvey (the brother of Alex Harvey), had been electrocuted and killed during a soundcheck in the Top Rank in Swansea on 3 May (tragically, his previous band, Blue Council, had lost their singer and bass player in a road accident). Peter Green had spent two weeks rehearsing with Stone The Crows, but stepped down two days before the festival. I only had time for a couple of brief rehearsals, but at the show Maggie went at it full tilt and the band sounded great. There were some nice gaps in which to improvise and Stone The Crows were a really solid band that included keyboardist Ronnie Leahy, who would later play on *The Steve Howe Album*. You have to just throw yourself into these moments, get a fairly good idea of the structures, then watch like a hawk to see when the opportunity to open up comes along. If the telepathy is good, just one look is all you need to stop, start, quieten down or raise the roof. Big cues are annoying because they're too obvious, too much about the person giving the cue and, besides, they totally give the game away.

Earlier in 1972, Jan, Dylan and I had returned to the house where Yes had rehearsed. I took my Martin 00-18 acoustic, Gibson Les Paul Junior guitar, BR-9 steel guitar, a few pedals and an EMS synth prototype keyboard. I recorded demos of part of the first track on the next album. I had a ReVox two-track tape machine, as used by many musicians – they worked well, were easy to operate and sounded good. Besides recording in stereo, one could bounce tracks across, left to right and right back to left, while building up the sound. It was far from the luxury afforded by the four, eight or sixteen tracks you'd get in a professional studio, but being able to build an initial track up at all was a big step up from recording to cassette.

I use the EMS prototype synth on the demo 'For This Moment', released in 1996 on *Homebrew*, for what became the Moog lines played by Rick on the released version. EMS are a very special UK company only really known by a select few. They created a wide range of very quirky and terribly British, scientific-looking instruments: twenty-two models, including the Hi-Fli guitar processor. All their instruments are now much revered but, most importantly, they have a highly individual sound. Built in cottage-industry fashion in Oxford, then later in Cornwall by Robin Wood and his team, they first started in 1969 and continue today. A slew of keyboard developments were taking place around the world, but it really started in places like Oxford. Solid State Logic followed, making world-class recording desks and computer-controlled mixing workstations. Of all the early electric keyboards, the Minimoog quickly gained popularity, followed by Mellotrons, Prophets, PPGs, string machines and sampling keyboards with discs with everything bar the kitchen sink on them. I looked after the EMS prototype for over forty years and it's now located where it can possibly be 'reproduced' and reborn in another age.

The title track for the next Yes album had been constructed by Jon Anderson and me while touring on the back of *Fragile*. At the start of the seventies I was living close to the river... the old River Thames. I'd written the chorus there and also a song that opened with the line 'In her white lace'. Here, Chris and I would sing counter-lines behind Jon. We both threw everything we had at presenting the band with an idea and the music to back it up. Early rock songs lasted for two minutes ten seconds, pop was later three minutes plus, 'MacArthur Park' was over seven minutes, Dylan's 'Sad-Eyed Lady Of The Lowlands' was over eleven minutes, but we were going to be longer, bigger, better(!), at more than eighteen minutes.

Through April, May and June 1972 we recorded *Close To The Edge*, that most quintessential of Yes albums. On side two was 'And You And I', a softer, more acoustically driven piece, and then all sorts of expansive orchestral-style arrangements developed from comparatively small beginnings. I started playing a little steel guitar, a Gibson BR-9 lap guitar I'd bought in New York on our first tour.

I also used the BR-9 on the third and last track, 'Siberian Khatru' – possibly meaning 'As you wish' in Yemeni – where it follows Rick's harpsichord solo. We opened many a show with this particular song. It has everything: riffs, themes, bridges and an unusual middle eight, big three-part harmony verses and Stravinsky-like orchestral stabs. In the end, it fades into a guitar solo that I purposely played while not listening to my guitar, just to see what would happen. When we heard back, we thought it was kind of weird but suitably interesting. On stage I would take some liberties with this slot, developing it differently on each tour. It became one of my most often rejuvenated solos, as I've enjoyed exploring the infinite possibilities over the thematic two 5/4 bar structure going on.

I play a Danelectro Coral Sitar guitar in several places during the album, which does sound sitar-ish and twangy. (*Homebrew 2*, track ten, 'Serpentine', is my demo of the middle instrumental harpsichord, steel and guitar section from 'Siberian Khatru'.) Though it had a great sound, I now use a Line 6 Variax 700 on stage, which has a sitar guitar as one of its many settings.

It's a shame that the closing minutes of 'Close To The Edge' contain a verse and chorus section played a whole tone higher than Jon Anderson discovered it was possible to reproduce live. A singer can hit notes in the studio that are nigh on impossible on stage. In the privacy of the studio they have multiple chances to reach high notes. Live, instead of F as the dominant key at the end, it became E flat. This, to my ear, is rather unsatisfactory. Even Jon Davison, Yes's singer since 2012, didn't want to sing it in the original key during the Album Series tour featuring *Close To The Edge* – and he has a surprisingly high vocal range.

This song 'Close To The Edge' had 'scenes' that we cut to: the intro is fast and ferocious, attempting to emulate John McLaughlin's Mahavishnu Orchestra, whom we all loved, then it rings out with the theme with loads of moving chords, on to the verses, plodding and stabbing with fretless bass and sitar guitar. We move about these structures till the drone comes in, before 'In her white lace…'

The drone was created by Rick and me, overlaying and planting mostly relevant notes at random on a tape, with occasional bass notes from Chris. Once set up, other chords from an electric piano enter while Jon sings the main song and Chris and I sing counter-lyrics underneath him, until we all return together to sing 'I get up, I get down'. A guitar line I'd written (once called 'Jim's Bossa Nova') was rearranged to provide Rick's structure during the church organ section, to which he added Minimoog lines. Of all things, we then play the theme from the beginning together, but now each note of the melody is a major chord, giving it an unusual franticness.

Rick takes a rapid-fire rock organ solo through a Leslie cabinet before all is revealed in the uplifting verse and chorus ending section with 'Seasons will pass you by', finishing off with a cacophony of birds. I think they're electronically simulated birds from a Moog, layered over a guitar and keyboard pattern in 6/8 time.

I remember a playback of the *Close To The Edge* test pressing at the studio, heard on a rented hi-fi system. We felt it was a job well done by all concerned, although we didn't know about some right shockers that came soon after.

It was time for Roger Dean to design his second album sleeve for us. His *Fragile* sleeve had created big waves in album design circles and among our listeners. It was clear his imagination was running wild. Here he took advantage of the gatefold sleeve to explore drifting islands and surreal landscapes, combined with structures inspired by nature. (For later designs, he'd include creatures/people/lifeforms.) The bubble Yes logo first appears on *Close To The Edge* and has stuck with us ever since, re-coloured and re-textured many times. Over the years Roger has become a good friend. He's also designed sleeves and logos for Asia, Anderson Bruford Wakeman Howe, several of my solo albums and my solo logo, but mostly he's known for his artistic presence accompanying all visual aspects of Yes's best works. Thanks a lot, Roger!

Phil Carson at Atlantic asked us to contribute a new track to the second volume of *The Age Of Atlantic* compilation series, called *The New Age Of Atlantic*, released in July 1972 with various tracks by Led Zeppelin, Buffalo Springfield and several other Atlantic acts. We chose to record Paul Simon's song 'America', selected from a shortlist of songs that we all liked. Much of the arrangement was invented from the themes, but instead of sticking to the original shape of the song we drew from what was there and then put our stamp on it. It turned out to last ten minutes and thirty-one seconds, including a longish, southern-rock-style guitar solo, which I mostly wrote with a strong Delaney & Bonnie influence alongside my own lead lines. In 1992, I met Paul Simon at a Florida hurricane disaster concert where I was playing with an Asia line-up. I asked him if he liked Yes's version of 'America', and I'm happy to report that he said he did. He accepted that the song's guitar break hadn't been written by his good self, and I later registered it as a separate piece entitled 'Southern Solo'. In fact, I also pay tribute to both Duane Eddy and Chet Atkins in this guitar break.

I consider 'America' to be a kind of lost recording. It's been included on a few Yes compilations but often as an edited single, missing the break and the intro. In its full glory, the recording stands up very well. The intro and ending movements feature subtle key changes and there's much light and shade from Bill and Chris. Rick and I forge ever ahead. I especially love Bill's Mellotron part on the very end. Although the video we made miming to this song was a totally wasted opportunity – in that it's a mess, mostly due to the fact that we were having way too much fun – it seemed like it was OK to send ourselves up. It was so loosely conceived, just us in the studio with no visual direction or style whatsoever. We've played this song on stage at many concerts, and it's appeared on a few live albums too.

CHAPTER 8

Big Switch

Bill Bruford left the band, something that no one had thought would happen, but he was a true professional to the end.

Apparently, even before King Crimson offered him their drum seat, he had wanted to leave anyway. His musical polarity told him it was time to move on, and we had to respect him for that. His highly individual approach to his 'tubs' had become a big part of what Yes were musically. He never wanted or needed a hit record exactly and, like me, success had to be on his own terms. Commercial considerations weren't in the mix.

In *Yes: The Authorised Biography*, by Dan Hedges, Bill says, 'Any time spent in a rock band not progressing is wasted time. I see it as a matter of survival… I didn't want to do these vocal harmonies and the business with the bass…' I guess Bill was the most free-spirited of all of us. He'd fight for what he believed in but, if the direction seemed wrong, then he'd be off. I can't now bleat on about how unhappy I was at the time, but it was sad to lose him when we were making considerable progress. We stayed friends and have collaborated musically at various times since, including with Anderson Bruford Wakeman Howe and Yes's *Union* period, as well as his several appearances on my solo albums and our project *Symphonic Music Of Yes* in 1993.

Alan White had been around the Advision sessions in the months before Bill's departure. A friend of Eddie's, he was a talented and well-respected drummer. He'd worked with numerous bands and had a claim to fame in working with John Lennon on *Imagine* and at John's famous Toronto concert. I later found out that Ainsley Dunbar was hoping for the call but there had seemed little time to think it through. Alan was asked to do the near impossible and learn our setlist in four days. Everything that happens in Yes is like this – no bridge too far, no request too great, no sacrifice too big. The continuation of Yes was vital. We never knew what was coming next. All too often we needed to consider what to do now in an attempt to avoid a bigger upheaval than the last one. We went straight off to start our third US tour, on 26 July in Edwardsville, Illinois, going right through to 21 August in St Louis, Missouri, at the Kiel Auditorium. Alan White was furiously learning more about our music every night. This was just the beginning of the live schedule: although we had the next two weeks off at home, we topped the bill at the third Crystal Palace Garden Party on 2 September. More UK dates followed before we hurtled back to the US, starting our fourth tour in Miami on 15 September and going right through until 20 November.

I've always known that we worked hard but now, looking again at those 1972 tour dates, I realise how many concerts and tours we actually did. It really is hard to believe, let alone comprehend. The most shows Yes ever did in one year was two hundred, in 1969. The opportunities were there and 'Go for it' was the management's attitude. A big part of what drove us on was to achieve our place alongside other British rock bands invading the USA. It's such a huge country, you could tour more or less constantly if you wanted to (or if you're crazy enough). I was very fortunate to get a lot of exposure (often of me blaring away on stage) in photographs on the front pages of music magazines, in particular on the cover of *Melody Maker*. The magazines often sent their journalists across the water to review our show at places like Madison Square Garden. It was free exposure that helped build our stature in Britain.

Without so much as the shortest of breaks at home after the fourth tour finished, we played two nights at London's Rainbow Theatre on 15 and 16 December, plus the Hardrock in Manchester a day later. These Rainbow shows would become *Yessongs*, the concert video (our first and only released video for some time). A UK company called A1 OK Productions filmed the second show with producer David Speechley, director Peter Neil and editor Philip Howe – my brother. That sounds cosy, which it basically was, although (of course) there's a 'but'. The editing was thought by some to put me in the spotlight, especially in 'Yours Is No Disgrace', the film's encore. Besides, Jon didn't like the shot of his foot. Nevertheless, the film certainly captures the musical excitement working between us. It opens with 'Seen All Good People', the second part of which rocks like mad (although I'm sure the live show had opened with a different song).

We were then ripped off by a million-dollar distribution deal. After A1 OK completed the film, Carlin Films offered the money for all rights in the video for US, Canada and South America. With a $100,000 advance on signature, the remaining $900,000 was to follow – except it never did. We never got paid, years went by, dust settled over facts and figures, the statute of limitations passed and we saw not one penny more, ever. The concert film was released on DVD with interviews and my *Beginnings* film, promoting my first solo album, also made by A1 OK. This was a nice package on which royalties are in fact paid to us. Learning that working with family or friends on projects with Yes could cause problems seemed shocking at the time, but then there is some professional perspective that's lost when personal relationships are involved.

Despite our busy schedule, I somehow found time to work with David (now Dee) Palmer in London, performing his composition 'When Wenceslas Looked Out' with Philomusica. The small orchestra was led by William Armon at the Royal Academy in Piccadilly and I played classical and electric guitars. Only a cassette tape exists of this charming performance, which followed music by Schubert, Bach, Handel and Mozart. I have not done anything like that before or since, really, and the concert may well have marked my first solo appearance.

When it came to Yes, there was a slightly sinister machine behind us, pushing us to earn more and more money. We were hungry too, mainly for success and recognition but, of course, a few bob in the bank was nice. We had our families to think about. How could we stabilise our home life while tearing around the planet? How could we also watch over our business affairs to see that things were in order, especially while we were abroad? The trust we placed in our management and the legal and accountancy firms we employed led to good and bad things. It's well known that most musicians are not born businesspeople and this can result in finances slipping between the cracks or falling into the wrong hands. We were only just starting to realise the responsibilities of being directors of our own company. Hey! What did we know? Nothing much, is the answer. There were many occasions when differing views and misunderstandings caused big problems.

Our UK accountant David Moss famously said to us that we couldn't even manage a sweet shop. This was probably true, but also probably not really funny. I once pondered, 'Why bother earning more money if it all goes in tax?' I wanted to earn just enough to live comfortably and that was it. I'd mistakenly imagined that all of the members of the band would want to build up a nice healthy reserve of money in our joint business account but, oh no, this was not to be. The income always got paid out, plus some even overdrew from the account. They needed extra for bills, or to pay for their recording studio; some needed advances some just spent excessively and didn't care so much about paying company bills or to pay tax on time. Quite a nightmare.

Merchandise was sold on tour and in the early days we heard promises about the revenue such as 'There'll be more income to follow later...' or 'The accounting is slow...' More never did arrrive; money usually got lost in the next tour start–up float or disappeared to pay more bills.

Financial clarity evaporated when we became a big operation. Would we ever get smart? Well, anybody who worked with Yes will tell you that it can be a little devilish inside the actual creature itself. The legal and accountancy issues erupted into fully fledged problems and we've always had to carry on through the years by coping with financial, copyright and trademark issues. Nothing is ever easy, though it might look that way from the outside. As with most bands, nothing is ever likely to be 'hassle-free'.

We had one lawyer in Los Angeles looking after legal matters for most of the time, Stan Diamond, who recently retired. His partner Jim Wilson has taken us on. We've had several accountants, big West End firms, massive West End firms and the same in Los Angeles. The back catalogue is managed from the UK by Jeremy Forsyth, who's kept it ticking over rather well, whilst the current operation moved its affairs to Mark

Donalfeld in New York, after decades of LA-based accountants. There's a whole separate book to be had there.

The band itself would also move around with time. By the early eighties Jon, Chris and Tony Kaye had all moved from the UK to live in Los Angeles, while Alan went to Seattle. Jan and I stayed in the UK, which was enjoyable and right for us.

Much of this was still in the future when, in early March 1973, Yes casually boarded a plane with Roger Dean for Tokyo, heading out to play what would be the first and only Yes tour of Japan for decades. It was an unusual experience, seeing a place where so much of its culture and style was so different. As a new vegetarian, suitable foods seemed hard to find, although in reality there were macrobiotic restaurants dotted about, as I was to discover on my return trips to Japan with the help of friends Hide and Kana Hayashi. They often took me out for lunch or dinner. Later they kindly invited me to eat at their home. All the food in Japan is of a high standard, it has to be said.

The concerts went well and we quickly got used to a quieter audience of well-behaved folk. It was slightly alarming at first, but we learned that Japanese audiences have a great hearing capacity: they get absorbed in the music and know what it should sound like. Yes always worked through Mr Udo's agency, who would look after us so well. Everything was taken care of – the travel arrangements from airport to hotel, to the station to catch the Bullet train (surely a modern miracle although it's been in service since 1964), then from hotel to venue and back after the show, following a delicious backstage dinner.

We played from 8 March in Tokyo until the 14 March in Kyoto before leaving Japan for Australia and New Zealand, closing that tour on 31 March. It really felt special to be playing somewhere for the very first time, moving from one world-famous city to the next. We were like tourists. We returned to the US just three days after playing in New Zealand, and it seemed really exciting on the West Coast. There was a sense of ease as we started in San Diego on 4 April. Then we went right across America to West Palm Beach, Florida, on 22 April, playing 'Close To The Edge' and other songs from our new live album *Yessongs*, released that month. This was an expanded set of recordings based on the video of the same name, some tracks featuring Alan White on drums, as in the video, and others with Bill on drums. It captured the crossroads we were at in terms of drumming styles. I can't imagine Bill drumming on *Tales From Topographic Oceans*. Yet the approach Bill employed feels to me like it was the major stimulus for the rest of us. It's obviously that old illusive group chemistry.

Yessongs was a highly successful triple album worldwide, selling amazingly well in Germany. We had attempted to mix the three discs like a studio album, and it took months of work, downstairs at Advision Studios. We vowed never to repeat the experience. In future, one independent engineer would be hired to mix the show with input from members, which meant it remained fairly democratic, needing only band approval prior to mastering and release. This freed us from intensive collective labour – and we've since released umpteen live albums this way!

The Anderson/Howe songwriting team had been busy on what was to become our most controversial collection of songs and both the only real concept album and the only double studio album (to date). One member of the band had trouble with all this material yet went on to make six concept albums himself! Our lyrics could be vague but they do hang together, based as they sometimes were on our lives and our vital new interests. Many of these values and beliefs would run through the band's career, defying the critics.

We didn't want to retread familiar ground: Jon and I knew this was a golden opportunity to explore the outer reaches of our possibilities. Music's heritage also interested the two of us. We had the confidence to see beyond mediocrity. Repeat 'la-la-la' choruses were definitely out, predictable developments avoided, we were after the unusual instead of the blindingly obvious. Not your sell-out album then!

We rehearsed in an abandoned cinema that ELP had rented in Fulham and renamed Manticore. The stage didn't seem quite the right place to be working but we did manage to get a rough shape of each side before we moved on to Morgan Studios, Willesden, for four months. You might have heard that we had life-size cardboard cows and real bales of straw in the studio. This is true – we thought it brought a little of the countryside to our environment – alongside the three-sided, tiled bathroom that was erected for Jon to sing in (no loo, shower or taps though!). Morgan had recently installed the latest and greatest 3M incarnation, the M79 – a twenty-four-track tape machine (bye-bye sixteen track). This had a surprisingly long tape path from one spool to the other, via the record and playback heads. It wiggled and jiggled up and down, like a film projector, and was quite troublesome.

Before a take we practised, tightening up arrangements and pinning down parts. Once we'd put something down we'd break and head to the control room to listen to our efforts. This was a test of how each musician could focus on their own part: 'Is it right? How can I improve on it or perhaps play less and detail it later?' Also, one needed to have an opinion about the overall aims: the parts, the shape, light-and-shade and the all-important tempo, besides whether the arrangement was right.

Big Switch

At times, after Jon had given his all, directing Rick, Chris and Alan towards the high level of musicology we hoped to achieve, he'd take a break. I would then step in to steer the band on the piece we were working on. Jon and I would occasionally discuss privately how we both thought it was going. This enabled us to plan solutions, bring new ideas in with unity and dispel some of the doubts that often returned to Rick, Chris and Alan.

The only exit from the control room was through the studio – which wasn't usually the case in other recording facilities. One day, after we'd been rehearsing, we wandered into the control room, expecting to see Eddie, as he hadn't passed us through the studio. There was no sign of him. He'd vanished. 'Eddie, man, where are you?' we asked. At last we heard some rustling under the desk, Eddie was underneath, editing tapes on his Stellavox mini two-track tape machine with his headphones on. 'What are you doing down there, Eddie?'

'Oh, I'm just editing some mixes back together that I slashed by mistake with a razor blade, thinking they weren't masters,' he explained casually. 'I just needed a blank spool.'

We went into shock/horror mode. 'The mixes we did yesterday?'

'Yes, those mixes,' he confessed.

Amazingly, the tapes eventually played fine.

We also had to copy parts of the end of the second side because there were several problems with stereo guitars being out of phase. They just kept disappearing when played back in mono and we had to we shift the left-to-right aspects to fix the phase reversal. It was a nightmare. As mentioned earlier, when an instrument is recorded in stereo, its signal path must remain phase-correct. If not, it will disappear in mono, either partially or totally. Mono-checking was usually done in mixing but on this occasion we only noticed it as we concluded the final mixes. With that fixed, the four final master tapes suffered one more drama when they fell off the roof of Eddie's car. He had placed them there while he got his car keys out of his pocket, forgot about them and drove off! They duly slid off the car and into the kerb, but, as luck would have it, survived intact.

November 1973 saw the release of *Tales From Topographic Oceans*, Yes's fourth album with me and the band's sixth album. The press had a field day. On the one hand there was flattery. Andrew Bailey in London's *Evening Standard* wrote, 'Without doubt this is Yes's most significant work to date', and, around that time, Robert Shelton wrote in a review for a live London show, 'The third movement alone… will be studied twenty-five years hence as a significant turning point in modern music.' Please allow me to quote one more music journalist, William A. Murray, who went a step further: 'But by far the most outstanding is the extraordinary guitar work… which reaches levels of accuracy and emphasis that really are formidable.' Thank you! I don't need the compliment, but I'll ride the wave. On the other hand there were many howling critics. Our pub-dwelling, keyboard-player friend was on the same wavelength as some of the music press who criticised us and it wasn't long before he joined in. Indeed, in 2016 he was still going on about it! On a BBC TV programme about concept albums, I watched with predictable horror as he pronounced that all the lyrics on *Topographic* were rubbish, even after Yes had recently featured *Tales From Topographic Oceans* in our Album Series tour. I love singing these songs with Jon Davison and Billy Sherwood. We have enormous love and respect for every word and note of this epic, one-of-a-kind concept album. So – love it or shut it!

The original *Tales* tour was our first with full-on staging by Roger Dean. Aided by his brother Martyn, this would be the first full production in what became an iconic partnership with the band. Comparatively simple but effective fibreglass mounds lit from inside surrounded our pedalboards and microphone stands, alongside dry ice and Mickey's mirror-ball effects. We'd open each show with all of 'Close To The Edge' then, after an interval, we'd launch into all four sides of *Tales*. These shows were played in a relentless schedule. Following UK dates from 16 November in Bournemouth through 10 December in Edinburgh, we began a US leg on 7 February 1974, in Gainesville, Florida, ending on 28 March in Baton Rouge, Louisiana. We picked up back in Europe on 11 April in Frankfurt, Germany, and finished up on 23 April in Rome, Italy. We played an astonishing number of back-to-back shows during this tour. Days off were a rarity. Initially, all four sides of *Tales* were played each night, but then every show would drop a different side.

Quite recently Paul Secord, Yes's webmaster in Seattle, sent me a list of how many of the sides of *Tales* were played each night across the entire tour (Forgotten-Yesterdays.com was the source – we hope they were correct). Out of the total fifty-four concerts, all sides were played on the first twenty shows, with only one show missing sides two and three. The next eight shows featured all four sides, then one show had sides three and four only, followed by one show with all four sides, then two shows where we played with only sides three and four. In all, twenty-one shows missed playing side two, so only one show missed side three, 'The Remembering', which is considered the most bizarre side. It's really surprising that side one was missed at all but side two was missed on a total of twenty-five shows. Needless to say, this decision was strongly influenced by Rick. Side two was actually the 'keyboard feature side', which had several 'swishy sea'-style movements, in which the band drifts from one held chord to another whilst the keyboards float atop. These areas got troublesome on stage, hence their demise.

Having seen our gear being thrown about by airline baggage handlers on the way to the US for our first tour, we didn't want to repeat the experience. Over time, trucks or tractor-trailers were instead used to move equipment from show to show. The schedule would be mainly decided by where the trucks could reach in time. The next consideration was our own travel schedule, which could be by car or plane, depending on the distances. By the third US tour we were renting a jet to make travel consistent, one place straight to the next. There are small, private airfields all over the US where we could get off a plane and straight into a car waiting for us on the tarmac. No check-in, no security, easy luggage transport, easy guitar movement – it was the ultimate luxury travel mode.

Our first experience of travelling that way came in the UK, after a show in Edinburgh. Not wanting to wait overnight at the end of the UK tour in December 1973, we booked a plane to whisk us back to London. It was dark on the runway as we approached the awaiting Hansa aircraft. We were all a little scared, a sensation not helped by the fact that the plane looked like an Air Force fighter jet (it was indeed the civilian version of a fighter). It got us back to London in lightning speed. We never travelled in another Hansa and rented a BAe 125 business jet on other UK and European tours.

In the US, we found far more enjoyable jets to buzz about in, like the Dassault Falcon, Gates Learjet and the Grumman Gulfstream II. We all once flew in the four-engine Jetstream plane that belonged to Warner Brothers. Other days we'd fly in a Gulfstream I, a turbo prop, but only when the GII wasn't available. The other rental option was an extended Learjet – the unstretched model only accommodated five passengers and had very little luggage space but, to compensate, it took off like a Ferrari, climbing steeply – about 45 degrees – as it surged skyward. The Gulfstream II was everyone's favourite as it was bigger inside and quite plush. We could eat lunch or dinner and that meant we could leave straight after the show to get to our next destination. We could depart New York in the morning, fly to Washington and do a show, then leave straight away for North Carolina – we'd be in three different cities in the course of one day. Private flights meant that just about anything could go on. If Chris was late – what, Chris late? – the plane would wait for him and the rest of us could do our own thing, smoking, drinking and messing about, watched over only by our own flight attendant.

This came at a price, of course, and it was a colossal price at that. But nothing else came close to matching the sheer convenience and Chris and I believed it was worth every penny, enabling us to precisely reach any location in comfort. There were always going to be costs moving all these people around the country, but this way we had control over our own space, schedule and we retained our privacy. It would be a difficult luxury to lose. Taking off while sitting on the bench seat in the rear of a jet's tiny cockpit was thrilling. It all looked so different from that vantage point: the pilot's hand pulling on the throttle, radio messages coming over, like 'Proceed to sector ten', while the clouds were straight ahead. Landing was exciting too, seeing the runway approaching from afar and then directly in front of the front windscreen as the aircraft touched down on the tarmac. Up in the cockpit the pilots were in total control of the beast, guzzling up gas in the most extravagant way known to man. For many years I bought a plane magazine called *Interavia* dedicated to all things flying. It featured futuristic designs, statistics and great photos – it was sort of airplane eye candy. My goodness, flying was such a different experience then. I guess that's partly why I've now totally lost my wanderlust.

The trials and tribulations of producing *Tales Of Topographic Oceans* and mounting the tour resulted in Rick's first departure from Yes, in May 1974. Who could follow in his footsteps or possibly even supersede our departing member? As with an orchestra, if there's an opening then it must be time for a fresh recruit.

We spent two weeks playing with the great virtuoso Vangelis in a studio barn in Buckinghamshire. This was a memorable experience. He produced a wonderful rich sound with lots of echo repeats and reverb, casually sauntering across his array of keyboards. Confidence exuded from him physically and even more so musically. We were, at times, immersed in and almost dwarfed by, his consummate and complete rendition of a tune. He'd even show us how to play particular things on the drums or guitar. However, he didn't believe in playing things the same every time, while Yes relied on musical parts that would come around again. This was the way we worked, finding parts that linked the music; our unique arrangements defined us, we didn't jam a whole lot. In essence, the chemistry with Vangelis wasn't right.

I learned quite a lot of different things, not least of all that we each have the right to play alone, together creating the whole sound, leaving space, quietening down, then building up to reach a place close to musical Nirvana. That was what individual performance is about, demanding but also rewarding.

I called Keith Emerson but he wasn't interested: he had a great band – why would he leave? I said, 'We've got bigger vocal harmonies, more guitars(!) and we are really going places.' His response was simply, 'No, thanks.'

Big Switch

Our attention turned to Refugee, a band that was just getting noticed. They included two previous members of The Nice, Brian 'Blinky' Davison on drums and Lee Jackson on bass and vocals. Their keyboard player was Patrick Moraz, an impressive and rather flamboyant European, with a style of dynamic jazziness that was quite a bit more adventurous than either Rick or Tony had been. He had an array of keyboards and the personality to pull off using them. He joined Yes and this was the start of a three-year period that encompassed our next album, our 'solo album' period and, across the other side, several more tours with the band. Live, he was a secret weapon, deployed to attack preconceptions, displace loyalties and perform as inspiringly as Vangelis might have done.

Work on putting together new material took a different turn around June 1974, after Eddie Offord bought a twenty-four-track mobile recording system that needed a home. Chris had a big house in Virginia Waters, Surrey, with a basement level that had empty rooms he was preparing for his own studio. This would comprise a playing area and a smaller control room. Eddie's gear was assembled here, followed by sufficient keyboards, guitars, amps and drums for recording.

It was a smaller and tighter environment than we were used to, but manageable. Dinner was served upstairs at a long table in a vast dining hall. The driveway was choked up with Range Rovers, Bentleys and Rolls-Royces belonging to the others. Jan and I had our own ideas about cars. We both drove NSU Ro 80s, futuristically designed and featuring the infamous Wankel rotary engines, their gears operated by an electric clutch made by Porsche. First manufactured in 1967, I'd seen one in Germany around 1969 and had thought at the time that I'd like to own one when I had the money and had passed my test. We enjoyed these nice but rather unreliable cars for a few years.

Mazda eventually bought and developed these engines for their RX-7 range.

We began recording what was to become a diehard favourite, *Relayer*. Jon and I had written 'To Be Over' while 'Sound Chaser' and 'The Gates Of Delirium' were group compositions. As all the songs had thorough arrangements and bits added to them by all the band members, an overall group split was devised to appreciate all the ideas. We were on the trail of a hard-edged, driving, complex and sensitive, yet explosive, sound.

I played Fender guitars exclusively, in particular my 1955 Telecaster. The front pickup had been switched to a Gibson humbucker so I could still achieve a thick, round sound when needed. We worked together in a mood of defiance, we stood by every note – we'd finally found the freedom that success was meant to bring and now it was all or nothing. We continued incorporating loud and fast sections with soft and slow sections, decorating the songs with our own personal explorations.

Relayer is the first album on which I play a ten-string pedal steel guitar, the Sho-Bud Pro 1. These single-neck, steel guitars have three pedals for upward string movements plus two knee bars for lowering certain other strings. I'd bought this model in Nashville and had taken some time getting to know the tuning and how to use its melodic scope for the central piece of the guitar solo in 'To Be Over'. An early sitar guitar tune is nicely repeated at the end, alongside tubular bells and strange vocal phrases.

The opening track, 'The Gates Of Delirium', took the form of a twenty-minute structure again but with a new approach to the tonality. It was a tough and gritty affair, lots of 'Stand and fight' and 'Surely we know', executed with loads of bravado. The contrasting closing passage, 'Soon', is a gentle dreamy song for which I returned to my regular Fender 'Stringmaster' Dual

Professional steel guitar, using just a volume pedal feed into some echo repeats. This clear Fender sound is characteristic of Santo (of Santo & Johnny fame), a steel player who has been an inspiration to me. Their recordings of 'Sleep Walk' and 'Venus' are particular favourites.

Contrastingly, 'Sound Chaser' must rank as one of our most exciting and complex pieces, with plenty of thrills and spills. I was in the mood for a flamenco-influenced rock guitar solo. I took a few artistic liberties here, with some screeching diminished chords and biting, twangy lines! The point where Patrick joins with the string chords really took some working out.

'Sound Chaser' and 'To Be Over' have not been performed since 1977 but we hope soon to change all that. I have arranged, performed live and recorded a solo acoustic guitar arrangement of 'To Be Over'. The studio version is only available on the US *The Ultimate Yes: 35th Anniversary Collection* on CD three, accompanying acoustic versions of songs like 'Southside Of The Sky' and 'Roundabout'. Since then 'To Be Over' has become a staple part of my solo guitar setlist.

The *Relayer* tours showed off a sizeable Dean stage with scenery and lasers to great effect. The design architecture was unlike anything anyone had seen before. It built dramatically towards the end of the set, with pulsating lasers stretching out through the smoke across the venue and moving scenery opening out to enact the arrival of a UFO. Fortunately, the band was playing good and hot and we steamed through another tour that started in Columbus, Ohio, on 8 November 1974 and continued to St Paul, Minnesota, on 17 December. We began the tour a few days before the release date of the album, as we often did. This meant the audience wouldn't have heard the music. There were risks involved with this approach, such as bootlegs of the show appearing before our record was in the shops and some fans maybe struggling to understand the new tunes. Critics could be unsympathetic at a loud live show.

Yes played shows in the UK from 15 April 1975, in Newcastle, through to Stoke-on-Trent on 17 May. This run included our London show at the Queens Park Rangers football ground in Shepherd's Bush on 10 May, which was filmed and, inevitably, bootlegged. The film shows us in peak performance mode, ploughing through the set with the ease of a well-oiled machine. Seals & Crofts and Gryphon were also on the bill, both acts we all really liked. Gryphon toured a few times with us (and also played on 'The Nature Of The Sea' from my *Beginnings* album). On 17 June, we started another US leg in Denver that continued until 24 July at the Roosevelt Stadium in Jersey City. We ended up back home for the Reading Festival on 23 August with The Mahavishnu Orchestra and Supertramp. Phew!

During time off, I played a solo spot at a show with the wonderful classical guitarist John Williams at an all-stars guitar concert in London. I much admired individual guitarists for the freedom playing solo gave them and the strength it showed to take the stage alone. I knew it was in my DNA and these fleeting, one-off performances taught me just how much I had yet to learn.

CHAPTER 9

On And Off

At this point in the story, we reach Yes's solo album period.

My first solo album, *Beginnings*, was released in November 1975. This was recorded at the same Advision Studios where Yes had often recorded, with a short overdubbing experiment conducted with Eddie's mobile equipment in the garage at our Hampstead Garden Suburb house. Much of the music had been roughly recorded on my ReVox quarter-inch, two-track tape machine and on writing cassettes that later trickled out via my *Homebrew* releases. The musical range was just about as wide as I could imagine it, including rock, folk, country and orchestral, with both songs and instrumentals, no holds barred, most styles represented somewhere.

I've always tried to learn as much as I could about the process of recording. The way a guitar sounds is determined by so many different factors: how you play, what you play, what you play on, what microphone is used and in what position, where and how loud the guitar is in the mix and what frequencies are added or cut during the mastering or pressing (as was the case on vinyl). It remains an elaborate journey that sound makes to reach the listener. Stuff can happen all the way along the chain.

Being in solo mode and responsible for everything gave me an exciting feeling. Just like Chet Atkins in his own studio, I was now directing the proceedings. I wanted to hone my skills and be able to make better records in the future. Each album would be an exploration of the music I enjoyed and/or wrote. There was obviously less pressure than there was with the band although, if trouble came, it would be on my shoulders, of course. Later on, I'd produce all my own solo albums but, since Eddie was on board to co-produce and engineer, I'd try to make the best of the collaboration. An element of fun came with working with him. One afternoon he burst into the downstairs studio and did a cartwheel across the room, dropped into a chair, opened his bag and produced a bottle of whisky and a duck call. He took a swig from the bottle, blew the duck call and just said, 'Hello!'

Many of the tracks began by recording a decent rhythm guitar live with Alan White or Bill Bruford on drums, when we'd play through the whole arrangement. Conversely, 'Lost Symphony' was played live in the studio with everyone, as was 'Beginnings' and 'The Nature Of The Sea'. 'Ram' was built up from a click track and featured my first banjo part (actually it was a banjo 'guitar' – strung, tuned and played the same as a guitar).

In my mind, the lead vocals would be sung by Clive Skinner, my friend from Bodast, but it never happened. When we got nearer to recording the vocals, Eddie told me he needed to take a holiday for a couple of weeks. I didn't have time to reschedule and began working with the studio's in-house engineer, Jeremy Stenham. This kept everything moving along and I decided to take on the challenge of singing the lead and harmony vocals of these very personal songs. It would have been great to have had Clive singing lead as he was a truly original character whose voice was warm and spiritual. Tragically, he was to pass away only a few years later.

I have to say that Patrick Moraz performed miracles in orchestrating 'Beginnings' and playing harpsichord on the album's title track. He also conducted the orchestra and played some great keyboards on other tracks too, notably the Mellotron on 'Will O' The Wisp', one of three tracks to have lyrics written by my wife, Jan. Roger Dean created a lovely sleeve combining a photo of me and my guitars. I took an early selfie of Jan, Dylan and myself, which was superimposed in the foreground of another photo I took of a Devon hedgerow. This stretches across the central gatefold sleeve.

A twelve-minute, three-track promo video was filmed, featuring a duet version of 'Beginnings' with Patrick Moraz on harpsichord and me on classical guitar. 'Ram' was also re-recorded and features in the video. It begins with me playing the basic guitar part and then more 'me's appear to jump out of me as I play, taking up a new instrument as each is introduced, an effect accomplished by overlaying films. For 'Breakaway From It All' a documentary-style clip was shot in which I go walking about in London, shots mixed in from a cattle auction at a village market. The film was made by A1 OK Productions, who made *Yessongs*, with my brother Philip editing. It was shown on the BBC music show *The Old Grey Whistle Test*, shown in cinemas with *Yessongs* and included with the DVD release of *Yessongs*. It felt good having a film to promote the project. It's been held in limbo for years, marked for inclusion in my long-awaited solo DVD compilation.

All the other members of Yes also released their own solo albums, which might have seemed like either huge statements of musical freedom or of total group defiance, if not for the fact that we had agreed things up front. We had decided that we would come back together afterwards – and be stronger for it. Atlantic Records released all, except for Patrick's album.

Yes had meanwhile been getting even more recognition at home, having previously won Top Band, Top Writers (Anderson/Howe) and Top Arrangers in the 1974 *Melody Maker* readers' poll. In 1976 I was honoured to be voted top guitarist for the first time in the annual awards. The chrome-framed award still hangs in my guitar room, reminding me of this pivotal moment: recognition for my individual playing – very nice. We had already accumulated many gold and platinum discs from Atlantic Records, and in the future Asia would receive plenty of similar awards. There were many other UK music papers with their own polls in which we featured during the seventies: *Sounds*, *New Musical Express*, *Disc and Music Echo* and *Record Mirror*. I don't display them all, but *Beginnings*' silver disc is also on my wall. I did have all the discs photographed by my dear friend and go-to photographer, the late Miki Slingsby, so they are at least catalogued. Miki photographed fine art for high-end galleries and collectors, my *Guitar Collection* book in 1993, George Harrison's guitar collection and many other fine guitar books.

Everything else was eclipsed on 23 September 1975, when Jan gave birth to our second son, Virgil. Dylan and I rushed to the hospital to find mother and baby were doing fine. It was Dylan who chose his brother's name, at our request – he was a fan of TV's *Thunderbirds*. All I can say here is that Virgil went through all the usual learning curves and developed his individual skills on the piano and drums, writing music and becoming a DJ. He was as fun and lovable as could be possible. His daughter, Zuni, was the love of his life. He tragically passed away on 11 September 2017. Nothing had prepared us for this. Our love for him and his legacy will remain, forever.

CHAPTER 10

Regroup

Yes had a nine-month period of collective inactivity before US touring began again in Roanoke, Virginia, on 28 May 1976, with short gaps until Fort Wayne, Indiana, on 22 August.

We co-headlined with Peter Frampton, who was riding the crest of an enormous wave with his live album *Frampton Comes Alive!* and the talkbox single 'Show Me The Way'. It was big stadiums and amphitheatres all the way, including JFK Stadium, Philadelphia, on 12 June. This became famous as the audience was so large the organisers lost count, but estimates ran to over a hundred thousand fans. Peter and I were old friends and I was delighted at the recognition he was receiving. He'd worked hard and deserved a big break.

These high-intensity bouts of touring taught us plenty about ourselves. There was no textbook for guidance. You are at the mercy of suddenly being well known – keeping it all together and dealing with everything that comes with fame becomes a test of character and self-control. What if you get burned out from late nights, parties, gatherings in hotel rooms and early flights? It's at this point that artists often start getting reckless and bedraggled or seriously messed up, then they let themselves and everyone else down. 'No thanks,' I thought. 'Surely that's no way to treat an opportunity.' Mad stuff happened on these tours: crew guys used to get loaded and trash things, there were run-ins with promoters and police and security incidents. What with all the over-the-top, spaced-out human wreckage that came with the touring, it wasn't surprising that the last chord of the last song on the last night was highly anticipated. Going home was on my mind throughout the tour. There was the golden egg of survival – sanity and love.

When we returned to the UK, it was both time for me to enjoy being with family at the beautiful London house close to Hampstead Heath extension, and to get better cars. The NSU Ro 80s were running out of steam. Ferraris appealed to me, along with Maseratis (particularly the Khamsin), but instead we chose a very traditional British make, a Bristol, hand-built in very low numbers. These hailed from Filton near Bristol and were developed by the Bristol Aeroplane Company, who'd started out making engines in 1914. After World War I, and with design plans from BMW, they began car production. The Bristol 400 was their first model, followed by 401 through to 411. In 1976 they produced the 412 Zagato, but in the end we went for an attractive blue 411, one of the last of the range, a handmade, grand-touring coupé called the 411 Series 5. Its Chrysler 6.5-litre engine went like the proverbial rocket.

To some, the Bristol might have looked quite anonymous, while others might have thought it slightly pretentious but, for those in the know, it was an extremely high-quality, individual car with smooth aerodynamic styling, a luxury interior and credible links with motor-racing history. Behind its front wheels were panels that raised up, one hiding a spare tyre and the other the battery. These kind of clever ideas prevailed throughout, although it came with very expensive servicing costs and was not for the faint-hearted. To start it, you needed to stroke the accelerator to give the choke just the right amount of fuel and it was a truly thrilling car to drive. A few other British guitarists have chosen these cars, among them John Williams, who bought a 411 Series 4 about the same time as I did and I believe Oasis's Liam Gallagher later had a 603 model.

I kept this car for seventeen years, putting only 55,000 miles on the clock. It was driven only occasionally and at first took some getting used to. Bristol kindly stored the car for two months while I was away on the band's next jaunt, in Switzerland, and I knew it would be in safe hands. I joined the Bristol owners' club and went to meetings where I entered the car for an annual competition for 'Best in Group' and one time I came second.

Jan wanted to upgrade her car as well and spotted a Mercedes-Benz she liked, a 350 SLC, another two-door coupé. It turned out to be extremely practical and lots of fun. It was trouble-free — turn the key and off it went. After eventually selling my car back to Bristol for a profit in 1992, we both subsequently drove only Mercedes-Benz cars, for their reliability, safety and comfort.

When the band returned to recording, we didn't feel we had to stay in the UK. Yes were free to go anywhere we liked. For several reasons we were drawn to Switzerland and, after visiting Mountain Studios at the casino in Montreux, it all fell into place. ELP were recording when we visited. They played us a few tracks with the studio monitoring almost at maximum. No wonder musicians lose their hearing — but it was the trend to play back tracks at enormous volume, as everything sounds great when it's really loud. Listening back at sensible levels — often quite softly — is much more common these days, as it's more useful and safer all round.

Patrick was sort of at home in Montreux, as he hailed from Switzerland. We could rent chalets or stay at a nearby hotel and thought perhaps we'd even drive our cars over from the UK and have a completely new environment to work in. The exodus took some planning but everybody was eventually accommodated near the studio/casino complex beside a beautiful lake.

We began rehearsing what would be *Going For The One* in part of the casino that later became the Count Basie Hall, just along the road with the French mountains opposite and the Swiss mountains behind, providing a stunning, panoramic view. Switzerland was a picture-postcard location. Driving up and down mountains, eventually in the snow with chains on the tyres, turned out to be loads of fun. There were long afternoon Sunday lunches during which Chris would make the choice from the wine list. There were plenty of distractions to keep everyone amused, even though we were supposedly working.

After rehearsals we moved into the studio, which had its control room at ground level and a small but nice playing space upstairs. We also rented part of the connecting casino below to set everybody up in a big semicircle. We had parted company with Eddie Offord and John Timperley took over, a former engineer at the BBC who also had other good credentials. He did a fine job. How it was that we didn't drive him totally crazy is another thing. We began work with Patrick Moraz still on keyboards but after first two weeks he felt it wasn't working. He wanted us to be a bit jazzier. 'Nope, that's never going to happen,' we told him. We did make a big effort to get going again with him, before realising it was all over.

It was very strange to have to change keyboard players, having already begun a period blocked out for recording. We weren't about to start a search-and-rescue mission to find a new keyboard player at this point and we asked ourselves if sufficient time had elapsed for the split with Rick Wakeman to have been healed. Accounts varied, but it proved to be the case and, with Rick returned, everyone got a clearer picture of the album. Work on the tunes intensified and, as tricky pieces evolved, we set about developing them in our habitual quest for excellence. 'Awaken' would be the last Anderson/Howe song of the seventies. Here I played pedal steel, Rickenbacker electric twelve-string and my Fender Telecaster. 'Turn Of The Century' had a delicate first half on which I played an acoustic Guild guitar and autoharp. I played my Fender steel guitar on 'Going For The One', my red Stratocaster on 'Parallels' and, for 'Wonderous Stories', I used my Portuguese guitar and played some jazzy Gibson L-5 guitar at the end.

Using the L-5 was a homage to Wes Montgomery. He was born in 1925 in Indianapolis and didn't take up the guitar until he was 19 years old, yet he is one of the few players who can truly be called visionary. His playing abounded with incredible ideas. Few have reached his level of musical coolness and versatility. A towering improviser, he mixed octaves, single notes and chords, played with his thumb and developed a beautiful tone, particularly on his mid- to later recordings. His sense of harmony was startling, taking every opportunity and employing great rhythmical strength within his ideas. He adopted the Gibson L-5, which personifies his jazz tone, but he also played a Fender Jazz bass on his album *Full House*, demonstrating that there were no obstacles in his mind, only fluid, soulful and stupendous playing.

In 1963 I had seen Montgomery at Ronnie Scott's club. I went with Doug Ellis, who worked at Selmer's and was supplying Wes with a Selmer amp for the gig. I saw Wes leave his dressing room at the back of the club and head for the stage and I was immediately struck by his huge smile. This persisted throughout his brilliant performance. To this day, I have never seen a smile stay on a performer's face through a whole show in that way. Each tune he played confirmed his command of the instrument. He traded lines in a blues style more that evening than he did on record and to witness his spontaneity and those large hands playing calmly while whipping up a storm of notes was awe-inspiring. The comedian Spike Milligan was there that night and he became uncontrollably excited as he interacted with Wes. I really don't know why. This minor distraction changed nothing for Wes, who merely continued playing.

The Artistry Of Wes Montgomery is possibly my favourite recording, and I have copies in all formats. 'Polka Dots And Moonbeams' is romantic guitar at its best. His compositions are perfect vehicles for him, especially his studio recording of 'Four On Six'. He made many records, from earlier Montgomery Brothers albums to double-bill projects – such as the one with Jimmy Smith – and then on to big orchestral albums as in *Bumpin'*. Playing live, Wes was so well composed, completely aware of his surroundings. Performing to a crowd is a different animal to working in the studio, a kind of day of reckoning or a calling from within, where you've had to put your neck on the line. Either way, stay calm if you can. I don't find it particularly entertaining to watch a gyrating, mobile musician. I'd rather sense emotion than just see motion. It takes absolutely years to train yourself to get in the right space for your music. It's all in the mind, after all.

Back in Montreux, Nigel Luby, who was Chris's tech, together with cameraman Tony Richardson, filmed some of the recording sessions in our playing area. Jon had an easel for some painting he was doing, while others had personalised their own areas with amps, keyboards, drums, percussion, guitars and bass guitars. The filming was never edited properly into a presentable form but over the years it's leaked out on bootlegs, occasionally showing some of the silly stuff that went on. Were we losing sight of reality?

We worked in Switzerland for all of seven months, including Christmas 1976, with only short breaks back in the UK. It was great to see the whole family come out, when Jan, Dylan and 1-year-old Virgil stayed with me in a lovely hotel, now called the Eden Palace au Lac, overlooking Lake Geneva. We took up half a floor, nine rooms in all: a lounge, kitchen, three bedrooms for us plus one for the nanny, a recording den with a ReVox, microphones and playback, a playroom for the boys and a storeroom. We next rented a house close to Chillon castle, which was also near the apartment of Claude Nobbs, who worked for Atlantic and ran the Montreux Jazz Festival. The live recordings from the festival each year were an incredible legacy of Claude's work.

Going For The One radiated lots of positive energy and gentle beauty, perhaps due to our attention to detail — including making twenty-seven mixes (or dubs, as they say in the US) of the title track. Reels of tape collected around us as we attempted to perfect it. I remember saying for a quite a while that mix number two(!) really had all the necessary qualities. Would they listen again? I asked. We did and, lo and behold, there it was, some twenty-five takes earlier.

The ideas for the sleeve went into outer orbit. All but one member wanted Roger to paint the design but there was a misunderstanding or something that resulted in Storm and Po of Hipgnosis offering us various designs from images they had stockpiled. It was far less personal and sympathetic a design by comparison with our previous work from Roger. They had done the kind of thing they do, but it didn't please all of us —

certainly not me. I've no hard feelings, though, as Hipgnosis were as helpful as they could be. We were simply in the wrong place. The two LA skyscrapers were the background of the image, the foreground was the back of a naked guy! Weird or what? After its release, a billboard featuring the album appeared on Sunset Boulevard in LA, but with a twist – now the guy had trousers on. This was done so as not to offend the fine folk who walked or drove down Sunset; after all we wouldn't want to offend anybody, would we? Let alone pimps, drug dealers or loose women…

We relocated to the UK when the album was complete, took a short break and then headed to our favourite rehearsal facility in Lititz, Pennsylvania, to prepare for the tour that coincided with the album release in July 1976. Roger and Martyn Dean created staging that cleaned up our stage presentation. Usually our equipment was untidy, higgledy-piggledy, at different heights and shapes, but they designed wide screens each side of the set, covering the guitar and bass amps – a nice, balanced look.

I used my single-neck Sho-Bud pedal steel guitar for 'To Be Over', with its ten strings tuned to Nashville E9. It was a challenge to play, not least because I also had a Telecaster around my neck. The tour started in Toledo, Ohio, on 30 July and ran right through the rest of 1977. The US leg, with Peter Frampton, ended in New Orleans on 9 October, before we played UK and Europe from 24 October until 6 December, closing in Paris with another huge sigh of relief.

Concorde began flying around this time, starting on 21 January 1976, the British and French supersonic jet coming out of service on 2 October 2003, by which time I had flown across the Atlantic in it fourteen times. It really was the best passenger plane. Asia and GTR members also enjoyed its space-age leap across the 'pond' in around three hours or so. I once heard that Vangelis hadn't felt very well while flying on Concorde one day and needed to lie down. The only place he could do so was the aisle that ran down the centre of the plane.

Concorde's styling was so sleek and powerful and Mach 2 was the fastest speed at which any public plane flew. It would rise into the sky dramatically, then straighten off to follow its flight path to New York – and later Washington, its only other scheduled destination. The blasting, booming engines could be heard over Devon about ten minutes after it took off from Heathrow. Even inside, despite soundproofing, it was quite noisy. The cabin was slim, like that of a private jet, but long, like a giant cigar tube. It was very costly – financially and ecologically – more expensive than regular first class. It was the height of supersonic passenger travel. I still have one ticket, for 10 October 1977, seat 7B to Washington, and some brochures that include facts about the aircraft: its cruising altitude was between 50,000 and 60,000 feet; Mach 2 was about 1,320 miles per hour, speeds reserved previously only for fighter jets; its nose drooped 17.5 degrees for landing; it was designed and built by British Aircraft Corporation and Aérospatiale in France; it was powered by four Rolls-Royce Olympus 593 engines; it was 203 feet 9 inches long with a wingspan of 83 feet 10 inches; in one minute it travelled 23 miles, twice the height of Mount Everest.

We'd sometimes take a private plane from the final show of a tour in Miami to New York so we could catch the morning Concorde flight home. We wrote off the added expense of Concorde as a necessity to meet our demands – we had to arrive expediently and to get home ASAP. It was reputed that I bought a seat for my 175 guitar but I'm sure they always let me take it on board, unlike the rules on regular planes where it was once necessary to purchase a seat for the guitar. The alternative was the airline would ship it in the hold, which meant leaving it with baggage handlers and who knows what would happen then?

The last time I tried to take my 175 on tour by hand was on a flight to the States on Virgin Atlantic airways, around 2010. A Virgin employee said, 'You can't take that on board.' I assured him it would be no trouble and that it was a precious instrument that the cabin staff could pop into a wardrobe. No, he wasn't having it. I eventually took the guitar out its case and showed it to the other travellers.

'Look,' I said, 'this is an extremely fine instrument which doesn't travel in the hold, for goodness' sake!' The Musicians' Union have rules about taking instruments on board, but it's common to find airlines unsympathetic and unaccommodating. If you come up against some empowered employee who doesn't know all the facts, it can be hell, as it was on this occasion.

The employee insisted I couldn't board. What was I to do? I had to get this flight so I reluctantly handed it over. It travelled in the pressurised hold and they returned it to me at the gate in LA. I wrote to Virgin in no uncertain terms and did receive their apologies.

Never again would I try to travel by plane with that guitar. I bought another 1964 ES-175D from my friend Paul Sauerteig, one nearly as good as the original 175. Airlines now stipulate that you can't have a seat without a boarding pass and they won't issue a boarding pass for an instrument, only for a person. It's over – ship it or leave it.

I've also been party to several other altercations on different matters at Heathrow and Gatwick airports. In the pre-Eurozone period I'd have to declare items bought abroad at the Customs hall. Arriving with a watch that had been discounted from

Switzerland, I declared it to the officer with the receipt. He looked the watch up in his book of duties payable and claimed my receipt was fake. I explained that I knew the shop manager and, yes, he discounted it.

'OK, but you must pay the tax on the amount in the book,' the Customs officer told me.

'No,' I said, 'just on the amount I paid.'

This went on for some time, back and forwards while streams of people from all over the world just walked by, as if unnoticed by this officer. I pointed this out to him and he bailed out, changing shifts with a colleague, who took one look at the receipt and calculated the appropriate import tax due. Another time, one of these chaps started opening wrapped presents from my case. When he got his hands on a present I'd bought for my darling wife, I fumed, 'Don't open that', but he did anyway. After all, he was only doing his job.

CHAPTER 11

The Near Impossible

Yes had finished touring *Going For The One* at the end of 1977 and had until August 1978 to write, record and release our next extravaganza, *Tormato*.

Right, let's get sleeve designs out the way first.

The original title was 'Yes Tor', the name of a big rock standing on Dartmoor, a protected moorland in the county of Devon, in the south-west of England. Storm and Po took photos of this ancient stone, adding to it a group photo taken in London's Regent's Park and a guy with divining rods overlaid on top. Apparently, they threw it on the floor thinking it was no good, then they trod some delicious tomatoes onto it. There was our sleeve, done, dusted and fairly dodgy. Inside it was nicer, with maps and stuff.

A very good engineer named Geoff Young continued with us from the backing track sessions at Advision to RAK Studios in St John's Wood for the overdubs. Outside was the increasingly large array of vehicles driven by the band members, the Rollers and Bentleys fighting over prime spaces in the leafy streets. Inside, the new polyphonic Moog had its day, battling it out with my Gibson Les Paul Custom – not an encounter designed in audio heaven. These two featured instruments from the keyboard and guitar departments never showed any sign of being compatible. Fortunately, the Telecaster and Hammond worked better on 'Release, Release', 'Madrigal' utilised harpsichord and classical guitar and 'Onward' – one of Chris's best songs – had an orchestral flavour with Andrew Jackman and occasional Les Paul from me, as did 'Don't Kill The Whale'.

I'd been learning to play the hurdy-gurdy, an ancient French street instrument that was very popular in Paris in the 1600s. It has one melodic string crudely stopped by pressing individual, wooden-pitched stops, while a drone is created on another string by a circular wooden disc that also revolves on the melodic string. Medieval by nature, the resulting sound is unimaginably olde worlde and eerie. Well, I had the crazy idea I could overdub this on 'Arriving UFO'. The mic was checked and the tape rolled to the section where I wanted to try it. I began turning the wheel to cue the wonderful cacophony, making a really spooky racket. 'No way,' was the immediate reaction of my bandmates. 'Never again.'

There was a similar reaction from Rick 'Can't take a joke!' Wakeman when I smuggled in commercially released eight-track cartridges that we swapped for the eight-track tapes inside his double-manual Mellotron keyboard while he was in the toilet. He continued recording without checking his keyboard and we looked on from the control room with great anticipation, waiting for him to press down the keys. To his horror, absolutely the weirdest stuff came out when he did: Seals & Croft, Frank Zappa and other artists in a mashed-up racket. Each key he pressed fired a different song from the many different artists we'd loaded into the Mellotron. Not the slightest bit amused, Rick had a complete meltdown and went storming out of the studio. All good fun... well, for most of us anyway.

I've been quoted as saying that none of us can possibly remember how to play most of *Tormato*. The material was certainly tricky to reproduce on stage and much of it never surfaced in our regular stage shows after the initial tour. For instance, 'On The Silent Wings Of Freedom' was actually often tried at tour rehearsals but it would just fall apart. 'Future Times'/'Rejoice' was similarly unsuccessful. It's apparent to me now that the atmosphere during the album's recording sessions transplants to the stage – as with 'Open Your Eyes' or 'Magnification' – and would seem to block the live performances. The improvised sections didn't jell and the songs somehow didn't sit comfortably enough.

That said, the success of our stage show was greatly increased by Mickey Tait's idea for us to tour in the round on a revolving stage. This was a huge draw, a new environment that brought about different ways to perform, and it carried on for several years, becoming a Yes attraction, although it wasn't without problems. The stage revolved four times clockwise then four times anticlockwise, when the cabling for our sound and lights invariably got tangled up. One night the motors failed and the crew had to push it round for us. Our flight cases were positioned like a barrier and beneath the stage it was another world. Cages held equipment off the ground, the crew sat in small perches and everyone avoided sitting in the very centre, as all the bass frequencies met there and were absolutely deafening.

With the album scheduled for release during September, the next series of concerts opened in Rochester, New York, on 28 August and ran until 8 October in Oakland, California. We concluded the year with three shows back home at Wembley Arena between 26 and 28 October. A further huge chunk of touring began on 6 April 1979, in Kansas, Missouri, and went on until 30 June, closing in Miami, Florida. This tour was captured on a video and later DVD release that was recorded in

Philadelphia. It's quite rough but demonstrates where we were at this point in Yes's lifespan, as a no-frills production.

These days we only tour for six weeks at a time. Being on the road and dealing with all the responsibilities that come with it just gets too much for us. I'd hear others grumbling about how the relentlessly demanding schedule cut right through their desire to play our music. Six weeks is the optimum length of time – we get warmed up, get going and stop before it's not fun any more and too tiring to maintain standards.

In the seventies, we'd travel in an entourage by limo and private plane, as was fairly normal for bands like us. But even without tiring connecting flights, queuing or having to explain to people who we were, the tensions and pressures of these much bigger tours would spill out and there were a few bad moments in our dressing rooms. An argument between Jon and Chris turned nasty one night, prompting Chris to do the unthinkable and pour a glass of orange juice over Jon just prior to showtime. Lateness was a regular problem for Chris, which not only caused arguments but also contributed to time wasted for all of us.

I always liked playing in the UK and Europe but it was undeniable that we had more interest in the US and Canada and that's why we toured there more often. The fans were more outwardly enthusiastic, often coming back to see us twice in one year. They were noisier, shouting and screaming compliments during the songs, with party-style banter contributing to the general racket. They intended to have a good time and showed their approval of the band by knowing all the lyrics and applauding favourite segments of songs. The US was the home of the 'superfan', after all. These folk can often be likeable but occasionally some expect more interaction than we'd be prepared to offer. There is a balance that they mostly keep, although some get disgruntled when they can't spend more time with us. Fortunately, most just enjoy the tour and support what we do – so, bravo.

The way that an audience listens to us says plenty about them. We'd independently reach a conclusion about the reaction, quite often depending on how our own performance had gone, although we each often had differing views about that, too. I preferred not to discuss a performance immediately afterwards as things could get out of hand. The right time was the next day at soundcheck.

As the tour ended we drifted apart. Our individual pursuits were leading us into different directions, so much so that Jon and I weren't writing together. It just wasn't happening, the pot was empty. 'Awaken', the song we wrote for *Going For The One*, was the finale. The lone harpist and the lone guitarist were no longer jamming together.

Between the two *Tormato* tours, I'd started recording some tracks for my next solo record, *The Steve Howe Album*, its title a bit of a take on *The Yes Album*, I guess. There was a small studio in Kensington called Redan Recorders where I laid down some of the tracks. I distinctly remember playing the tubular bells on 'Diary Of A Man Who Vanished' and recording the six-string bass guitar on 'Pennants' there. Claire Hamill sang 'Look Over Your Shoulder' rather brilliantly.

After the second *Tormato* tour I took the tracks to RAK Studios, where Yes had recently recorded, with Greg Pryce Jackman engineering, to overdub and mix the album. Greg's brother, Andrew, who'd arranged 'Onward' for Yes, agreed to arrange 'Double Rondo' from a cassette tape of themes I'd written, for an orchestra, and record the second movement of Vivaldi's D major lute concerto for a string section. These were both recorded at the famous Studio 3 at EMI's Abbey Road

Studios, where 'All You Need Is Love' was created. When I have the opportunity to play with an orchestra, it fills me with excitement. Staying calm and clear throughout is vital, so no distractions are allowed. The Vivaldi is rather slower than normal, but this allowed for the sustain to ring on from my electric guitar.

As with *Beginnings*, drumming was divided between Bill Bruford and Alan White. I sung only on a short section in the middle of 'All's A Chord' and most of the rest was instrumental, apart from Claire's lovely contribution. I enjoyed producing myself, although having Greg was a big help. He has great ears and knows all there is to know about the recording process. Andrew steered the orchestral performances perfectly, conducting both pieces. Patrick Moraz had developed *Beginnings* from ideas I'd written, but Andrew dug deeper into arranging my music. He brought so much to the themes, particularly in the finale of 'Double Rondo', where the orchestra swells up to 'call the tune' one final time. Andrew invented a breathtaking canon that I really enjoy, a crescendo that sends shivers down my spine. The album employed what I call my jamboree approach where anything went, as it had in *Beginnings*, *The Grand Scheme Of Things* and *Elements* too. I wanted to stay only loosely in a particular area, expanding its framework.

Towards the end of 1979, Yes unwisely attempted to record a new album in another country with no prior writing or rehearsal. Jon and Rick had been putting together some tunes for our next album but there were issues. Chris and I struggled to get parts for these songs: we felt a little self-conscious and didn't understand the vibe in the Parisian studio we worked in. The songs were different from anything we'd worked on before. Chris and I were puzzled about the direction that the band was taking. We also didn't connect with the chosen producer, Roy Thomas Baker, nor his seemingly heavy drum sound. He played up his role, using his own jargon like 'takey-poos' for 'let's record a take'. We even went with him to collect a brand-new Trans Am car that he ordered from a Parisian dealership. It drove like crap, bits rattled and even fell off in no time at all. We took a lot of breaks and had a lot of dinners.

During these sessions chaos broke out, with our resident comedian repeatedly throwing peanuts over the drum kit and cymbals. This started with a song that we must have been growing tired of playing. The noise of the peanuts falling across the surface of the kit was amplified by the multiple microphones and transmitted to our headphones, which made them sound ginormous. The mess took a while to clear up each time.

We travelled back and forth between Paris and London. The hotels near the studio weren't great and it was cold and noisy. Rough lead vocals were recorded but seemed to have little shape or dynamic and some of the songs were slightly 'Schlager' in a rhythmical sense.

The subject of these tapes came up decades later when I was working with Rhino Records, who re-release Atlantic material, while we were compiling Yes's fortieth-anniversary boxset. They wanted to include whatever we could find. All I had to hand from my archive of the Paris recordings were the backing tracks, each lasting five or six minutes. I edited them down to three or four minutes, omitting much instrumental repetition. No final vocals, melodic ideas or improvised lines had ever been recorded, but they were compiled with other Yes titles and featured as unreleased bonus tracks.

'What happened next in Paris?' you might ask. Well, an accident provided the solution to the impasse. Alan broke his foot – he was skiing, I think. Work was immediately brought to a halt and we got out of Paris pretty quickly to seriously rethink our situation. Many matters would still be left unresolved at the end of the process, including our musical direction, but pressing financial issues also arose. Trying to communicate via accountant, UK solicitor, US lawyer and manager left much to be desired.

'Could we even run a sweet shop?' came back to haunt us.

At meetings we'd even despair that, while we talked, Pink Floyd were probably generating much bigger revenues. Understanding the principles of business seemed fundamental, yet the logic of that approach wasn't evenly distributed throughout the band. After so many good years, here we were trying to evaluate why we needed money in the Yes bank account. I'd always assumed this account had deep reserves, but now it appeared they had been depleted.

A simple solution was settled on: an agreement would be made between us, the aim being to adjust imbalances and to ensure that inequalities that had 'come about' would be fixed. Not everyone agreed, but in the end it happened, because it *had* to. No one member of Yes was worth more than anyone else. We'd risen together and we were each entitled to an equal and even share of the profits.

This equality took several years to achieve and, even then, further imbalances would 'come about' and continue to plague us as we went along our merry way.

Alan, Chris and I were left with the impression that the band was going to reconvene to rehearse new ideas in a room at Redan Recorders. The room we occupied was small and very basic, but affordable. We could at least relax and stay for three or four weeks. Strangely enough, though, only three of us actually worked there: Jon and Rick never showed up.

After a couple of weeks, Jon did appear to play some of the new songs he'd written in Barbados. While Chris, Alan and I had been blazing away in some prog-rock fashion with fast riffs, stomping drums and some really big, heavy structures, Jon's songs were light and wispy with a sort of flower-power breeziness to them. Major chords and pretty, singalong choruses prevailed. The three of us thought, 'That's weird, two different directions.' Jon left that same day and no further work together took place. We three continued to meet and construct more songs, realising we needed to stick together and fill the holes left by Jon and Rick, who always followed Jon's lead.

At this time, The Buggles – Trevor Horn and Geoff Downes – were high in the pop music charts with their song 'Video Killed The Radio Star' and I was surprised when Chris suggested I listen to their album, but he really felt it was 'quite progressive'. It was, in fact, very quirky, with big keyboard pictures, great production and thought-provoking lyrics. Perhaps this pair could be real contenders for Yes. Oddly, they'd already contacted our management looking for representation and we seized the moment to invite them to the rehearsal studio to say hello and, possibly, broach the idea of them joining. We all got on really well and their equipment was delivered and we started playing together. There was instantly something there, something we hadn't felt for a while – hunger and excitement. It felt like there was a great potential for our future.

Over the years I'd watched as the many changes in our line-up made us stronger. Indeed, when no changes occurred it seemed we became weaker. I'd like to think not, as longer periods together should have brought value to our work. But between *Close To The Edge* and *Tales*, and from *Going For The One* to *Tormato*, the shape of each second album with the same line-up signalled that someone was unsure. This meant change was inevitable.

About half the break-ups were musical, but others had much more complex causes – a mixture of personality clashes, financial disagreements and leadership challenges. To exploit our internal battles was never the inspiration behind writing this book but it's hard to gloss over the absurdity of some of the confrontations. There were those who may have believed they ran, controlled or directed Yes, but if they did, they were only fooling themselves. There have always been loud voices and quieter voices in Yes, confrontational or non-confrontational members. Officially the band was/is a democracy, where each vote counts and the majority wins.

The politics of rock bands are loathed by all, yet they determine many an outcome. Someone might so vehemently disagree with a planned idea that we had to respect their individual feelings and hold back. We could each then refuse to accept a particular plan, assuming it wasn't just one person disagreeing with what was being offered. Management would have a vote too (how anything was ever agreed is a mystery). There were many individual calls to management discussing the strengths of one argument over another.

This could have been a filter for opinions, but became divisive when another member's views were portrayed wrongly. 'He's happy to do that,' would be the report but later, from the horse's mouth, you would hear, 'I don't want to do that.' Inconsistencies would repeatedly upset us, causing certain people's reputations to become tarnished. Who could we trust? We were learning different things about each other, but left much to our advisers. Our new-found success had put us in our own firing line.

The professionals sorted out plenty of things. Management encouraged our growth by finding sufficient work to fill up the year. Accountants received their fees, paid the bills with our income and recommended we save a little for a rainy day. Solicitors finalised deals and protected us with and from the written word – usually with far too many of the words for us to fully understand what was being decided. Record companies paid advances, distributed the recordings and accounted quarterly. Publishers collected the songwriting income and passed it back to the writer at the agreed percentage. Agents booked the tours, organising the routes with the promoters and accounted to our accountant. I mention these people to demonstrate the complexity of the band's operational structure. Each professional provided their services to the fullest extent. Not many were thanked. Some left us disgruntled while others lost it altogether. But, remember, the problem at hand was mostly us.

We were the creators but could we act accordingly and properly run our companies? We had a classic tendency to veer off into irrelevant areas during business meetings. We eventually made a rule that there would be no alcoholic drinks or smoking of any description while we met to decide things. This lasted for about five minutes. There simply wasn't a clear enough division between art and our business affairs. We rarely managed to tidy up one area without influencing another.

In the mid-seventies we suffered a major decrease in our writing income due to a deal that had led to us being 'double-published': two publishers were receiving percentages from our songs and this alone lost us a massive share of our rightful income. Add this to the cost of our big stage productions, private planes and stylish hotel arrangements and it's easy to see how our touring profits and record royalties were

The Near Impossible

eaten up. As if that wasn't enough, our personal spending was eclipsing our income. Somehow, we always got over the hurdles, but that merely meant we were closer to approaching the next one.

In 1980, the new line-up presented us with a golden opportunity to reset our business structure and make a break with the past. Good teamwork and shared writing meant we were beginning to chart the group's direction and reinstating its standards. It was run to the end of my first ten-year 'term of office' in the band. The second decade would go from 1994 to 2004 and, at the time of writing, I'm about to complete my third decade, 2008 to 2018. Yes will then be 50 years old. I have been part of it for nearly thirty of those fifty years. The first decade was monumental in establishing the sound of Yes around the world, with my guitar-playing to the fore. Back in 1980 we thought, 'Let's close out the decade with a life-fulfilling, great record. Let's make every note and word count and every beat and space tell its own story.'

After more time preparing at Redan we went to the Townhouse Studios, owned at that time by Richard Branson, in Shepherd's Bush, London, to record *Drama*, which was released in August 1980. We worked in Studio 2, notorious for the stone room area that Phil Collins and others made famous with crisp, compressed drum sounds that contributed so much to their end product. We began by working with Eddie Offord, Chris insisting and believing that the partnership 'would be like the old days'. Well, it wasn't and nor could it be like the old days.

On one occasion, Eddie walked into the control room while we were playing back a mix, assumed it was coming from the multi-track machine and began moving faders, adding delays, panning and deceiving himself that he was altering the sound. As it faded out, we shouted, 'Eddie, it was a mix!'

Eddie left after three weeks. One fateful afternoon he told us, 'There's more interesting things I could be doing than presiding over the control room desk.' Things were going nowhere and he needed to be in the control room the whole time. But matters reached a head when I arrived at the studio and the restaurant staff asked me to stop Eddie cooking an unpopular London pigeon – deceased but not dressed for dinner, bubbling away in a saucepan. 'Right, that's the last straw. You're fired!' I told him. 'Officially fired! Get out of here, now!'

Eddie packed his and his girlfriend's things from the penthouse above the studio where he'd been living and left. Since the end of the *Relayer* period he'd been 'sorting himself out' after getting pretty messed up on the road. Eddie was a really skilled engineer, mellow but also a bit crazy. Contradictions abounded. Picture him pushing a motorbike through the lobby of a hotel into the elevator, saying, 'I'm just going to fix it up in my room.'

We really started having a good time at the Townhouse when Hugh Padgham began engineering. He was already on the way up, and by now his CV must be enormous. We laid down all the backing tracks then started overdubbing. To stay on top of the schedule (we were thinking: 'Tour ahead'), we started running two and then three studios at once. I focused exclusively on guitars, moving into Roundhouse Studios, Chalk Farm, for three weeks, where Ashley Howe (no relation) engineered the sessions using an array of my favourite guitars, amps and effects. I had a thoroughly good time and returned with the tapes to the Townhouse, where the master tapes were synchronised with the slave tapes I'd used. As we listened back to my parts, a mixture of delight and shock engulfed the room.

All my leads were highly developed and I'd played everywhere where I thought a guitar part was needed. I was delighted with the brightness of my sounds, although almost everyone else wasn't. I thought I'd found the most appropriate sound I could, be it Gibson, Fender, Gretsch, Rickenbacker, steel and acoustic (although it was Trevor who played the acoustic guitar on 'Machine Messiah'). The guitar tracks settled in and only one of the parts I'd recorded didn't make it to the mix, from 'Into The Lens', where a slightly mad steel guitar part, nicknamed 'the buzzy bee', was overruled. It had a kind of zigzag slur but was forever silenced.

'Tempus Fugit' was a particularly exciting, high-speed track with descending and ascending guitar lines moving across different keys, lines inspired by one of Charlie Christian's guitar parts. His importance can be summed up by saying that all jazz guitar players from the fifties and sixties are part of the post-Charlie Christian era. He was the first electric single-line guitar player to emerge and join the ranks of the jazz greats. This, if you like, is where the electric guitar really took off, insofar as guitarists had previously usually played only chordal rhythm work.

Born in Dallas, Texas, in 1916, Charlie Christian was discovered by John Hammond in 1939. Possibly the best place to hear him is on the recordings he made with Benny Goodman. It is in the quality of these recording that his sense of musical organisation is most evident. This team-up actually had a hit record with the tune 'Solo Flight'. The refreshing ideas he brought seemed to indicate he was destined to became a jazz thoroughbred but, sadly, he passed away at the height of his career on 2 March 1942, due to tuberculosis, leaving behind a road map that everyone could follow and add to. With his humble Gibson ES-150 and amp, he facilitated the elevation of the guitar to the front line. Segovia was busy with the classical repertoire, Django was finding great success and Charlie was busy inventing a new sound that bandleaders could build around.

The guitar's acceptance and popularity increased at an incredible rate after him. Christian's imagination had been developed mostly from the horn and piano players surrounding him in clubs and during recording sessions. One of the most striking things about his playing was the length of his lines. Back then the guitar was seen as a folk or blues instrument and it was Charlie Christian who made sure it was taken far more seriously.

Back to *Drama*, and the mixing, at Sarm East, was really intense. Trevor and I were left to mix most of the tracks as the other guys went on holiday, which we had all initially planned to do. Instead, the two of us stayed put and worked with Gary Lanham and Julian Mendelsohn, both great engineers. We tried to squeeze every last drop of goodness from the tapes.

This had to be a whole and complete Yes album and Roger Dean returned to deliver a perfect-fit sleeve. He produced deep colours and jagged shapes – it was very textural but had a looming forebodingness of darkness, like old River Thames herself. Inside, the gatefold sleeve photo showed us up close, leaning against the glass sliding doors between the control room and the stone room of Townhouse Studio 2.

Not long after the album's completion, we headed for Lititz, Pennsylvania, and Tait Towers, to rehearse a new set that contained several *Drama* pieces and classic seventies tracks. We had plenty to do, as the touring began in the month of the album's release, August 1980. We started at Maple Leaf Gardens in Toronto and ran all the way through to the Rainbow Theatre in London's Finsbury Park on 17 and 18 December.

We had only three weeks off, between the end of October and the middle of November. The new songs were great to play on stage, which helped us in the US. There the tour went off without so much as a glitch, to the extent that we polished off three highly successful nights at Madison Square Garden in New York. With these dates, Yes set the record for the most sold-out gigs – seventeen – by any band at the venue, up to that point.

The UK was a little different, with several bouts of heckling and noisy shouting from diehards who missed Jon and Rick. In addition, some members of the group were contributing less than satisfactory performances due to their indulgences in habits or vices. Without naming names, I can state that the perpetrators rarely cleaned up their acts long enough before they went back to their old ways, much to our dismay. It was a testing time for us all, particularly for Trevor. He'd suggested that we change the keys of a few older songs but, unwisely perhaps, we refused. We put him under enormous strain, expecting the near impossible without properly listening to what he was saying. It would be the same in 2008 when Benoît David tried to explain how he could perform better with us, but we didn't change or properly accommodate his requests, as in 'Turn down the stage volume!' The level of the backline amps and the monitoring for the drum rig was a highly sensitive area that caused endless problems for all our singers.

The Yes boxset *In A Word Live* highlighted some of our strengths at this time, as we played two other songs live on this tour that were not released on *Drama*. 'You Can Fly From Here' was revisited in 2011 with Trevor, building it into the twenty-six-minute extended epic title track of our *Fly From Here* album, re-released in 2018 with Trevor singing lead vocals. My 'Go Through This' was the other one, which, as a rediscovered studio recording, may be released in the future.

Drama stands out in my estimation as a true classic Yes album. If you haven't listened to it, do. It speaks oceans about Yes music and the melodic adventures we loved, a kind of accumulation of the previous decade, I'd say. We were just a rock band fundamentally, with a bent towards individuality.

With as much technology as possible, we took to the road, with Geoff's massive keyboard setup, Chris and I with all the guitar and bass gadgets and effects we needed and Trevor playing great rhythm guitar. With a Clair Brothers PA and Tait Towers staging, often in the round, the shows were really exhilarating. On the last night of the tour there was a predictable panic, as no prizes for guessing who arrived forty-five minutes late... er, Chris, of course. 'It's only Chris,' said his wife. This was absolutely no consolation. I'd been waiting around for him throughout the previous ten years. The tour ended with us waiting for him yet again, one final time.

In early January 1981, Trevor Horn, Geoff Downes, Chris Squire and Alan White came to our house to discuss the future. It was an ill-starred meeting. Chris and Alan announced their intention to collaborate with Jimmy Page (who apparently wasn't on the same page – no pun intended), Trevor needed to get the next Buggles album recorded (although Geoff was less clear about whether that required his full attention), I was available to continue with Yes and, in the end, it looked like only Geoff and I would be remaining in the band.

After giving it some thought, I said to Geoff, 'Replace three members? No way.' I was over with juggling musicians to re-form another Yes line-up. I couldn't go through that again right away. I'd been there, done that and bought the T-shirt! Little did we know at that point, but we would encircle each other again in the following decades through different line-ups of Yes and Asia. Yet the decision to discontinue Yes was not an easy one. I was helped by how I was feeling mentally, which had been, in turn, strengthened by the eating and well-being principles that Jan and I had followed since we went vegetarian in 1972. At this point, that was the end of Yes — at least until the gauntlet was picked up in 1982.

CHAPTER 12

Launch Pad

Within a couple of months of the decision to abandon Yes, I met John Wetton.

John had been performing throughout the seventies with groups like Family, Uriah Heap, UK and King Crimson. We agreed to spend a few days at the Redan rehearsal room. We blared away, firing off riffs and jamming on simple structures while checking each other out, to see how we got along and if we could write together. We might have touched on a few of our eventual co-written songs.

We asked Simon Phillips, an excellent drummer, if he wanted to try out with us. He had impressed us when we watched him with Jeff Beck a few days earlier and he arrived at Redan with a riser and a full-on kit that occupied half of the room. When he played it was phenomenal. He wanted to write songs too and we agreed to meet at our house in Hampstead Garden Suburb. Here I had a small drum room with an eight-track recording studio on the top floor. We set about laying down a couple of tunes and added a few overdubs. It had been quite promising but other, seemingly disconnected, matters weighed in and before long Simon stopped working with us, but without hard feelings either way. I have these two recordings in my store —

one 'untitled' while the other became one of the songs on the album we would soon record.

ELP weren't doing anything, so John and I invited Carl Palmer to Nomis, a rehearsal facility in Shepherd's Bush, near John's home. I rented a double storage cage there, for my guitars and amps. We played one afternoon in mid-1981; it worked well and made us feel confident about starting a new band.

John and Carl had it in their minds that we'd be a guitar-trio-style group. This was, in a way, flattering, but in my head I was hearing the interplay and texture between guitar and keyboards. I told John and Carl that Geoff Downes had a lot to offer with his keyboards and writing. He had the notoriety of Buggles and his Yes wings. We played with Geoff at Nomis and, although it went well, auditions didn't stop. Strangely, we continued to look for yet another musician/writer/singer to further augment the line-up. We auditioned Robert Fleischman and Trevor Rabin(!), both at Ear Studios in Shepherd's Bush. Finally, after meeting up with Roy Wood it became apparent that we had our line-up already with just the four of us. We started preparing ideas and rehearsing and our management looked around for a record deal. We had the same infrastructure that supported Yes, the managers simply moving operations to back my new, as yet unnamed, group, as did Yes's agents and publishers. It did seem like a good idea to have a new record label working for us, with a fresh sense of opportunities. We were free to negotiate – after all, we weren't going to be called Yes.

'Asia' was chosen (as I remember) because it was the last remaining name on a list of ten after all the others had been knocked off; definitely better than, say, Scunthorpe, I thought. We had no intention or desire to emulate, copy or be compared to Yes. We each of us wanted a different direction to free ourselves from the confines of our previous groups and to stand out with a more rock/prog/pop style of music. We would be less reliant on long instrumental sections and, instead, we would take a more direct route, in order to appeal to a wider audience. There was definitely a hint of stadium rock in our thinking. Mike Stone agreed to produce us, having been the main man behind Journey, Queen, Kiss and other highly successful bands, and helped us keep the more straightforward style. The band members brought added value in the form of the musical credibility of our previous bands, leading people to think Asia would be similar to Yes, King Crimson and ELP, although we clearly weren't. Much of what Geoff and John wrote together was in a nice contrast to what John and I wrote. The first album would be a successful attempt to keep most of the fans happy and ourselves happy, for most of the time.

We set up in Marcus Studios, Kensington, to do backing tracks, before moving to the space we'd liked most, Studio 2 at the Townhouse with its stone room. Mike Stone ramped up the atmosphere with funny repartee that echoed his rock'n'roll lifestyle. He knew when we were 'on' or 'not on', and his confidence made us feel at ease – he was a hands-on engineer and producer with great flair. Good producers can be channels to communicate through and arrive at a common place on time and within budget. It doesn't always happen in practice.

The sessions pushed ahead with all the main tracks recorded (except the eventual single), including 'Over And Over', which would later be re-recorded for our reunion, *Phoenix*, in 2008. 'Ride Easy' (Wetton/Howe) would be the B-side of our first single.

There were a few fractious moments between the team, usually after dinner when we started getting hazy about exactly what it was we wanted to hear from someone else's instrument at any given time. We might be trying different ideas out, deciding later which was best, with the producer's guidance, of course. Occasionally, it was Mike's role to clear the air and decide what was happening, and then it had to be *his* way, if you please. Great ideas came about through collaboration but the songs themselves had to stand up, ringing with conviction before we dressed them up. Music can only be as deep as the belief it holds; songs without a story or any particular reason to exist provid no reward for the listener.

With most of the songs recorded, David Geffen at Geffen Records, who'd signed us, reviewed our progress and said he wanted just one more song to be a really strong, standout single. Fortunately, John and Geoff had one more in the pipeline. John ran through the verse chords with me, saying, 'Beef these up a bit.' The chorus rolled along nicely with interesting bass routes. It didn't take long to lay down the backing track to 'Heat Of The Moment' and then detail the song. I powered up the intro and verses with my Gibson Les Paul Junior through seven different amps for seven tracks of grungy, distorted guitar. I played a cleaner arpeggio part on my Telecaster during the choruses and a koto (a Japanese stringed instrument) in the middle eight that doubled the keyboard line. The guitar solo across the fade was played on the same Les Paul Junior. John sung all the vocals (elsewhere, Geoff and I provided harmonies).

Mike would happily have mixed alone but we insisted on being involved. Each evening we'd arrive about 7 p.m. and have a listen to the mix as it was. Usually, just about everything seemed right but, occasionally, we'd rebalance some guitar and keyboard moments before approving the fades and, eventually, the running order. Each track sounded better than we thought they would and we all got a little happy about it — always a good sign. It was a solid album that I have fond memories of making. There was a lot of excitement about the crafted production of our songs that really helped form a bond of respect and equality between the four of us. 'Time Again' and 'One Step Closer' are among my favourites, 'Here Come That Feeling' and 'Without You' come close too; also 'Cutting It Fine', which was sketched with Simon Phillips and has more of a live approach to the electric guitar – an ES Artist model – with an acoustic intro. Some musicians don't listen to or enjoy their recordings but I review mine periodically and derive insight and pleasure on occasion. More importantly, I'm delighted that other people enjoy the way I play the guitar: that's the real reward.

We then wisely invited Roger Dean to design the artwork. This gave Roger a chance to show he could adapt to new demands and reinvent himself, as it seemed we were doing. His logos were brilliant at locking in the association between a band and its name.

The eponymous *Asia* record and CD – my first ever CD and vinyl release – came out on 8 March 1982. We rehearsed for two or three weeks at the venue of our first US show in Potsdam, upstate New York, on 22 April. This almost drove us stir-crazy! It was close to Lancaster and Lititz and the advantages of Tait Towers staging and Clair Audio equipment, but we overestimated just how long we needed to rehearse. Staying put didn't feel right and we were itching to do shows. We didn't want to sit around or be over-rehearsed – or so we thought.

The shows eventually kicked off and we got a terrific reaction every night. Besides playing tracks from the album we also played two unreleased songs, both recorded later for our second album. 'Midnight Sun' had a full band arrangement and 'The

Smile Has Left Your Eyes' found John and Geoff in duet mode. John featured his bass guitar-playing on 'The Man With The Golden Arm', on two April dates at the start of the tour. I played various tunes from my solo repertoire in my nightly guitar spot: I did 'Clap' quite often but also 'Ram', 'Double Rondo' or 'Surface Tension'. There were no big problems on that first tour. It was our honeymoon period, with champagne breakfast.

Something far more important was happening back home: Jan was about to give birth to our first daughter. The tour dates had been scheduled in the hope that the baby would arrive before we left but she was born two weeks later than expected, on 28 April. I was about to board a plane from New Haven, Connecticut, when I called the hospital from a public phone to hear that Georgia had been born and both Jan and our tiny girl were doing just fine. I was elated when my flight left and the pilot announced the news. All the plane's occupants congratulated and toasted us with champagne. It was a shame I couldn't have been home at this time but Jan managed the whole thing brilliantly. I had to wait a whole month, until 1 June, to see them both in person, but photos were sent to me by our friends Alex and June Scott. Getting back was super-exciting, as we were simply overjoyed by our growing family.

After a two-week break at home we resumed touring on 14 June in Toledo, Ohio, and continued through until 8 July in Denver, Colorado. We then took a well-earned break for about three months. From 5 October we played through Europe, opening in Brussels and continuing in the Netherlands, France, Germany, Spain, Italy and Switzerland. This first Asia tour closed with two amazing shows at London's Wembley Arena on 27 and 28 October.

'Heat Of The Moment' did us proud, particularly in the States, where it climbed to US No. 7. In Europe the first single was 'Only Time Will Tell', which didn't chart as high. This song was the second single in the US and did fairly well, giving us massive airplay. Hey, we were the first 'supergroup' of the eighties, after all. This sort of hype didn't do us any harm, was encouraged by the PR people and so we obliged and played along with the idea.

The fact that Asia were succeeding and climbing the same path trodden by Yes was deeply satisfying for me. The band had quickly demonstrated its popularity in the US and we thought perhaps we could open up Japan and Australia for touring and records. It felt like a bit of a second coming for me. The band Tomorrow had broken through to some degree in 1967, then it was Yes that broke through in the seventies, going on to wider success, and now it could be happening all over again for me with Asia.

It was important that the Yes royalties kept ticking over, flowing from the previous ten years' work with all the splits and percentages paid out quarterly. Nevertheless, the agreements on the actual rights would forever be up for interpretations, re-analysis and reinvention.

My popularity as a player was holding strong, as reflected by my winning *Guitar Player* magazine's top guitarist category for five consecutive years (the first to do so) from 1977 through 1981 in the premier US publication. They had kindly featured me quite a bit during the seventies, with several front covers, often with interviews stretching to many pages inside. Mostly, and perhaps surprisingly, this was about music, and I say this because, in the many hours spent doing interviews, I was chit-chatting about the musician's life – touring, 'living the dream' and answering dubious questions about why members had left Yes and even 'Aren't you millionaires yet?'

As with TV, when interviews were good, they could be very good. I've enjoyed good interviews with thought-provoking questions which are more like conversations, where an actual response to an answer is greeted with respect. Suddenly, people were interested in what I thought, not only about my music but my opinions about hundreds of other minute topics and whatever I said went into print. I do say to myself, 'I should be so lucky,' but it's also worth remembering that I was just one part of a group and it's because of that group's success that I was enjoying far wider popularity. That being true, I know the success I've had has increased my confidence and my belief in myself as an artist. Those goals I set myself years before were all about what sort of guitarist I would become. I wanted to refine and develop my playing to achieve the highest possible standard. I wanted to encourage my inventiveness so I could rise to whatever challenge I was presented. While listening to great guitarists I often thought, 'How can I combine their approach with mine?' I doubt there's any musical sound I've heard that hasn't influenced me in some way or another.

Steve Morse, the most deserving of musicians, also achieved five consecutive years of nominations. Actually, in 1981 I was amazed when I heard *What If* by Dixie Dregs, Morse's southern country-jazz rock group, brilliantly produced by Ken Scott. Steve Morse knocked my socks off with his astounding dexterity and the way he could switch to subtle lyricism. As the record ended, I vowed to reach him. I had to. I did too, the very next year.

Amid the repeated success there was little time to consider how lucky Asia had been, how fortunate I'd been or how delicate the future was going to be. Juggling life with work is never easy and, by 1982, Jan and I had our three wonderful children growing up while my touring schedule required demanding, tiring and prolonged periods of separation. We needed gaps – long gaps – to properly reconnect. We felt happy about the lifestyle we'd created for ourselves and the freedom it offered us. I mainly remember being happy that love was all around us, our unit seemed protected, and our parents were around too. The children's good school was just around the corner and between term times we could take nice breaks. Times were good – in fact, very good. Nevertheless, the achievements I enjoyed in my music career couldn't hold a candle to the time I spent relaxing with the ones I loved.

Having experimented with various different methods of learning about altered states of mind, near the end of 1982 I finally decided on one particular approach to meditation. Altered states can be evoked by breathing exercises taken from Zen ideas, Tao thoughtfulness, Buddhist thinking, Indian horizontal relaxation, and different chanting or mantras. One exercise even involved revolving on your backside and another breathing in and out nine times for nine seconds with each breath but none resulted in me losing my awareness totally. I made a free-will choice and have happily spent the last thirty-six years following the methods of transcendental meditation. If you can find something that's right for you, stick with it and see what develops. Naturally evolving methods accumulate their benefits gradually. I was always curious about the mind's potential, not so much scientifically but more in application. We come heavily programmed with all these amazing functions automatically occurring inside. With some practice, directing our focus engages the mind so that other things don't interfere, offering a few moments of nothingness that prepare you for the next task at hand, possibly the whole day ahead or perhaps just the concert you're about to give.

CHAPTER 13

Perils Of Empowerment

Following the sudden success of Asia, there was a mad rush to start on our second record.

We should have rested a bit longer, collaborated more and discussed its direction but Geffen's A&R guy John Kalodner stepped in and pushed for an album containing as many potential hit singles as possible, putting pressure mainly on John Wetton and Geoff, as they had written our previous singles. Kalodner believed they had the Midas touch.

As winter drew in on 1982, we put together plans to record in Canada at Morin-Heights, outside Montreal. The studio was pleasant, albeit fairly remote, next to a lake with mountains in the distance. I stayed in a little cottage within walking distance of the main house where there was catered food and, just across the car park, the studio. John stayed in the house on a permanent basis while Geoff, Carl and myself came and went as we saw fit. We were all there for backing tracks and splintered off when overdubs started. Although Mike Stone was producing, we had our dear friend from Advision, Paul Northfield, the resident engineer at Morin-Heights, engineer all the recordings. Paul lives in Canada and now has a top producer's CV. This sort of allowed Mike to play things differently. He wasn't as hands-on as before but rather wafted about overseeing everything, leaning towards his producer side. This should have worked fine but... here's why it didn't.

The first issue was that, while the setup was everything we could ask for at the time, we were in a fairly remote part of Canada and some cabin fever was inevitable, I guess. Although the Howe/Wetton song 'Lying To Yourself' was recorded – with vocals added later by Bob Clearmountain – it didn't appear on the album and, indeed, the choice of songs made to record and overdub for the record didn't include anything by me. I pressed on anyway, as I can easily enjoy 'being the guitarist' without writing for a band or project. It's weird, but not being involved in the writing actually keeps me unbiased and clear: I'm not rooting for my songs.

In this case, I obviously pushed hard enough to get 'Lying To Myself' recorded. It was originally titled 'Barren Land' and John rewrote the lyrics. In its early form the song told of the plight of the American Indian (now referred to as the First Nation Americans). It might be hard to believe but John Kalodner was seriously worried about the lyrics.

'It'll be too controversial,' he said.

'Bullshit!' I replied.

Either way, 'Lying To Myself' lay on the shelf until it was rescued as the B-side of 'Don't Cry', the first single from our second album *Alpha*, which was still being finished off as we geared up to tour again. John contributed some nice vocals and Bob Clearmountain asked him to come into the control room to listen to the final vocal take. A strange mini-loop began. John listened and said, 'Play it again, please.' It played again, then again and again, with John repeatedly making the same request, 'Play it again.' An unusual atmosphere settled over the control room, a sort of 'lost in space' vibe. We were there, but was

John? Bless him! Eventually, he agreed it was good, so the final mixing could go ahead. We much enjoyed working with Bob, a genuine professional whose sound was as clear as his name suggests, besides which he was pleasant to work with.

Another thing that was not great about this recording session was that, once we had ploughed through the bulk of the songs on *Alpha*, we realised it was quite commercial – not terribly prog – with many repeated choruses and few instrumental sections. Paul Northfield and I collaborated well during the guitar overdubs, though some were heard only softly and others lost in the mix, including some short introductions that were completely cut. This is the first time I can recall so much editing and poor mixing of my guitar parts, and I couldn't help but feel my role was being undervalued.

I had a Super 8mm camera with which I captured a clips of 'Life in Morin-Heights', some included in an Asia DVD. One clip featured the huge lake adjacent to the studio that we used as an echo chamber, with a microphone on one side picking up the speaker playing back guitars on the other side. It sounded vast when added to the tracks via an echo return. Once all the tracks were done, we left Mike Stone and Paul Northfield to mix, giving us a tiny break before rehearsals would start for the scheduled US tour.

Lititz was our destination for three weeks of rehearsing, again more time than we really needed, and we all became restless. Then mixes from Mike arrived for our approval. I remember us gathering in an apartment, one rented to us by Clair Brothers co-founder Roy – I think it was mine, actually. The mix went on the turntable, the level was adjusted and… we began to worry. Without our influence, Mike had created a kind of wall of sound with the guitar and keyboards mixed together in a bit of a mush, resulting in a lack of distinction. Some guitar fronts were missing – never to be replaced – and I wasn't by any means alone in feeling disappointed. We all felt let down. We demanded a remix of the entire album. Reluctantly, it was done, although it didn't seem to make a big difference overall and tour deadlines and release schedules determined that, however it sounded, *Alpha* had to be released to the world on 8 August 1983.

The upcoming tour was entitled The Asia Invasion (not exactly what we'd call a tour now). I had bought a car to avoid as many flights as I could and to ensure I was no longer part of an entourage. The car afforded me a vital degree of privacy I didn't get even with the luxuries of private jets. I didn't drive it myself, instead hiring younger friends of friends from Lititz who saw it as an adventure, an opportunity to see the US from city to city. I still travel by car whenever I can.

I had a Mercedes-Benz 300 turbo diesel estate car that was dubbed 'Steve's ambulance' (David Bowie also travelled in one) due to it being white, and it soldiered on for around 300,000 miles. Imported to the US and stored in various locations around Lititz, it was sometimes transported coast to coast when an empty truck had to go anyway, enabling me to have the car on the West Coast if the touring started there. It was returned to Lititz after tours, often driven across the US by my hired hand. The main drawback with owning a car in the US as a non-citizen was storing and moving it when I wasn't in the country, besides the insurance and servicing. I now use rented cars that are replaceable if they break down and are easily returnable at the end of a tour.

Our live work began at the Blossom Music Center near Akron, Ohio, on 27 July and continued until 7 September. Since 1978 I'd been playing through Fender Twin amps with two 12-inch speakers but on this tour I used two 15-inch speakers instead. This caused me a bit of concern as the sound was quite different. I was playing four Gibson ES Artist guitars: the sunburst had been the main instrument on the 1982 tour of US, UK and Europe, then there was a black model detuned for 'Heat Of The Moment' and, finally, a custom blonde and a tobacco sunburst as spares. We had more space now as Geoff was behind us on a rostrum that stretched right across the stage. He'd run up and down to reach different parts of his keyboard setup. Carl was centre-stage, flanked by John and me, and, as he played with ELP, Carl revolved during his drum solo near the end of the show.

We played songs from both our albums and I performed a solo piece. To all intents and purposes, we looked good but as we went along some of our musical arrangements began to fall apart. 'Who was right, who was wrong?' we'd ask after the shows. There were variations in the arrangements, such as repeated choruses or extended solos, that differed from the tracks on the album. 'We do this on record but do that on stage,' we'd say and hope that tomorrow night all would be fine. Well, this didn't work. Before the New York show some of the band gave an interview — never a good idea — and went on stage disorientated and rather out of it, so to speak, and the standard of performance suffered. Now, if you screw up, try not to do so in New York. The word gets out, just as it does if you're playing great.

Much has since been said that suggests things happened differently, but Geoff, Carl and I eventually told John that we were unhappy with the mistakes in the show. We depended on each other 100 per cent. We were only as good as our weakest link. Surely we could pull it together if we agreed we had to? But we had to agree there was a problem in the first place. We decided to stop touring after Pine Knob, Michigan, on 7 September, cutting all future shows that were planned till 31 October. This seemed like a bad move – and it certainly was. It wasn't made public, but John Wetton had effectively left Asia due to our lack of support for him.

While the tour was in the New York area, I had a musical reality check when I jammed with Steve Morse at My Father's Place, a club at Roslyn, Long Island. I had taken a cab to arrive for the soundcheck of that evening's performances by Allan Holdsworth and his band and the Steve Morse Band. Allan opened the first of two shows, followed by Steve. I joined Steve on two encores: one a Jeff Beck tune I'd just learned at the soundcheck while the other was most probably a 12-bar blues. Steve then opened the second performance, and again I joined him for his encores. We went down sensationally well both times. I felt like music was properly 'running through my veins': it was challenging and really connected with my spiritual side. It was like Asia played at one level but that night I'd ascended to much higher levels of performance that involved telepathy, excitement and finesse. I'm pleased to say that I've stayed in touch with Steve Morse since then. He invited me to appear on his album *Industrial Standard* and remains one of my favourite guitar players. I'm delighted he's found an even wider appeal playing with Deep Purple. I will always particularly admire his sound.

It was strange to hear Allan Holdsworth when I told him how fantastic his set had been. 'It was terrible. I didn't play well at all!' he said. This was sad to hear because he *always* maintained an utterly amazing, beautiful level of guitar inventiveness. I nevertheless knew how introspective performers can be. It's good to set your goals high and attempt to maintain those standards throughout your life but, in reality, so much changes on the night due to any number of factors in any individual show. Yet with practice and through focusing effectively, performers can control their state of mind, make the most of the opportunities available *and* enjoy themselves. As Ronnie O'Sullivan has said about playing snooker, a game I love, 'You have to enjoy it to do it really well.'

Asia were committed to play several shows in Japan, predictably entitled Asia in Asia. Management pointed this out when Geoff, Carl and I talked things through with them. How could we do this after what we'd been through? How could we keep the group going? It was suggested that Greg Lake replace John in Japan and then we'd see how it went. If he fitted in, he could continue to fill John's role with lead vocals, bass guitar and bass pedals. It turned out that Greg was available but had a few rather extravagant requests: a week at a famous health farm and some new amplification, paid for by us. This was greeted with a degree of outrage, but Greg charmed us into providing him with these and other natural comforts to make a rock star feel OK. It was all compensation for the pressure we were putting him through. Next we had to make key changes to accommodate his lower pitch, a semitone here, two semitones there. To change the keys of so many songs could only work for me by using a guitar detuned by two semitones, another by a whole tone and, more often, using the semitone-down, black guitar already in play. The show we started preparing was also going to be filmed and broadcast live. Oh, my goodness! A new guy in the band, recording, filming and broadcasting – nerves of steel were required.

We did most of the rehearsals in a three-week stint at a Yamaha music centre on the Japanese coast overlooking seaweed farms floating in the bay. We each had a small chalet overlooking the sea, but at night there were no outside lights. We rode bikes and I did a little archery, a hobby I tried back home but had quit as it strained my wrists. We got on with the job at hand, often bemused by Greg's mannerisms. He was a really great singer, a fine guitarist and bassist, and displayed all the grandeur of a rock star, rather frozen in the seventies. He was a larger-than-life character, partly due to his size, but equally because of his expectations. Amusingly and classically, we were working with someone who acted on impulse: after we'd repeatedly asked him not to break off songs for any old reason, he persisted by stopping us yet again, turning to his tech and saying, 'Oh, John, make a note for me. I mustn't forget to call so-and-so.' We were livid at the time, but to survive one has to tolerate and occasionally enjoy the quirks of others.

The shows and the final recording, filming and broadcast went fairly well, considering. It is what it is: Asia in Asia. A week or so after we'd finished with the tour, I was back home and at 1 a.m. in the morning, Greg called. 'It was great, let's write together, let's make an album.'

The next day the rest of us talked and it was clear that Carl rather regretted getting Greg in the band. He should have known better but it has to be said that Greg had, in fact, helped us out of a very tight corner. Now, however, it was time to rethink things.

At this point, John Wetton opened up discussions, via management, about returning to the band. We were delighted and agreed to start planning a third album. For two weeks we worked at John Henry's rehearsal facility near Holloway, London, playing some of the material that later became *Astra*. I thought it was going well until a meeting was called at the management office. Rather nervously, John Wetton said, 'Steve, I can't work with you any more.'

He appeared to have the undivided support of Geoff, Carl and management.

'Oh, so I guess this is final, then?' I said. 'Oh, well, good luck.'

As I upped and left the building, I couldn't help but think to myself that perhaps I was luckily avoiding more trouble and doubt, and that I was better off out of it after all.

I did some loose but productive session work for Trevor Horn and his label ZTT. These included playing with Frankie Goes To Hollywood and Propaganda, the German synth group. After 'Relax', Frankie were huge and work was under way on their first album, *Welcome To The Pleasuredome*. I played acoustic Dobro guitar in the breakdown section of the title track. On 'Two Tribes' I'm 'part' of the bass riff – by which, I mean Trevor picked elements from performances of the riff played by different musicians and then looped them.

Welcome… featured mainly top session players but more of the band's own performances made it to their second album, *Liverpool*. It was great, but lacked a lead single to propel it up the charts. My appearances with them and on the Propaganda album were great fun. I always enjoy the vibe of going in sort of cold to a session and then being able to pull something out of the bag in the shape of quality guitar.

I got to talking to Steve Hackett and we soon discussed writing together and forming a band that would combine the styles of Genesis and Yes with perhaps a bit of Asia thrown in for good measure. It was mid-1985 and we mostly met at his house in East Twickenham, south of London, playing our acoustic guitars face to face on various tunes and songs that we hoped we could collaborate on, mixing ideas from each of us. I brought demos from my studio while Steve had some CDs and cassettes of his music to play for me, although he didn't have a recording setup in his house. We got quite a lot of co-writing done this way, initially over a three-month period. We also talked about who could play in the band, who could produce it and who would release the album we were writing.

We tried out the various musicians we'd discussed, settling on a line-up featuring Max Bacon as lead vocalist, Phil Spalding on bass and harmonies and Jonathan Mover on drums. Phil had been recommended to us, Max was in a band Steve knew called Nightwing, and Jonathan had hounded Steve to audition him. Our eventual stage shows would also include Matt Clifford on keyboards. We rehearsed solidly at John Henry's. Not only did we have a bunch of songs we believed in and a band assembled to play on the record and for touring but Sun Arts, who had managed Yes, Asia and now this new group, had sniffed out a deal with Geffen Records, the same label that had so successfully released Asia's records.

While all this was happening I got a call from John Kalodner. 'Steve, will you play on the next Asia record?' he asked. 'Overdub on it for us and we'll pay you $75,000.' I thought for a minute. How was Steve Hackett going to feel about this?

I said, 'It depends on the music. Maybe. Send me the songs and I'll take a listen.'

Two cassette tapes arrived. I'd already played 'Rock And Roll Dream' at the aborted rehearsal and the other songs were slow, dragging on somewhat. These, I hoped, were not a fair indication of their material. There was way too much of it in general and, besides, there were too many sad and ponderous numbers. I made up my mind to turn down the offer. Kalodner was disappointed but I didn't care. As often as possible I follow the music that calls me, rather than a sound or mood that repels me.

The new band I was working with would ultimately become quite a big production, something that Steve was wisely cautious about. A record deal was one way to front the costs.

Now we were no longer idly ticking over in someone's front room, we rented a bigger rehearsal room and set up as if we were on stage to play for none other than... John K. He was back in the picture, as Geffen Records had an interest in this follow-up to Asia. We played for thirty minutes and took a break. Steve overheard John being asked what he thought: '50 per cent of everything they played was good,' he commented, 'but the other 50 per cent was rubbish!' We played a couple more songs – slightly reluctantly – and Mr A&R left. Never mind – we had other things on the horizon that were hopeful.

Talk turned to Clive Davis, founder of Arista. Geoff Downes had a song called 'The Hunter' that Clive had heard and liked and he played it to Steve and me with the thought that we could record it and that he would be our producer. This underpinned an assumption that we would sign to Arista Records. All seemed to be going fine until we started getting some grief from John who, despite his reported comment on our material, believed we were signing to Geffen; besides – he'd paid for the bigger rehearsal room! Of course, he'd made us feel bad with the 50 per cent nonsense and had made no clear commitment to sign us. He couldn't have his cake and eat it, not this time. The deal went ahead with Arista Records and we were off and running.

Part of Richard Branson's empire at that time was the Townhouse Studios in Shepherd's Bush where Yes had recorded *Drama*. The Townhouse had their new studio, Studio 3, equipped with digital multi-track machines. We settled in there for quite a while, listening to our sound as it developed on their cutting-edge equipment. The backing tracks were laid down, then overdubs and vocals, layering the tracks for a big, full sound. Digital tape, unlike analogue, sounded very clean and could be thin on the bass end. This was early days with the technology too and there was a degree of experimentation, with us as the guinea pigs – we discovered one day that the bass track seemed to have entirely disappeared overnight.

We had individual reverb units, compressors and noise gates strapped across every sound source imaginable. Contrastingly, at Sarm West, where Trevor Horn did most of his production, instruments sounded pinned down to the ground and were close-miked with only a few sources bathed in reverb. Our group – called GTR, as an abbreviation of 'guitar' – was venturing closer to the tried and tested stadium-rock sound – more Asia than Yes or Genesis.

'When The Heart Rules The Mind' was the lead track on the album and the first single from *GTR*, released in July 1986. This was fun to write and record. Lots of ideas were used in this song, making it our best shot for a single as it was radio-friendly in an edited format. With a strong lead vocal from Max, harmony vocals from Steve, Phil and myself, strong riffs and a searing synth guitar melody, it switched to acoustic guitars in the breakdown section, after which it rose up again to fade on some chant-like guitars. It was the quintessential GTR track. 'You Can Still Get Through' had some tight stuff going on and 'Toe The Line' was simply beautiful.

Steve and I wanted to use guitar synths instead of keyboards as much as possible, although they sounded exactly the same, unless they were matched with a good guitar sound. Complicated sync adjustments had to be made as the midi programming signal that controlled the synth was delayed by up to 30 milliseconds. The guitar had to be delayed too to make up for the lag. Adventurously, we hired a Synclavier synthesiser guitar and Steve tried for much of an afternoon to get it to trigger correctly but it was seriously oversensitive and rang on after he lifted his fingers, making all sorts of noises. I had no more luck with it than Steve. Early synth guitars glitched, requiring considerable control to avoid sounding like a screeching elephant. Neat fingering and careful picking was essential... or else.

Roland made the Synclavier and they favoured a system that didn't only use midi but came with a slew of internal, editable sound patches that were in sync and quite unusual. Their blue-coloured 300 unit was monophonic and had no midi connection. It only produced its own sounds, and only one note at a time. The Roland 700, meanwhile, was polyphonic, allowing a bigger chordal and harmonic range.

In the end Geoff had to play a few of the less successful guitar synth parts on his keyboards himself. The band got to approve the final mixing, which was done with us in the room, committee style, the two Steves trying to have most of the say. Alan Douglas engineered and provided supposedly impartial ears – though he had his own taste in audio terms. He was an expert at drum sounds and a fine Scot.

Steve and I did a two-week promotional tour before the real tour of the new album began. His wife came along too and a division formed between the two of them and the rest of us. We were noisier and they stayed on different floors to avoid being disturbed, should Max and Phil decide to strike up with a song or two early in the morning. Things happen when sweaty musicians are in close proximity to one another, things are said in ways that can best be described as indiscreet. From time to time, I liked to clown around a little unashamedly too. A little light-headedness releases built-up tensions. That was OK when it was just the blokes mingling but now extra tact was needed – and was in very short supply.

The US leg of the tour opened at Stanley Theatre, Utica, on 21 June and ran until 31 July at Sunrise Theatre, Sunrise, Florida.

Perils Of Empowerment

We continued in the UK at Manchester's Apollo on 11 September, finishing at Hammersmith Odeon before one European date in Munich, Germany, on the 22nd. I believe this was recorded and filmed but there was a major problem with my sound as I was playing through two amps which were recorded out of phase – basically, my guitar disappeared in the stereo mix. Pretty hopeless!

The band performed well together with Matt Clifford on keyboards for those parts we couldn't easily play live and those Geoff had done. This meant the shows were well orchestrated and fairly disciplined. Matt was the joker in the pack and it didn't take much to set off giggling and banter. His terrific keyboard-playing and arranging made him a natural go-to guy. We delved into material from our back catalogues and Steve and I played a duet based around 'Time Runs Slow' (later appearing on my *Turbulence* CD).

It worked visually, with Max centre-stage, taking care of the announcing, Steve and I stage left and right, Matt and Jonathan behind us, with Phil closer to Steve. Steve had a steadfast playing stance and moved his guitar back and forwards a little. I wasn't dashing about much either, although my head would nod a bit and I pulled some odd faces, which was fairly normal. Max and I fed off each other and we began to get animated – sort of rocking out. This was about enough for me until one night, when Steve wore a new pair of cowboy boots with his trousers tucked in and we thought, 'Right on!' Later in the set, much to our surprise, he lay down on his back and wiggled his boots in the air. Right-bloody-on! It was a crazy time, indeed. Steve and I are, by the way, still good friends, often sharing the same stage with our own bands.

On 19 July we recorded the King Biscuit Hour Presents GTR show at the Wiltern Theatre, Los Angeles. This was finally released on CD in January 1997 under the same name. The original *GTR* CD was re-released by Cherry Red in 2011, when it included a DVD.

Just over a month before the King Biscuit show, on 2 June, Jan gave birth to our second daughter, Stephanie Jane. Dylan, Virgil and Georgia were so thrilled to have another sister, especially as Jan brought Steph home from the hospital just a few days after she was born. Dylan was then 17, Virgil 11 and Georgia 4 years old. Jan certainly had her hands full.

As with the years 1981 and 1985, the years 1987 to 1988 would turn out to be a period of transition, in which my new group was realigned and rebuilt. For a variety of reasons, I found myself playing without Steve Hackett but with Max and Phil. Songs flowed from the three of us after Steve said he wouldn't come down to Devon to try things out. We took that to mean a 'No' to playing with us and understood the situation didn't suit him so well. Jonathan came over once to record some drums, but as the rest of us lived in the UK we could give more time to it. Drum machines were deployed.

Sun Arts sent a few of our demos to Arista but they didn't want to pick up the band. I had written a lyric that included the line 'With heather in your hair'. This was queried as they appeared not to like it – I've never understood why.

At this stage the band wasn't necessarily going to be called GTR although, if a replacement for Steve Hackett was accepted by a label, then maybe something could be worked out. The batch of recording we did at that point was recently included on Rhino's *Anthology 2*, on CD three, with my dear son Virgil on drums. I had recorded him at our studio and mixed with Will Worsley. I had a great time putting these tracks together for release, so special thanks to Max, Phil and, of course, to Virgil.

A well-rounded musician and songwriter from California called Robert Berry entered the picture to collaborate on a batch of new songs. He played rhythm guitar, harmonised and sung some leads. We tried out some of his own tunes and ideas, which added LA ambience to the party, although Max clearly felt strongly about his position as lead singer and Robert appeared to threaten that. But with Robert now on board, we got past the first hurdle – the label backed us and agreed to pay studio costs while we carefully pieced this thing together. In *Rock Family Trees*, Pete Frame cleverly plots the connections of members of many different bands in a visual form. He refers to this band as 'Nerotrend' but we actually called it 'Nero And The Trend'.

We'd just finished most of the backing tracks when everything suddenly fell apart. In a moment of utter stupidity, Sun Arts offered Robert a gig playing with Keith Emerson and Carl Palmer, who quickly became three. We were out in the street, literally. I dashed to Sarm East Studio to make quick mixes of the tracks recorded at Marcus Studios, ensuring there was at least something to listen to in the future. The master tapes went back to Marcus Studios awaiting payment but Arista totally dropped the studio in it by refusing to pay the bill. These tapes were never to be finished – no mastered vocals or guitars, just guide backing-track parts that needed to be overdubbed and properly mixed. The tapes required further investment if ever they were to be released or used for presentation. I would later be offered them for £20,000, reduced to £10,000 but, although it was sad to ditch them, there was to be no turning back.

I was still wondering what role I might have in Yes. 'Owner Of A Lonely Heart' had brought them considerable US success and many Yes fans of today discovered them as a result of their eighties music, but they had failed to follow up on the single's potential, releasing just two albums in the eighties while bringing comparisons with Asia. Now both groups were expected to deliver hit singles. This was not something that had been in the original premise of Yes or its early history. Sure, 'Roundabout' charted and helped launch the band but it followed the developing style of the band in being complex and highly original. Yes was always primarily an album band, anyway. As Asia had done, Yes had now opted to grab attention by adopting a more conventional rock/pop style. I would play 'Owner' many times, until we decided more recently to leave it out. We don't feel we own that song in the same way that we own our songs from the seventies, nineties and noughties.

I remained surprisingly busy on the sidelines. My 1988 diary tells me, with some degree of accuracy, that on Monday 18 January, at 4 p.m. I played at Air Studios for George Martin on an album he was producing for Andy Leek. Interestingly, I was booked to play acoustic guitar, something I always found quite attractive. On electric guitar was Alan Murphy, who I'd met several times before. It was relaxed and the session band played live with Andy on the piano.

My diary also shows that four days later I went to Yamaha's London office to inspect their take on the synth guitar. Back in January 1985 I'd played the SynthAxe, which was shaped so oddly that I almost broke off its headstock. Just after the *GTR* album was released I bought a Stepp DG1, a digital guitar with its own sounds and midi control. The Synclavier setup didn't appeal to me, nor was it practical. My early experience with the Sears guitar synth should have put me off for life but I still searched for something better. Meanwhile, Roland pressed on with practical, affordable guitar synthesis. Better than my encounters with the technology of guitars was my first meeting, around this time, with Martin Taylor.

Perils Of Empowerment

I played a solo guitar spot at the Spectrum in Philadelphia on 27 April for WMMR, the station championed by Ed Sharkey, with Cheap Trick, Greg Allman and Paul Carrack.

Between 17–19 July I played for Stanley Clarke and Stuart Copeland on their Animal Logic project at Westside Studios in London. On the last day they wanted me to solo over a section that already had many different instrumentalists soloing at the same spot. 'Could Steve Howe do better?' was the challenge, I guess. It was left for them to decide at the mix.

Meanwhile, throughout the year, I was recording a third solo album, *Turbulence*, my first all-instrumental record. Many of the backing tracks were recorded at Advision Studios once more, with Bill Bruford on drums (and GTR's Nigel Glockner on one track). I continued with Tim Weidner engineering at a London basement studio owned by Billy Currie (of Ultravox fame) called Hot Food in Kensington. I felt at home with the guitar-based concept and had written 'Hint Hint' for our daughter Stephanie. The results certainly sounded of the era but it was tight and quite adventurous. I guested on Billy Currie's *Transportation* while at his studio. He had some good ideas to develop, plus we wrote the track 'Traveller' together. I've played with most of the best keyboard players around and Billy Currie was among them, standing out in particular for his stylishness and originality, not to mention his viola-playing. Think: 'Oh Vienna'.

I completed my own album mixes at Sarm West Studios with Renny Hill, another fine engineer I've enjoyed working with. I'd become very preoccupied working on the record but I was about to get a surprise. One day in January 1988 my wife Jan arrived at the studio to collect me to go for dinner. It transpired that this was no ordinary Friday, it was our... anniversary! I'd forgotten! I duly said I was sorry and eventually I was forgiven.

I met an expert in library music, Tony Cox at KPM Music. They provided accompaniment for TV and film productions – an area I knew little about – which was usually sponsored and compiled by music publishing companies. KPM was part of EMI and the two of us discussed putting together music for a CD. This would then be sent to producers and directors for potential inclusion in their projects. I had a number of back-burners in my stock of music, short ideas that went nowhere fast, usually incomplete or unfinished snatches of songs. I learned about the style required for library music and was encouraged to hear that short, sub-versions or underscores were what was needed and the more I delved into it the more fascinating I found it. I got a bundle of my ideas together and finished them up at Hot Food with Roger Howorth in September. The music wasn't available in the public domain at first, but not only did many of the tunes go on to be used in future band projects, they also eventually formed parts of different volumes of *Homebrew*. A few copies were later sold on the internet and another CD followed.

I was asked by Miles Copeland, then manager of the Police, to contribute an instrumental track to a compilation featuring nine other guitarists, including Hank Marvin of The Shadows, that became the *Guitar Speak* CD. This was released and the *Night Of The Guitars* tour began on 20 November at Colston Hall, Bristol. I joined the tour for the first UK leg. It was great: we each had our own spot and jammed on a few songs at the end. We all got on well together, travelling by bus and enjoying soundchecks, shows and dinner afterwards.

It amused me that Miles, talking to the audience at the beginning of the show, described us as gods or from outer space! My spot opened with 'Sketches In The Sun' played on the Danelectro twelve-string I used on the *GTR* album. Then I performed 'Sharp On Attack', the track I'd recorded with the house band for *Guitar Speak*. I had enjoyed making the studio version, with its many banks of guitars backing up the 175 and some quick time changes between 3/4 and 4/4 played by Nigel Glockler on drums. Hank didn't come on the tour but Leslie West certainly did. Once on stage he usually turned his amp up to 'eleven', but he was a gentle soul, I found. 'All Along The Watchtower' was the end-of-show jam.

On 11 May 1988, I met someone very special, Paul Sutin. His first album, *Serendipity*, was very much a new-age outing. He asked me to work on his new album, *Seraphim*, which I overdubbed at Sound Suite Studios, Camden Town – where Asia had briefly worked at the very end, while recording 'Masquerade'. Paul and I hit it off. His music was meditative and soothing, and I got right into it. Some of the tracks, such as 'Passione Magica', were mostly improvised, others were pleasantly tuneful. Our friendship has developed and we've become a great team.

CHAPTER 14

No Yes

It seemed like only a few months after everything fell apart with GTR that I got a call from Jon Anderson asking me if I had any songs.

'Yes,' I replied. 'I've got six on a cassette. Do you want to hear them?'

I invited Jon to our house on the edge of Hampstead Garden Suburb. We had a few laughs as if nothing too insurmountable had happened and he left with the cassette. I still have a copy and the demos formed part of the first volume of *Homebrew*, released in 1996. This was to be the start of some really convoluted recording experiences. I can't tell you everything and you wouldn't believe the half of it if I did, but I can say it was simply a mind-boggling time that began with the recording of the ABWH album.

Jon had had enough – for a while, at least – of the Los Angeles Yes setup. Chris, whom Jon clearly loved, had been getting harder to work with. The members of each new incarnation of Yes needed to stand on solid ground, as they completely relied on each other. This quality is an essential key that can unlock any band's progress. Reliability and trust are the glue that bind musicians together to create great performances. Lack of it had played havoc throughout my career.

Jon was steering this project, but his relationship with Sun Arts, our management, was – as usual – a bit too cosy. He began work on the tracks in various locations, including Montserrat, where he convened with Bill Bruford and Tony Levin to record their parts. Tony had come well prepared, as he always does, but apparently Jon needed convincing. They had a few words but, of course, it settled down once it was clear Tony had learned the titles. I flatly refused to attempt guitar parts in the Bahamas, instead recording all my parts at Air Studios, London. The tracks were developed with Matt Clifford on keyboards and Milton McDonald on guitar to form the overall structures.

I took about forty guitars to the studio, storing them in a vocal booth. Two digital twenty-four-track machines were synchronised to get forty-eight tracks. That was plenty of tracks but also plenty of 'wind-up' time – when the machines had to locate their positions and then synchronise. This process wasn't automatically muted and all too often the manual mute on the playback system wasn't pressed. I'd hear the horrid slurring up of two tapes, which was frightening and sickening. Chris Kimsey, with Chris Potter engineering, got the job done and I was happy with what I played in those two weeks.

Sadly, instead of staying as a homespun, British-sounding album, *Anderson Bruford Wakeman Howe* was farmed out to a mixing team who were very popular at the time but who appeared to have no idea about the internal instrument balance that we'd developed over the years, a crucial part of Yes. The album opens with a strange overture, several minutes of musical folly, and, although I'm credited as a writer, I had nothing to do with 'Themes'. This was evidence of that old chestnut, the 'group-writing split', which can work, particularly if you don't write anything. My songs were also given a group credit. Several outside writers were involved, including Geoff Downes, Max Bacon and even Vangelis.

Despite the flaws, much joy can be found within these recordings, as they seemed to connect with our actual lives. I knew it definitely had something, but quite what, I wasn't too sure. The style of mixing wasn't to my liking. Parts and textures could have been balanced more effectively. 'Vultures In The City' isn't on the album. It became the B-side of the single 'Brother Of Mine' but in its extended form it was quite something. Unfortunately, its editing left it lacking. This also appears on the original *Homebrew* release.

The album was complete and what we had was no mere 'band'. It was Yes but we couldn't call it that. Chris Squire, along with Trevor Rabin, Alan White and Tony Kaye, claimed the use of the name and we weren't going to challenge that but even when we said we would be offering 'An Evening Of Yes Music' on our tour posters, it very much upset the LA organisation. A document with thirty clauses was sent, threatening us really, but it was found to be worthless as many of the clauses attempted to outlaw things that were permissible not just by us but by anyone – most notably to simply play Yes songs. Anyone could do this, of course, as the songs are in the public domain. Emotions ran high as attempts were made to undermine us but we continued to put together our touring schedule. Some promoters took a bit of a liberty in local advertising: they would fail to use our official poster, or modify it by enlarging the size of the word 'Yes', but that was their call and hardly our fault.

We embarked on a huge US tour, starting in Memphis on 27 July 1989, and running until 10 September. We started up again in the UK on 21 October in Edinburgh and played until 21 November in Milan, Italy. We had to cancel the final six shows due to Jon's voice giving up on him. He usually sung night after night but the length of this tour put extra strain on his vocal cords. Partly as a result of these cancellations, another tour was scheduled which took us into 1990, opening in Barcelona after two days' rehearsal, then Madrid on 23 February, then on to Japan where we rested for a few days before three shows in Tokyo, followed by one in Osaka on 5 March. The first of the Tokyo shows was criticised by many fans, and rightly so as we were noticeably jet-lagged.

On 10 March, we flew to Vancouver, Canada, to open on 12 March. This led down the West Coast until 16 March, when we flew to New York, playing Radio City Music Hall the next day. This was an AIDS charity event for Arista Records, featuring a who's who of the music business, among them Barry Manilow, Dionne Warwick, Whitney Houston and Elton John. Quite a shindig. While I was having a touch of makeup applied (not a common practice for me), many luminaries wandered in and out of the dressing room — superstars galore, but really only one band: us.

We went on to play regular Yes venues, including the Philadelphia Spectrum, and finished off back in New York to play Madison Square Garden on 23 March — another high point. During the tour we also recorded a live DVD at the Shoreline Amphitheatre, San Francisco, show. Unfortunately, Tony Levin fell ill around the time of the filming. Bill recommended the very talented Jeff Berlin who was fortunately able to stand in on bass, although he obviously didn't have the sound we were used to. Nevertheless, he did an admirable job. At the Spectrum, ABWH had received a fifteen-minute ovation after playing 'And You And I' and nothing stood in our way.

Chris might not have been there but the Yes momentum was. Still, this wasn't sufficient for Jon and Sun Arts.

They wanted us to *be* Yes and the merger began without the approval of Bill, Rick or myself. The ball was rolling and everything was uprooted and, to be frank, became quite ridiculous. Arista bought the rights from Atlantic to release our music in a deal involving all sorts of agreements between ourselves, buying in, buying out and, of course, an advance for the combined members of ABWH and LA Yes to record an album created by musicians from both camps.

As this was being sorted out, ABWH had been recording tracks in France with Tony Levin. Jon's chosen producer was Jonathan Elias, whose biggest achievement during the sessions was getting pieces of mine married up with pieces of Jon's. I had demos of songs like 'Big Love', which became 'I Could Have Waited Forever', and tunes from *Turbulence*, unreleased at that time, that were moulded into several of our titles on *Union*. The denseness of the twists and turns in creating the album were unimaginable. I hardly know where to start.

Well, in France near Marseilles there was a villa that had been owned by Jacques Cousteau, the famous underwater photographer. It had studio space, outbuildings, a tower and accommodation of sorts. I believe that when we were there it had just been bought by a famous racing car driver. I drove there in my Mercedes two-door G wagon and did some decent off-road driving on this big estate. Lunch and dinner were often had outside on the veranda overlooking a valley. We had our own small chalets but, for some reason, I slept for a week in the villa which was old, cobweb-ridden and very creaky. These distractions, while attempting to write and record, undermined the whole concept of thinking it would be good to go somewhere else in order to create. But we now lived in different parts of the world and needed to meet on neutral ground. Some of the band had thought a holiday location was an ideal place to work.

The ABWH contingent had already started what we thought was going to be our second album and our quota of material on *Union* was larger than that of LA Yes. Some collaboration was evident – Chris sung harmonies on a couple of our tracks and Jon added his voice to a few of their songs. Then the tapes began to move about the world.

Sarm West in London was used for guitar overdubs and I filmed them on a Sony V8 camera. The footage revealed that Jonathan Elias's production approach was often repetitive. 'Do another take, Steve,' he'd say, without explaining exactly why or what was wrong with what I'd done. So I'd try a bit harder to win him over to my ideas, in the absence of Jon. The tapes journeyed on to LA, where I was on holiday with Jan, Virgil and his friend Eli, Georgia and Steph in Santa Monica. We'd rented a house from Andy Summers for a month and, towards the end of the break, I recorded vocals at Cherokee Studios, as well as counterpart vocals, none of which appeared on the finished album. Jonathan said Jon didn't care for my vocals, except almost as a send-up, insofar as the closing track ended with me singing about 'give and take'. Oh, yeah, give and take – that it wasn't! This was a totally wasted opportunity. I'd added warmth to the vocals, mainly singing in a bass register that offered balance to Jon's higher tones. Then there was the five evenings with the family I'd given up to sing in the studio. I often chased Jonathan on the phone, trying to anticipate where the album was going to be mixed as it moved from LA to New York and all around the bloody houses.

The one track that didn't morph or change in any way was my twelve-string acoustic guitar solo, 'Masquerade'. The head of Arista at the time was an executive called Roy Lott and it was he who asked me to contribute a guitar solo, picking the final one from three I sent. It was similar to 'Australia' on Yes's US thirty-fifth-anniversary release and 'Solitaire' from *Fly From Here*, in that I recorded and produced all three myself, stylising the tracks around my sound. I was delighted when 'Masquerade' was nominated for a Grammy in 1992. I was invited to the ceremony and experienced the extravagance and pampering that the big stars get on these sorts of occasions. A few years later, Martin Taylor would ask me to produce his solo guitar for his album *Artistry* as he liked the guitar sound on 'Masquerade'. As with that track, we took his songs to Gregg Jackman to finalise the sound at Sarm West Studios – which is where we're pictured on the sleeve.

Roger Dean was called in to grace *Union*'s sleeve with landscapes from afar and package the 'two-camp' album seamlessly. He also designed *Turbulence*, both records coming out in 1991, with Kia Krause doing some of the computer-generated designs. I asked Roger for a new logo that really only worked on this release. It has more of a squared-off, Eastern European look, rather than the traditional 'bubble' effect. My own album was released on Relativity Records and sold well, not least because it was released during the massive reunion tour. ABWH had truly become Yes who now became an eight-piece band with several managers, lawyers and an enormous crew of people set up to take us on the road again.

Several weeks of rehearsals took place at Pensacola on the southern coast of Florida before we opened the shows on 9 April, closing the first leg on 21 May before starting again in Europe on 29 May in Frankfurt and finishing with two shows at the NEC in Birmingham on 25 and 26 June and three at London's Wembley Arena from 28 to 30 June. This second leg was marked by a better sense of discipline and control and the music was a little cleaner and tidier. In the US there had been plenty of playing up to the audience and spotlight-stealing. When individual members had their own spots, a couple of them chose to pose and, in my opinion, overdo the performance level, reminding me of Spinal Tap!

The band had conflicting ideas about the presentation. The LA contingent thought they'd be on stage the whole time, while ABWH expected the line-up to switch about and that not all eight of us would be performing the whole time. 'What would everyone play the whole time?' I asked, not unreasonably. In the seventies I had left space, a period of relief, between full-on sections. I kind of liked these moments but, sadly, on the *Union* tour these were often filled with Trevor's ideas. 'Awaken' pretty much took the biscuit. How could I make a return if another guitar part had been sandwiched between my parts, filling in the gaps?

A week into the tour a meeting was called to discuss why I was upset. I wasn't happy with what was going on after I improvised on opener 'Yours Is No Disgrace', when Trevor took over. I suggested that this part didn't need so many scrappy, scratchy noises and discordant sounds, weird and wonderful as they were. They simply weren't working for me. Trevor agreed to leave them out and things progressed more smoothly – most of the time, anyway.

Yes returned to the US, playing big shows with around 10,000–20,000 people per night. We opened this third *Union* touring leg in Tampa, Florida, on 5 July, finishing at the familiar Shoreline Amphitheatre in Mountain View, California, on 8 August. Whenever it was possible to do so, we used the round-stage presentation, with our own Tait Towers, second-generation, super-revolving stage. The brainchild of Mickey Tait in the seventies, it was now bigger and smoother. As before, this required suspending the PA from the ceiling and housing the crew more comfortably below deck. Once again, the bass response in the very centre of the circle was dangerously intense.

On Chris's suggestion, Eddie Offord returned to record some live material for a DVD. After the main show had been taped, the band piled into the dressing room when Eddie appeared, walking towards us, waving his hands and saying, 'It was great.' He added a caveat, 'Er, the tape ran out while you were playing "Lift Me Up" and the backup also ran out...'

'What?' yelled Trevor.

Obviously, this was an important moment in the show for Trevor, but we were all pretty mad about it, too. Mistakes happen, but they had to be minimised wherever possible. The DVD was released some time after the tour ended.

We took a five-month break. I enjoyed a rest and got on with other things for a while. Geoff Downes asked if I wanted to overdub on a new Asia album and guest the next year on tour with them. The guys were recording at Advision Studios, which had moved to Brighton. I headed south from London and overlaid five tracks with my guitar parts. I dabbled with this work more than committed to it, which I felt was clear in the mix. Geoff and Asia's singer, John Payne, got on with finishing up the album.

There was still one more *Union* tour leg to play, this one in Japan. We opened in Tokyo on 29 February 1992, followed by shows in Osaka, Nagoya, Yokohama and then Tokyo again to close on 5 March before flying home. I would make another trip to Japan in the same year although not with Yes: as suddenly as it had started, this brand of Yes madness stopped completely. I left Sun Arts and started planning solo guitar shows in the UK, US and even further afield for the following year. Later, surprisingly, Yes would be asked to do another album.

In the spring of 1992, I rehearsed with Asia in London. On 16 May our equipment was shipped to Japan and I headed west to our studio where Martin Taylor arrived to record his *Artistry* album, with his son James assisting. This was the most enjoyable of sessions. Martin was on terrific form, playing masterfully on the tunes we'd selected, some standards and great originals. 'Polka Dots And Moonbeams', a favourite of mine, opens the album, and 'Cherokee' is really quite unbelievable. Linn Records released the album and it's still available today.

Using alternative equipment Asia played a warm-up show in Worcester on 27 May before leaving for Japan four days later. We opened in Osaka on 4 June, then did two shows in Tokyo and left the next day. There were more rehearsals back in the UK before we played Folkestone and then London.

Then I worked on my next solo album at Advision in Brighton. On the last three days we recorded my son Dylan playing drums on all tracks. His years of experience had given him confidence and he was ready to take it on. I would return to the recording of *The Grand Scheme Of Things* soon but in a different country, Switzerland.

Mal Reading, who worked for NBC, had gotten me several quality interviews and come up with some other performance opportunities as well. We left the UK together on 23 July, heading for Houston in Texas, and the next few days were filled with radio interviews and a charity show. From there we flew to Dallas to talk and play acoustic on KZPS, followed by a couple of days in New York meeting the folk from Relativity Records and also Yves Beauvais from Atlantic to talk about Yes compilations.

After a few days back in the UK, I left for Geneva on 8 August for a week recording at Paul Sutin's studio. By now he had some high-end digital recording equipment, including an AMS digital desk and a forty-eight-track Studer machine. Renny Hill came to engineer and Keith West, who'd co-written a couple of songs, came over to sing some harmonies. Before leaving the UK, Nick Beggs performed most of the bass parts, perfectly complementing Dylan. Anna Palm plays some lovely violin on several tracks, as she has on many of my solo albums.

Asia then fitted in a one-off show in Bern, Switzerland, on 22 August. I returned to Advision on 1 September for over a week, preparing backing tracks. I was back in Geneva on 14 September for another week's work on my album, which was becoming a true labour of love. Paul Sutin and I may have been working on some of his tunes along the way, the fruits of which we would harvest later. Asia went off to play a couple of dates in Florida and Virginia on 26 and 27 September. We did a show in Redcar before a clutch of dates in Europe and a show in Cambridge on 6 November. Looking back on it now, the second half of 1992 was one of the busiest times of my life.

Fender wanted to give Hank Marvin a retro copy of the first Fender Stratocaster he owned, and on 13 October they assembled about ten guitarists of note, asking us to hide behind a curtain until the Fender rep and Hank came into the conference room. We revealed ourselves and handed over the red Strat. It was a really fitting gesture, as Hank was emigrating to Australia. Afterwards, there was a casual lunch and it was a great pleasure to sit at the same table as Eric Clapton, Jeff Beck and David Gilmour, alongside Hank. He was deeply touched to be reminded of the huge influence he'd been on us all.

There were more UK and European dates with Asia in November, winding up at London's Town & Country Club before we left to open in the US at Asbury Park in New Jersey, playing through until the end of the month. The schedule that Asia's management team had devised was not yet complete: we played in Florida – in Orlando, Naples, Tampa and Miami – before getting home on 14 December.

I was back at work recording at Advision and in Geneva in the new year before an Asia visit to Canada in February – the coldest tour I've ever done. I was still travelling in the old Mercedes-Benz 300 turbo station wagon that had transported me for many years. Lane Sieger drove it from Lititz, Pennsylvania, to Halifax, Nova Scotia, and stayed at the wheel through all the dates. The snow was deep and thick, another adventure in survival. We were on a freeway listening to the CB radio when we heard a trucker say, 'That little white station wagon is losing it' and then realised it was us he was talking about. We skidded around before Lane managed to regain control of the car. Being diesel, the car needed to be plugged into AC power overnight to ensure nothing would freeze up.

These shows varied a lot. One was on a military base. I'd done a few in the UK but here we were out in the middle of nowhere, playing all sorts of clubs and dives. A drunken idiot called out my name, using what I felt was a deeply inappropriate cliché, at least if flattery was his intention. I almost left the stage in utter disgust. In Quebec City we lost control of the car going down a hill and got a ticket. From Montreal and Toronto we went to the US and New Jersey, where we finished the tour at Poughkeepsie, New York. I've played there many times, and (as with hundreds of other towns) I only really remember it when I get back there. Looking back now it occurs to me that these are the kind of places that have been the source of much of the interest in the music I've played since 1971.

I got back to working on my solo album, flying to Geneva on 1 March 1993 to mix. I continued at Konk Studios, north London, where two of the songs with complex orchestration were finished. It's The Kinks' studio. I still see Dave and Ray from time to time. It's our neck of the woods too, now. Speaking of which, on 21 March, I headlined a concert along with Labi Siffre and Brand X at the Hackney Empire for the Dandelion Trust Woodland Scheme in support of reversing climate change. How slowly this moves. It was 200 years ago that the great discoverer Alexander Humboldt gave the same warning: 'We're destroying the planet.' Did I say slow? Static more like.

In early May, I spent four days researching and discussing my idea for a book of my guitar collection with Tony Bacon, a respected writer in the world of guitar books. This would incorporate beautiful photographs of my collection with anecdotes about the instruments. It required considerable organisation and hard work to collect the dates and information on the materials used in construction of the instruments as well as interviews to get my perspective, which has changed considerably over the years.

Playing solo guitar is central to my music and I started my first solo tour entitled Not Necessarily Acoustic – a nod towards Monty Python's argument sketch – 'Not necessarily, I could be arguing in my spare time.' I worked with Ian at the Ibis booking agency in Aberdeen, and we began in Scotland on 22 June, at the Queen's Hall, a delightful venue where I have played many times over the years. Doing press and radio interviews along the way, the UK run ended in Colchester on 10 July. Travelling around Britain was new and refreshing.

I talked about the music which was, as the tour name suggested, both electric and acoustic, and learned more about the timing of introductions and announcing song titles to get a flow going. I usually did two forty-five-minute spots that often overran a little. I usually started with classical guitar, my Kohno 10, then moved into some country-picking on my Martin 00-18, then my Martin twelve-string interspersed with some electric.

As soon as this tour finished I was back in Konk Studios, this time with Bill Bruford and Dee Palmer. Between us we had masterminded a project that became *Symphonic Music Of Yes* for the RCA Victor/BMG label. After much planning we started a month of recording on 12 July. Tim Harries was on bass; Alan Parsons produced the string arrangements written by Dee Palmer. Dee and I produced the overall project from start to finish. Although the recordings were mostly instrumentals, Jon Anderson agreed to sing 'Roundabout' and 'Good People' with a choir. When the record was completed with a Roger Dean sleeve, we were hot to trot, feeling like we were having fun.

The Grand Scheme Of Things, my fourth solo album, was released on 24 July and the following month I had a short family holiday in the Lake District, doing a little boating, as I recall. The hotel was fairly OK and there was a vegetarian restaurant nearby. We visited a museum commemorating the first pencil factory and explored the scenic rolling hills and lakes. In September we loaded up Jan's estate car with copies of my *Guitar Collection* book and a few guitars for sale and drove to Veenendaal, Holland, for a vintage guitar fair. I sold a young but very talented guy a Gibson F5 mandolin from the sixties. He played it real fine. I signed copies of the book and we stayed overnight in a motel, returning the next day by ferry.

I visited Fish, once of Marillion, at his studio near Glasgow, to add ideas that I'd demoed for his fabulous recording of Yes's

'Time And A Word'. For two days we detailed the track that was released on a collaborative album entitled *The Funny Farm Project: Outpatients '93*. Around this time I also played acoustic guitar for The Bee Gees on a song called 'Haunted House'. It was a pleasure to meet them, and they left me to record with their producer.

In October I went to Geneva to work with Paul Sutin on our *Voyages* album, which took a while to complete. I was mainly laying guitars on top of the tracks he prepared with his piano and production ideas. We went to great lengths to find the right approach and often used my Steinberger twelve-string electric, which had a bright, clear sound. I returned to London to appear on the James Whale show on LBC on 25 October. After a chat I played 'The Valley Of Rocks' and 'Clap'.

RCA Victor set up some promotion in the US for *Symphonic Music Of Yes* and Bill, Tim and I left spent two days in New York in November. We appeared on *Good Morning America*, live early morning TV, playing 'Roundabout' as a trio, with me singing and playing guitar, Tim on bass and Bill on drums. Interviews followed before we rushed back to London.

As if this wasn't enough, I started my first US solo tour in Solana Beach near San Diego on 22 November, also playing smaller venues like the Troubadour in LA and the Great American Music Hall in San Francisco, which was real nice. Having decided that the whole show would be fun, I had the freedom to play anything I wanted. We went on through Texas, up to Chicago, then took in the Bottom Line in New York, the Theatre of Living Arts in Philadelphia and the RPM in Toronto, finishing in Montreal on 19 December, just in time for Christmas. Touring the US solo was a new experience, with the noisier, looser audience sometimes driving the show onwards and upwards. At other times, it was as if the music couldn't breathe against the noise of an audience and, all too often, the background hum and general clatter of the bar.

The big upside was that my solo music was now being performed, which meant it was being heard by a cross-section of fans of Yes, Asia, GTR and ABWH and regular guitar fanatics.

CHAPTER 15

Not Necessarily Acoustic

During January and February of 1994 I stayed in the UK and in March I took another trip to a Dutch guitar fair, this time with a few boxes of *The Steve Howe Guitar Collection* with me, to sign and sell. The book was launched at Wapping Acoustic Centre on 7 April, with a 'guitar clinic' and a display of my instruments.

In the second week of April I visited Paul Sutin to work on our *Voyagers* album. This was a truly collaborative project – Paul's tunes grow with embellishments from my guitars into a celestial sound, melodically and rhythmically. Dylan added his brand of drumming to the tracks.

I started another UK solo tour on 19 April in Dundee. It was nice to be back in theatres in Scotland, among them the Henry Wood Hall in Glasgow, a distinctly different venue from the city's Renfrew Ferry where I played previously. One of the strangest gigs I've played, the Ferry was a floating venue on which I would also play with my band Remedy. The Glaswegians are a great crowd, rowdy but keen-eared. More town hall gigs around the UK followed and I finished with a London show on 12 May.

The next day I flew to New York to attend a weekend guitar show put on by *20th Century Guitar* magazine in Dix Hills. I stayed in New York to see label people like Steve Vining and Roy Lott from RCA and Arista. By the beginning of June, I was back in Geneva for a week or two, then I played a one-off show in Blackheath, London, on 18 June before returning to Geneva in July.

Between 10 and 16 August, Glenn and Doug Gottlieb visited me in Devon. They ran *Yes* magazine (coincidentally in Dix Hills, home of *20th Century Guitar*) and, as Gottlieb Bros., designed most of the tour programmes for Yes and for me, alongside my solo album sleeves (often in conjunction with Roger Dean). They carried out extensive interviews for a book about me that they were planning to write. Many cassette tapes were recorded as I rambled on about life and Yes but, when transcribed, something got lost in translation. It was then too hard to get it into shape.

I was also compiling my first live album on trips to Switzerland, *Not Necessarily Acoustic*. Toby Alington did the mixing and Tim Handley compiled the tunes, wrapping the sound of the audience into the finished master. This was released in the US later in 1994 on Herald Records, part of EMI, but on RPM Records in the UK. Live releases can be fairly straightforward to create, but this had become a highly polished and upbeat sixty-two minutes.

I played a solo spot outdoors in Romania on 7 September. I caught Jimmy Smith's set at the same venue, enjoying his excellent, inspirational organ-playing. The next night I played my spot, as did Dee Palmer, conducting an orchestral selection of rock band music. It was all a bit strange because Dee's manager had attempted to set up a symphonic music tour in the

States, inviting Bill and me. We kept time aside but it never came together… Promises, promises.

After three UK dates in Middlesbrough, Lancaster and Newbury I headed off to Canada at the end of the month for another solo tour, this one titled Pulling Strings. I opened in Toronto, before crossing the border into the US where I played a series of shows that wound up in Minneapolis at the end of October. As the tour title vaguely implies, I played over backing tracks for several songs, as well as doing strictly solo performances. Park West in Chicago was a particularly memorable gig. I used six of my favourite guitars that were usually stored in my hotel room after each show. If it wasn't possible to keep them with me, they could stay in our vehicle as long as parking was under video surveillance and the temperature was OK. The tour would provide the audio for my next live CD, released in 1998, recorded by Dave Natelle and Dave Wilkerson.

The year 1995 would be dominated my return to Yes, although it began on 18 January with a *Pulling Strings* solo tour in Japan, playing clubs in Tokyo, Nagoya and Osaka. The week before I arrived, Osaka had been hit by an earthquake and I almost cancelled all the dates, but the promoters assured me it would be fine. After my Osaka show, Dave Wilkerson, my sound guy, and I returned to our earthquake-damaged hotel and as we were sitting in my room, the light started to move, swaying more violently extremely left to right. The hotel had been hit by an aftershock. We looked at each other and headed for the door. Although the shaking subsided, we had to gather our thoughts on our survival and we couldn't seem to move at first – we were just transfixed. It was scary for us but Japan is used to earthquakes and usually they don't hit the cities.

Five days later I played Ronnie Scott's back home. No earthquakes in Soho!

In February I pulled together a batch of ideas for another library music project for Peter Cox at KPM Music. He suggested finishing them up at a studio he often used, run by Curtis Schwartz. Inside of a week all my titles, including two recorded at the facility, were finished. Since then Curtis has worked on almost all of my solo projects. We always work really well together – he's a sound engineer, Pro Tools expert, musician, writer and producer, yet he always stays focused on what's actually going on and which skill he's providing. He's put up with me too, so I say, 'Very well done'.

I did a one-off solo show in Vancouver, co-headlining with Terry Bozzio, who played the whole show on his enormous drum kit, solo, after which Rick Wakeman and I were invited back into the Yes fold at the same time. On 16 May we met with Jon, Chris and Alan at a hotel in Los Angeles. There was some sense of a reunion, but it wasn't clear straight away where it was heading. Chris was talking about a new manager who could get deals with Castle Records. Lee Abrahams – the early-days fan turned satellite radio executive – was there to expound the virtues of reforming this classic line-up. It was all very 'LA' to me – the illusion that anything was possible in Los Angeles. London would keep me far more grounded but here we were distracted from exactly how the business arrangements were being set up. Each line-up of Yes needed a reset: new manager, agent, business-manager-cum-accountant, tour manager, crew, front-of-house (FOH) engineer, lighting person and production designer.

I toured the UK with Pulling Strings, opening on 18 June in Swindon and playing fifteen shows in all, finishing at the Union Chapel in Islington, London. Ric French, my UK FOH engineer and tour manager, had to fix the PA systems at most venues, which couldn't cope with the delicate sound of a classical guitar projecting through their speakers. Any rattles or distortion were far more noticeable than they would be when a rock band drove the PA system.

I returned to LA on 11 July, hoping to finalise plans with Yes, and returned later that month to Devon with Annie Haslam, writing for and recording her voice on some songs for a never-to-be-released joint project. We'd previously been invited by Magna Carta Records to perform 'Turn Of The Century' for a Yes tribute album for which I had suggested the title *Tales From Yesterday*. This album, released in 1995, also featured Steve Morse playing 'Clap' and 'Mood For A Day'.

On 6 August, two days after Dylan's 26th birthday, I played solo at a little church in the village near us in Devon. This was always a special gig. Our ties with the area go back to 1970 and we have helped to restore the church spire. Later in the month I recorded a programme about my guitars for the BBC and played electric guitar on 'The Continental' backing track – they actually used my recording for the theme music.

I was back in New York in November to work on the Annie Haslam project, completing 'Lilies In The Field', with her keyboard player David Biglan playing and producing. This was released as a single around the time of an all-star New York concert with the same title that took place at Irving Plaza on 21 November arranged by us, Larry Acunto (who ran *20th Century Guitar* magazine and many New York guitar shows) and guitar collector Scott Chinery. Cheap Trick, Roy Wood, Justin Hayward, Phoebe Snow, Gary Brooker, Ian McDonald, Annie and I performed that night. We jammed out with 'Midnight Hour' to close the show, which was recorded but trapped in a format that was difficult to synchronise and mix. This was complicated by release agreements and mix approvals and in the end it was just too problematic to release.

I left the UK on 13 December for a solo tour of Argentina. Strangely enough, I had never been to South America before. Premier Talent agency, which booked most of my US shows, convinced me that Argentina was the best place to tour in the region – it was a sort of tester. I was well looked after, though Argentina had a few surprises in store. Vegetarian meals were rarities. Even when assurances were given that something was meat-free, it usually wasn't. The fans surprised me in a different way – they knew the music thoroughly. I was well received and got many good reviews, some of which were translated for me. I had a huge billboard outside the theatre in Buenos Aires and I actually got mobbed, with fans wanting to hug me.

I started in Córdoba where, when the power went out for a minute or two, I played Bach's Cantata No. 140 acoustically in the dark until the lights and sound returned. I closed in Mal del Plata where, again, I could sense that the audience had a strong connection with the guitar. They applauded many of the sections in the music and didn't want to go home at the end. I was feeling well rounded and musically independent by now and quite successful in my own small world of guitar music and songs. Still, it was good to be back home for Christmas in London.

In the new year, attention turned to Yes. It was time to pick up the plans we'd laid earlier. In a supposedly money-saving scheme, we were to record new tracks together and record a live DVD in the town of San Luis Obispo, where Jon lived in California. The new tracks would be recorded on remote computer recording gear running Logic Audio, set up in a building that had once been a bank. The familiar bank till was still there and the main space was big enough to set up the band with former offices used for the control room and drums. Working there entailed a long stay at a hotel by the freeway exit for San Luis Obispo.

I had my library music CD and other ideas in demo form as reference, knitted into 'Be The One' and 'That That Is', which constituted thirty minutes of music. I prefer 'Be The One' because its music was truly characteristic of Yes. It was a strange album to record, however. Chris's verses featured a high chordal baritone bass part and, as the music moved to different sections, I asked him to add a lower bass part. He didn't want to, even when I said I couldn't play electric guitar where the drums played without bass. 'You play it, then,' he said. Anything to get on with the job. I played a bass guitar tight with Alan, as Chris would have done, and got on with layering my guitar idea on top. There always had to be a warmth in our music, drawing in the listener. We are traditionally less abrasive than other bands, acoustic and electric and it was my belief that our sound should be sweet.

Jan brought Georgia and Stephanie over for a week, staying at the hotel, when there was time for exploring and trips. It wasn't Malibu but the weather was similar: hazy mornings and scorching afternoons. After the family returned to the UK, I went to Lititz to produce a special project at Right Coast Recording. This had taken considerable planning. Scott Chinery had asked me to record an album featuring his guitars, I pondered different scenarios and recommended that Martin Taylor and I prepare a list of material and select a few models from his collection of 750 guitars. Having beautiful guitars around was a familiar pleasure for me, of course, but this was way beyond anything Martin or I had ever had access to before. Many of the pieces were historical so they would feature period material when possible. Martin had a wide repertoire to choose from and we'd added several new original compositions to keep it fresh. Sixty-five guitars arrived, transported by security van from Toms River, New Jersey, to the studio, accompanied by a guitar expert to change strings and fix intonation. These guitars needed to be at their best when the red light went on.

Martin was mostly featured and he excelled everywhere. On 'Blue Bossa' he played a D'Aquisto rhythm part as well as a bass, then he added seventeen of the blues guitars Scott had ordered from arch-top guitar makers from around the world, each one taking a 16-bar solo. We played a few duets and I recorded 'Thought Waves' with two historic guitars and 'Tail Piece' with a whole lot of guitars, including a Bigsby steel guitar. We open with a nice duet called 'Two Teardrops' that featured Scott's most precious guitar, the D'Angelico Teardrop, and its tribute, the D'Aquisto Teardrop. The recording took just over two weeks. It was nothing but sheer fun, made easy by Dave Wilkerson engineering. A sampler of three tracks came out in a limited edition in late 1998, before *Masterpiece Guitars* was released in 2002 on P3 Music.

Yes went back to Billy Sherwood's studio in LA to mix 'Be The One' and 'That That Is'. All of us were there most of the time, which sparked a few debates. For my part, I sometimes wanted a better position or level on my guitar. It was the old push-and-pull technique, trade-offs made for adjustments, so no one player was allowed to dominate. The business side of things was another matter. Our affairs were structured through a Cypriot company – it was like wearing a blindfold most of the time. Castle paid the advance and funded costs we continued to incur.

The deal included recording the whole of our live show for three nights and filming the last night. We had to rehearse a load of tunes, about 140 minutes of music, which was a massive amount of work for just three shows. We played at the Fremont Theater, San Luis Obispo, on 4–6 March. In warming up for the stage shows we relied immensely on how much we'd worked together before and on how well we could pick up the pieces together. The amount of preparation varied from member to member, but much of it we simply already knew rather than charted or notated. On the upside there was a good feel, but the downside was those times we spent waiting for someone to load a CD, find the right spot and then check their part against the original. I often commandeered the CD player, leaving it paused near a bass part and ready to rerun as often as needed, a bit like a DJ.

We skimped on the video filming. I think the budget came in at only $6,000, when shoots like this often exceeded $400,000 in the real world. It was to prove to be a false economy, as fixing stuff later became very time-consuming and expensive. You always get what you pay for: if you pay peanuts, you get monkeys. Quite apart from any issues with quality, the sound match, or synchronisation, became a far greater concern.

Tom Fletcher, our engineer in the San Luis former bank, began mixing the live shows. I was due to spend four days adding a couple of harmonies and checking how it was going but in the end I was there for four weeks, as the first mix of 'Siberian Khatru' was all wrong. The parts just weren't balanced. I stayed to see it through, as I had with *Yessongs*, but never again, thank you. Although I got the satisfaction of knowing the mix was pretty good, it was 100 per cent a thankless task. We sometimes fixed or improved sections by taking say, four bars of keyboards from the second night and then pasting it into our third-night mix, as this was the filmed night with mostly all the right parts. These fixes sounded perfect but caused havoc in the video-cutting room. They're not at all apparent on the audio releases. The film showed one performance while the audio told a different story – rather as if we were miming at times. This could only be remedied by cutting away from the shot that didn't sync. A list was drawn up and some changes were implemented. I dislike even slight amounts of misalignment between sound and picture. It wrecks everything if you can't believe what you are seeing. Why should you?

With volume one of *Keys To Ascension* mixed, delivered and due to be released in October, Castle said we should start on the second volume. We were now deep into 1996 and recording new tracks at Billy Sherwood's studio to add to the remaining unreleased live show, which hadn't been mixed yet. A rough demo was almost used as the basis of 'Mind Drive' but I managed to get some of my material to complement the structure and to force a re-recording of the backing track, which we constructed around a click, laid down with guide parts to form the blueprint. Four other tracks were assembled in a somewhat similar fashion – 'Foot Prints', 'Bring Me To The Power', 'Children Of Light' and the instrumental 'Sign Language', which I'd written and to which Rick added two repeat chords that worked well. These titles do have their merits although, at times, there's not enough consistency in the arrangements for them to be solid, characteristic Yes tracks.

We handed over the mixing of volume two of the live show to Billy Sherwood, but we all had a hand in the mixing of the five studio tracks. In fact, it was Billy and I who shunted the new music along. He was engineer and co-producer but it often took more to get the job done. One Sunday, we were hoping to lay down the bass and drum for 'Bring Me To The Power' but neither Chris nor Alan could reach the studio, possibly because of the previous late night or some kind of soccer match. I mapped out the structure on a rhythm guitar, playing to a basic drum machine track, then Billy played a demo bass and quick drum part and we were on target. The bass Chris overdubbed later was drawn from Billy's attempt to emulate and think along the same lines as Chris himself, something he learned from respecting him and being around him and, as we were about to find out, collaborating with him. The pair later released two albums together as Conspiracy. Rick often did short keyboard sessions, some at lightning speed. Jon would conduct him and inspire different parts. Sometime Rick would have liked to find his own way through, but Jon's ideas flowed through Rick's hands and he did most things correctly.

Aside from developing the music, the band was feeling the after-effects of recent management upheavals. Due to a variety of issues, I decided I couldn't be in the same room as our new manager any more – nor could anyone else, really. Rick then left the band and there were to be no follow-on *Keys To Ascension* shows. It was time for a rethink.

CHAPTER 16

Twist After Twist, '96

It struck me that the demo recordings I had made over years had some merits of their own. No matter if I re-recorded them or developed the music with others, the originals had a vibe that didn't or rarely ever carried over to the more well-known versions. This was the purpose of *Homebrew*, which has notched up six volumes at the time of writing: to give an airing to the original versions from all areas of my output.

Volume one – titled simply *Homebrew* because I didn't know then if the series would develop – included ideas from GTR, ABWH and *Union* as well as some of my songs from the seventies. I was delighted when Caroline/Herald Records paid a decent advance for the US rights and, in the UK, RPM Records released it in 1996.

This project channelled my compilation experience and allowed me to sort of tell a story about what I write. 'Rare Birds' is 'Vultures In The City' as it really was, its mood and fragility intact. 'At The Full Moon' and 'Never Stop Learning' became parts of 'The Big Dream'. I also took the opportunity to release my instrumental recordings, which was the most important part of the project for me, showing guitar ideas and solos as they were being created and still in the process of being formed. Their development in whatever environment they find themselves in interests me. The further back I go, the more I see things that I hadn't noticed before, strange though that is. *Homebrew 7* is now forming in my mind and the project still excites me just as much as it did.

Whilst *Keys To Ascension 2* was being prepared for release, we left our current management and met the likeable Allen Kovac. He had a big management roster and was pretty down-to-earth. He said he'd speak his mind when he needed to. Apparently, Jon also wanted Alan to manage his solo career but Alan said he would only manage the group, wisely suggesting there would be a conflict of interests if he also looked after the individuals. After all, Yes was a tried and tested band, but none of our solo careers amounted to quite the same thing. 'Just make the little Jewish guy happy,' were his parting words – in other words, if we make money, he'd make money, which was fair enough.

Out the blue, Chris proposed that Billy Sherwood join the band and that we adopt songs recorded by Squire/Sherwood and convert them into a Yes album. As staggering as this was, the idea took root. These recordings featured lots of Billy's ideas, a few of which had space enough for me to play in and to some extent this happened, but overall there wasn't enough room to allow me to contribute to the sound of the album. The exception was 'From The Balcony', the main contribution by Jon and me, a fairly honest duet, simply voice and guitar. The rest of the tracks were heavy overladen and processed. The title track, 'Open Your Eyes', was the only one that came close to being the result of any kind of collaboration. I still didn't believe in this: like everything on this record, it is what it is, a Conspiracy album before Conspiracy. Or was that a conspiracy...?

Jon told me he thought keyboardist Igor Khoroshev ought to join us and he auditioned at Billy's studio, playing along with 'The Revealing' from *Topographic Oceans*. He went on to play on just three of the tracks on *Open Your Eyes*.

With the album recorded, we undertook promotional events, visiting the Moulin Rouge in Paris on 22 October, then the Wall of Hands – an exhibit of artists' palm casts at London's Rock Circus – the Howard Stern radio show, *Fox After Breakfast* show and, on 29 October, we did a record store signing at HMV. The following month we played a live acoustic set to 500 people at Tower Records on Sunset Strip, Los Angeles. Tower was considered by many to have been the best record store around and I often stocked up there with a good search through the aisles of vinyl and CDs. They had all the boxsets and other merchandise like books and T-shirts. The performance was rather marred by Chris being drunk. Indeed, he was only partially with us, so to speak, displaying his unmistakable trait of getting wasted. Nevertheless, we had a good laugh and the fans enjoyed the spontaneous banter that prevailed through the short set.

As 1996 slipped into 1997, we were preparing the CD for release and rehearsing for our forthcoming tour. The idea was that the new material would be heavily featured in the setlist but much of it wasn't translating well to stage performance. The band had never played any of this music together before and songs broke down as individual parts seemed to conflict with one another. It wasn't really that surprising when, in the end, only 'Open Your Eyes', 'No Way You Can Lose' and 'From The Balcony' made it to the final list. The rest of the set was filled with traditional Yes fare – songs from the seventies along with 'Owner' and 'Rhythm Of Love' from the eighties.

Initially, we were to play in June and July with Rick Wakeman, but this was cancelled. We eventually took to the stage in Hartford, Connecticut, on 17 October, with a band consisting of Billy and Igor, Jon, Chris, Alan and me. This tour went right through until 14 December, taking in Canada, Texas, the West Coast and ending on in San Jose in California. *Keys To Ascension 2* came out October, closely followed by *Open Your Eyes* in November.

When another Yes tour was cancelled early in the new year, Martin Taylor and I were able to play at the Carmichael Auditorium on 28 January, in conjunction with the Smithsonian museum, to celebrate their Blue Guitars exhibition. Scott's instruments were on display to promote the *The Chinery Collection* book. As with my own title, this featured Miki Slingsby photos and Tony Bacon's writing. We were also promoting the upcoming *Masterpiece Guitars* CD.

In early February, I recorded with Annie Haslam at Right Coast Recording in Lititz, trying different treatments of the songs we had done, including adding real drums after orchestral arrangements. Jan, Georgia, Stephanie and I were invited to Hilton Head Island for a week's break with our dear friends Skip and Roy Clair. While there, I played solo shows at the Elizabeth Wallace theatre on 15 and 16 February, then rested up on the beach — very pleasant and mellow.

At the end of the month, Yes started a UK and European tour at the Apollo, Manchester. Igor had been held up over passport issues, missed the warm-up rehearsal and nearly didn't make it to this first gig. Adam Wakeman, Rick's son, rehearsed with us, but in the nick of time Igor arrived. On to Bournemouth and Hammersmith, London, and then over to Paris, on to loads of shows in Germany, Switzerland and Warsaw, Katowice, Prague, Poznań and Budapest. There were another two weeks of European shows before we returned to the UK, finishing on 24 April with a second show at Hammersmith.

I had two solo releases in 1998, starting with my live *Pulling Strings* album. It had been recorded in Chicago and Minneapolis, mixed at our UK studio, compiled at Right Coast in Lititz and then mastered at Dinemec in Switzerland by Christophe Suchet – quite a journey for a live tape. Gottlieb Bros. designed a sleeve that looked rather like a ticket to one of my shows, which was a neat idea. My fifth studio album, *Quantum Guitar*, was an instrumental affair with only Dylan on drums as my support. The instrumental world lets me dig in deep to colour and layer tracks for their top lines. I used thirty-three different guitars on the various tracks, drawing comfortably from my collection. The sleeve featured a big chart listing the featured guitars and basses.

Some of the tracks were conceived in Malta as a suite, hence the title 'Knights Of Carmelite', a reference to the island's past. The original title of the project had been 'Quantum Steel', but I thought it might be too much of a departure to feature only steel guitar, although the second track, 'The Collector', mostly features that album. I included two well-known guitar tunes, 'Walk Don't Run' by Johnny Smith, made famous by The Ventures, and 'Sleep Walk' by Santo and Johnny, where I utilise Chet Atkins' arrangement to augment the original. The Shadows also recorded this. I'd always hoped to record these tunes and make them my own. The other original tunes also showed how nicely synchronised Dylan and I were.

Recorded entirely in Devon, with me engineering, the album was mixed with Curtis Schwartz. Again, Gottlieb Bros. returned to design my sleeve – and what a sleeve. I had sketched some ideas in which shots of guitars were partially seen, but they took my idea to another level (a quantum level!).

Over the whole of May, Yes toured South America, and in mid-June we toured with The Alan Parsons Project opening for us, beginning in Toronto and going across and around the US until 8 August, in Miami. I went on to take a family break with the girls in Schönried, Switzerland, at Paul Sutin's chalet above Gstaad, also visiting Milan on a spectacular train journey.

There were more Yes shows in October, in Japan. In fact, the total number of shows for the year was 148 – this was a seriously long bout of touring for a group that was now celebrating its 30th birthday.

I had been working on an album of Bob Dylan's forlorn love songs, with the working title 'Signals Crossed'. Bob Dylan's manager, Jeff Rosen, had sent me a tape as the project developed of the unreleased title 'Well, Well, Well' that Bob wrote with Danny O'Keefe. Singers had been invited to pick a song from a list I drew up of Dylan's titles and record themselves anywhere at my expense. Jon Anderson went off-list, asking if I could record 'Sad-Eyed Lady Of The Lowlands' as he'd always wanted to sing it. I took on three songs myself, appearing alongside Annie Haslam, Max Bacon, Keith West, Phoebe Snow, Alan Clarke, P. P. Arnold and Dean Dyson. I added Dylan – my son, that is, not the man himself – on drums and, towards the end of 1998, I moved operations to Switzerland. I compiled the various guest vocals at Dinemec Studios, Geneva, and added more guitars to backing tracks that I had recorded in Devon, each one with my guide vocal. The album was mixed at Mountain Studios in Montreux with Dave Richards engineering. Released by Eagle Records in 1999 – May in the UK and July in the US – it came out as *Portraits Of Bob Dylan*.

I never heard whether Bob cared for these versions, but I can accept that he might find that hard. His originals speak plenty about the way he recorded them, as do mine, but there's a world of difference between his live feel and my production style.

In mid-January 1999, Yes moved operations entirely to Vancouver where we rehearsed for four weeks. For the latter two, producer Bruce Fairbairn was in attendance, sitting on the floor recording bits of our new songs. Bruce had produced countless successful records where we were playing, his Armoury Studios, so when he told me we didn't have any hits I knew he was right. He was simply marvellous to work with. He talked the talk with great conviction, yet called me 'swami', possibly due to my laidback approach. He critiqued Jon's lyrics unmercifully, drawing lines through lyrics and saying, 'Change all these and show me it again tomorrow.' He really gave each of us his personal attention when we were overdubbing and steered the ship when dealing with the six of us collectively. He knew exactly how to make records but had to remind us how to.

During a break in March I returned to the UK and played a solo show in Amsterdam for YesFocus, the Dutch fan club, returning to Vancouver a few days later to continue with the band. We had rented apartments in a Vancouver tower block, mingling with tourists and locals in a city not entirely dominated by the car: people walked about, hung about, with a Starbucks on just about every corner. Months of work led up to the mixing. The first mix, of 'Nine Voices', a light and easy track to start us off, shone like a jewel. The next day, uncharacteristically, Bruce didn't arrive at the studio at midday. He didn't answer his phone.

Something was wrong, very wrong.

Jon went to Bruce's apartment with one of Bruce's friends. To the immense shock and sadness of everyone, they discovered Bruce had died in his apartment the previous night. For two days, we remained in the studio, trying to make sense of what had happened, retracing our steps, trying to recall what had been said. Could we have known anything was wrong? Bruce's wife and four sons were in our thoughts. Jon, engineer Mike Plotnikoff and I decided we would somehow finish what had been started and mix the other tunes, attempting always to consider how Bruce would have liked it to sound. We could only hope.

On 24 May, there was a memorial for Bruce at a theatre where friends spoke of him to a hushed crowd. Jon and I performed 'Nine Voices' and were heard in silence, resonant and heartfelt. Bruce was such an incredibly together guy who could laugh and sometimes raise his voice, always for the betterment of music. 'Nine Voices' and 'It Will Be A Good Day' were the songs that came out the best for me on the album that we called *The Ladder*.

Yes's touring regime kicked off once more on 6 September in Rio de Janeiro and, after Mexico City on 24 September, continued in the US. Jan and our daughters came to Phoenix, Arizona, for a week in October and the tour ended in mid-December at the Tower Theater in Philadelphia. Much-needed Christmas holidays enabled me to regain some sanity and energy and were a welcome break from the relentless schedule. And then we were back on the road, with UK and European dates that included two nights at the Royal Albert Hall on 19 and 20 February. We were in Portugal on 23 February, closing the European shows in Bucharest, Romania, on 25 March. This show was Billy Sherwood's last with Yes, at least for that period. Oddly, it was the same day he and Chris Squire released the first of their two Conspiracy albums.

We took a three-month break from April through most of June, which was wonderful insofar as it reminded me that life wasn't just about work. The family spent some time in Warbleswick, Southwold, in East Anglia, which was not quite as far east as Devon is west from London. Southwold has stayed more or less as it was in Victorian days and it was where Jan liked to go for weekend or longer breaks.

A whole new plan had evolved for Yes after Jon and I talked during the previous tour. We felt that the band needed to play extended songs again, especially now that Billy Sherwood was no longer a member. These really didn't require any extra parts and we were sure that just the five of us could pull it off perfectly well. Master Works became the title of the tour that began on 20 June 2000, in Reno, Nevada, where we rehearsed in a casino. Kansas were our opening act. To rapturous applause, 'Close To The Edge', 'Gates Of Delirium' and 'Ritual' – each nearly twenty minutes long – were featured alongside other classic seventies songs. These totally uncommercial titles reminded us Yes was an album band rather than a singles band. What a gift these songs were, setting us apart from most of the other successful prog bands. It was on this tour that we dropped Stravinsky's *Firebird Suite* as intro music and instead used Benjamin Britten's *Young Person's Guide To The Orchestra*. We have since used this more than *Firebird*, which we return to whenever it seems appropriate.

To say that Igor Khoroshev was a bit of a wild card was an understatement. He thought he had the gift of the gab and his artistic temperament reached superstar level, but he could certainly play the keys.

One night on tour, Igor even had a run-in with the police. He was released after spending an evening in jail, and after paying a huge fine. The news only leaked to the local rag and, fortunately for us, it was missed by the wider press. But time was up for Igor – we couldn't continue with him once the tour ended on 1 August, in West Palm Beach. This was all quite embarrassing for Jon and his wife Janee, who had been quite pally with Igor. At one point Jon had been planning to record with Igor.

Jan and our daughters joined me in West Palm Beach for a planned holiday at the Four Seasons Hotel, right on the beach. Lane drove the old Mercedes wagon for us, but Jan refused to set foot in it as it was now so tour-worn, and we rented something more practical. The beach was fun and we ventured around the area a little. We got some extra time as Yes had missed a show due to bad weather, which required the underwriters of the tour to reschedule. I personally lost three days in flying back to Cincinnati to perform the date, satisfying the contracts and being paid, before returning to continue holidaying. It must have cost the insurers plenty.

I also got on with new solo recordings with Curtis Schwartz. At the end of August, we compiled *Homebrew 2*, released later in 2000 with writing demos from the titles incorporated in *Union*, ABWH studio tracks, GTR and my solo albums. As before, Gottlieb Bros. created a design with my random photographs in great style. This series has been the most fun to do.

My next studio release would feature acoustic instruments exclusively. It was again mostly recorded at our Devon studio, on eight-track ADAT tapes, engineered by me. I selected the tunes from my unreleased back catalogue, some of the tunes Annie Haslam and I worked on, plus Yes's 'Your Move',

'Disillusion' and 'To Be Over'. It was the label's suggestion to include some Yes music and this gave me an opportunity to model the vocal lines with guitars over the backing tracks I'd recorded.

Somewhat adventurously, I booked myself a solo tour, In The Groove, that covered the UK, Europe and the USA, starting in Tilburg, the Netherlands, on 13 September and including the Queen Elizabeth Hall, London, and Renfrew Ferry, Scotland. By the middle of October I was playing in Buffalo, New York, followed by Cleveland, Chicago, Pittsburgh, Boston, New York, Philadelphia and Atlanta, with smaller dates in between. Yet again, I ended up in West Palm Beach. The Gottlieb Bros. extended themselves by producing another colourful tour programme that had a page dedicated to each of my solo releases. I played 'Dorothy' on a stereo arch-top guitar, a Yamaha AEX 1500 or Martin Taylor model over the backing track from *Homebrew* and my Gibson Les Paul Roland on other backing tracks, as well as the usual solo acoustic tunes. I was committed to building my one-man-and-a-guitar concept as far as I could take it.

Straight afterwards, on 12 November, I boarded a ship leaving Orlando for my very first music cruise. There were about sixty fans aboard, all eager to be entertained by my performances and workshops, and I also signed autographs at a meet-and-greet while the boat sailed around the Gulf of Mexico for four days. Small and intimate, this was fairly manageable, compared to the five cruises I've done with Yes. That said, when I got back on dry land I vowed never to do one again – but I have since gotten my sea legs.

In early 2001 I asked Castle, who had the rights to *Keys To Ascension*, if they'd like to release the seven studio tracks we'd recorded for the project separately. I assembled a running order, approvals were received and *Keys Studio* was quietly released later in the year. I was pleased that now the audience could see who we were, what we sounded like without the live show material weighing it all down. The forty-two minutes of new studio material might be as close as we have ever got to recreating the seventies feel and sound in our music.

Next, I turned my attention to the acoustic album, Curtis and I finishing off recording and mixing this huge musical undertaking for which I'd recorded streams of steel-strung and nylon-strung six- and twelve-string guitars, mandolins and mandolas, Dobro steels, Hawaiian steel, mandocello, acoustic bass guitar, koto and autoharp, aided by Dylan on drums and Andrew Jackman on the recorder for 'Your Move'. I knew exactly what the recorder parts were, as it was my idea in the first place.

I thought I might call it 'Wood Under Wire', but there was another record with a title too close to that and I settled on *Natural Timbre*. It was released on 14 May in the UK and 5 June in the US. The sleeve was done in-house at Eagle Records, my photos taken by Mike Russell, who took some of my best portrait shots ever from the GTR period onwards. He often worked in the world of advertising, doing as well as my friend Miki Slingsby had in fine art photography. Mike's death in 2011 from cancer was very sad. I've also enjoyed working with many other photographers like Bart Nagel, Dimo Safari and Mark Hadley. Meanwhile, Doug and Glenn Gottlieb's endless attention to Yes and to my solo photographic needs continues happily today.

Another plan was being hatched. Since Yes's 1970 *Time And A Word* had been the only album on which we featured an orchestra, we thought perhaps we should revisit it and, as we didn't have a keyboard player any more, we could once more use an orchestra. Keyboard-playing had partly become a way of accessing an orchestral palette anyway – strings, cellos, woodwinds and brass. But we'd have the real thing. This idea would eventually bear fruit as Yes's next release, *Magnification*.

CHAPTER 17

Grand Ambition

Yes stayed in apartments in Santa Barbara in California between 5 March and the end of April 2001. Jon Anderson, Chris Squire, Alan White and I began co-writing in the studio with Tim Weidner at the desk engineering the sessions. Tim had been busy since my *Turbulence* days, partly as Trevor Horn's main engineer.

I was delighted that Virgil came over and stayed at the apartment with me. We had some laughs cruising about in an awful Mustang that neither braked nor steered like anything we'd driven before. He witnessed some of the goings-on at Sound Design Studios, although I think things went a little smoother because he was there, tempering the distant storm.

Tim often found himself in difficult situations, but working with Yes is always difficult, truly. As Tim and I had worked together before we were able to update each other on to how to reach the next phase of the project without going nuts. It should have been easier now there were only the four of us but each of us pulled Tim in different directions, and some sessions required staying up all night. Usually, this is a failed strategy. Sometimes finicky members disagree with the path of least resistance. When I play, I like to decide when the idea has evolved sufficiently to say it's done. That's when it's in time, in tune with a good sound and all the right notes are in the right order, of course (as Morecambe & Wise reminded André Previn). I sensed interference, but just got some decent guitars down with Tim. Chris and I had really wanted Andrew Jackman to do the orchestration but Larry Groupé had credentials and was in LA so we went with him. He started describing the arrangements to us and all we could do was hope.

We moved to Trevor Horn's studio on Linda Flora Drive in Bel Air for the whole of May to complete vocals and do final overdubs. The house was perched on a canyon ledge with spectacular views, a pool and Trevor's recording setup (and would be, sadly, destroyed by the forest fires that swept California in 2017). It was a great place for the business of recording, with plenty of guest bedrooms and a cook to prepare our main meals. Rental cars had to wrestle with the steep terrain and tight parking positions, but we didn't go out much, working through the afternoon, breaking for dinner and then, if we were lucky, back for more recording.

It took loads of work to build the guitars near the end of 'In The Presence'. My 175 took the limelight but Jon felt more was needed so I used the Fender steel and whizzed about in the highest of registers and something jelled. It wasn't relaxed though: we had cabin fever and a tour schedule to juggle. These sessions ended with the orchestra yet to be recorded, meaning mixing was way off in the distance. This would require a major effort to steer, but steer I did.

After five weeks at home in the UK, Yes assembled near Lake Tahoe at Reno's Silver Legacy hotel and casino to rehearse for a unique tour. The album would be finished while we were touring and come out after it was all over – such was the way with Yes, always chasing its own tail.

We rehearsed our own parts and each night a different local orchestra would play Larry Groupé's arrangements which, for a short time, he also conducted. This was a challenging setup, to say the least. These mostly classical musicians would be at the daily soundcheck, sight-reading parts that fitted with ours (providing we all stayed together, under the conductor).

We opened the Yes Symphonic tour at the casino on 22 July as a warm-up and started officially in San Diego three nights later. We did the West Coast, Vancouver, then across to Chicago, up and down the East Coast and eastern Canada, finishing in New York at Radio City Music Hall on 8 September. It was very successful and well received, despite occasional problems with orchestras, some of which were better than others.

While touring, we were sent mixes of the album with orchestra in which we couldn't hear much of the band and certainly little or no guitar. I went into survival mode and faxed Jordan Berliant at Left Bank Management and Tim Weidner, whose hands moved the faders in a second-by-second revision of the mix levels to enable the guitar to be proportionally heard. This took weeks but they did come through for me – no one else had objected to the first mix of the album as much as I did. Sadly, on Jon's insistence the sleeve design wasn't offered to Roger Dean. What we got was a lacklustre dull and dark image that did nothing but disappoint both the fans and me.

After the tour ended, I was asked to stay in New York to do 'the most important of interviews regarding the imminent release of *Magnification*' but I declined. It just seemed to me that I'd been in the States forever. I flew to London on 9 September. On the 11th I was at a car wash where a conveyor belt dragged cars through the water spray and brushes while their owners watched TV in the office. OMG! Unfolding in front of my eyes were the events of 9/11, war on the US mainland, now forever indelibly printed in my mind. I'd just left the city. On *Magnification*, on the song 'Spirit Of Survival', Jon sings, 'Who's teaching the hatred... in a world where the gods have lost their way?'

At least I was in London. I called Jan immediately and arrived home twenty minutes later. We hardly moved for hours. We tried to reach friends in the US by phone but all lines were jammed. Jon and Janee were in Washington, where the Pentagon was hit. They couldn't get out for days. It was the official release date for *Magnification*. But nothing seemed to matter about the album after that day, a day of mourning forever.

In October, Yes and crew went to Vienna, Austria, to continue the Symphonic tour. This time we had two different orchestras, spending two weeks with each. This proved to be a blessing, as each got the chance to get their teeth into the music and they played more from the heart than the head. We opened on 25 October and then went on to Poland, Latvia, Russia, Estonia, Finland, Sweden, Germany, the Czech Republic, Switzerland, Italy, Holland, Belgium and France, before starting in the UK at Manchester on 28 November and playing London on 4 and 5 December.

I travelled by car between almost every gig, as per usual. My driver was Jim Halley, who'd previously worked with Yes as tour manager before managing my solo career. We worked out which bits were driveable and when I'd have to fly. Driving in Europe was trouble-free – borders often didn't exist, while others required only a quick show of passports and we'd be out of there. We used my Mercedes-Benz 300TE 4Matic estate car with the model numbers taken off, and with what we thought was the correct paperwork required for the countries outside the EU. In Germany, the car's rear axle started playing up and interfering with the '4Matic' system (which was supposed to automatically go from two- to four-wheel drive when needed). It was fortunate that Mercedes-Benz in Stuttgart accepted the car and fixed it in four days, leaving a sticker on the dashboard recommending that we didn't drive over 130 kilometres an hour.

Then there was Lithuania. We pulled up, showed the car's registration papers to border guards and they said, 'Oh no, photocopy *no good.*' After a while, we paid them money and suddenly, 'Everything's OK, you can go now.' Lucky for us, as we had a show that night.

Worse still was Russia. Driving from Estonia, we travelled along awful, bare, dull minor Russian towns on a straight road where, at every crossroads, there was a soldier or two watching suspiciously as we drove by, strictly observing the low speed limit until we reached St Petersburg. After the gig, the Russian promoter escorted us out of the city in the direction of Finland. He got lost for a while before eventually signalling for us to pass him and carry straight on. We came to two huge queues of lorry and trucks, all waiting to cross the border. No way were we going to join this line of trucks, some stationary, others moving at a snail's pace. Arrogantly, we drove down the middle of the road until we were stopped by a guard who asked, 'VIP?'

'Yes, VIP,' replied Jim, pointing at me.

The border guard directed us to a vehicle inspection bay. We got out and showed them our papers, but they were far more interested in the car and apparently what it might hold.

'Where's the money?' they asked us.

One soldier wanted to check the guitar and insisted on taking it out of its case. This was my Gibson 175. To my utter disgust, he strummed it. The whole experience was more than a little fearsome. It was time for a transaction. Once in their office, one of the soldiers said, 'One, two, three,' pointing at himself and his two colleagues. A $100 bill, then another, then one more were each taken from Jim's float and placed on the desk. As we left the building we saw the orchestra tour bus being evacuated for Custom checks. We got back in the car and departed the Customs area in a shroud of white smoke, a result of having to fill up with substandard petrol. Half an hour after leaving Russia, as we approached Finland, we at last stopped at a garage-cum-supermarket, bought good gas for the car and stocked up with goodies. We relished indulging in a genuinely free world again. This was to be the last time I'd ever use my own car for a tour.

The tour wrapped up the year and still in the pipeline was the release of the *Symphonic Live* DVD taken from our Amsterdam show with the European Festival Orchestra conducted by Wilhelm Keitel. Most of the material came from the seventies, balanced by a little *Magnification* material. My solo guitar spot was shot in really high quality with nice camera work and lighting, directed by Aubrey Powell. I played the second movement of Vivaldi's Concerto for Lute in D and 'Mood For A Day'. The European tour had been far more stable and fun than the earlier leg and the music held together through repeated performances with the orchestra. There was a stronger sense of camaraderie that translated on screen – possibly, then, this is the best Yes DVD available.

Workwise, the first half of 2002 was spent on projects outside of the Yes camp. I was back in Curtis's studio in early February, Geneva in early March, Martin Barre's Honiton studio in late March, back at Curtis's early June and otherwise working at our studio in Devon.

One of the outcomes of all this studio time was *Skyline*, my next solo release. This was instrumental bar the opening song, 'Small Acts Of Human Kindness', which was finely developed as an arrangement, and its closing reprise, 'Small Acts'. The album was a balance of my own start-up tracks and Paul Sutin's material, on which I collaborated. All the tracks received the same careful treatment and consideration. In many ways it was unlike any other album of mine. A number of tracks featured the 175 in clean mode and the Steinberger twelve-string guitar, which had worked so well on other projects with Paul Sutin, like *Voyages*. It was all gentle and improvisational, with classical guitar featured on 'Secret Arrow', backward electric guitar on 'Moon Song' and my Fender Precision bass on most tracks. The sleeve features pictures I took of a rainbow rising across the Vancouver skyline. This was the first of four releases on Inside Out Music.

I visited Martin Barre's studio on 16 March to master *Masterpiece Guitars* with Mark Tucker for its release on Twentieth Century Guitar as a limited edition and through P3 Music outside the USA. In early May I left for New York to attend another of Larry Acunto's *20th Century Guitar* magazine shows where I hung out with guitar people and played a spot on the Saturday night event.

I was in Nijmegen, the Netherlands, in late May to give one of my rare guitar workshops, stopping over in Stuttgart to meet an arranger before going to Geneva for four days, then returning to London on 31 May. From 5 June I was back at Curtis's studio, finishing off mixing *Skyline*, with the running order completed a month later.

Meanwhile, there was the background hum of developments regarding Yes's ever-changing line-up and touring plans. Yet another new chapter in the group's convoluted history was about to unfold. A major tour was booked and, with Rick Wakeman back in the band, the classic line-up was a reality once more.

After a two-week rehearsal in Seattle prior to the first show on 17 July at the city's Paramount Theatre, the tour then took a huge, circular route around the States, ending up back on the West Coast and closing in Las Vegas on 25 August. Jan and Steph came out to LA to see the Universal Amphitheatre show on 23 August, after which we returned to the UK together.

I had a respite in September and did interviews ahead of *Skyline*'s release in mid-October. Then I left for Orlando for rehearsals with Yes before opening another tour in Tampa on 24 October. We were certainly maximising our live potential, as this tour continued till 8 December in Mexico City.

I can remember these gigantic tours only as a 'point in time' or a 'feeling of effort and gratitude'. It was the cumulative effect of performing so many shows in one period. There were so many highs and lows – the band climbed up at the beginning of the tour and wandered downwards towards the end. By the mid-period and certainly towards the end, the shows began to run themselves, at least to some extent. They more or less had to. The band machine was oiled and greased for greater things but wear and tear, tiredness – the meals, the hotel nights and especially the travel – began to upset my balance and really got me down.

My suitcase was the only connection to normal life in a pursuit that became a case of the survival of the fittest. What went in the suitcase was, over time, stripped right back to the barest essentials, all contingent on space, weight and the need to discard anything superfluous or valuable that could go missing. Having been robbed of a few things from hotels and dressing rooms, I learned the lesson of leaving cherished things at home. It was only the music that made it all worthwhile, apart from the income.

The role we played in delivering our music gave us some small satisfaction made manifest by the feedback from the audience and the knowledge that we were 'good' and 'on' during the show. If the sound was good, then we could go places not found on any GPS system – somewhere inside the audience, whose enjoyment in turns fed our enjoyment. When it's at its best, this is what motivates us to keep going.

During the second half of January 2003, I was recording Dylan on his drums at our studio for my next solo release, *Elements*. These recordings encompassed rock, blues and jazz and developed into Steve Howe's Remedy Live tour in 2004. The line-up was assembled as we were making the record: Dylan recommended Derrick Taylor on bass guitar, I invited Ray Fenwick on second guitar and Virgil played keyboards and contributed harmony vocals. Gilad Atzmon was only on the record, playing sax, clarinet and flute.

As per usual, I began work with a drum machine rhythm on each track, before expanding the tunes. With only eight tracks available at our place, I would ingeniously maximise ways to overdub more ideas, usually through recording slave tapes that would later get synced up to the master in Pro Tools at Curtis's studio. I compiled the thirteen instrumentals and three songs that Dylan had now played and recorded Gilad's great saxophone riffs and solos, then Virgil's keys and vocals, adding Derrick's bass to all the tracks but 'Pacific Haze', where my bass seemed to fit best.

The album opens with the sounds of a Devon garden, birds, bees and woodpeckers crossfading into 'Across The Cobblestone', possibly influenced by that crazy night and morning at the farmhouse in 1970. 'Where I Belong' is a country-blues thing, and the only other song is 'Load Off My

Mind'. This has the structure of 'Milk Cow Blues', with part of the first guitar solo taken from Rick Nelson's version of that song, where the great James Burton cries out suddenly from the seventeenth fret of his Telecaster.

Some of the material on the album was wholly improvised. The shorter solo electric tunes, like 'Tremolando', 'Hecla Lava', 'Sand Devil' and 'A Drop In The Ocean', had been recorded back in 1999, directly from a Roland GP-100 rackmount guitar processor to MiniDisc in Vancouver. 'The Chariot Of Gold' was a song before my guitars took it over, and a version may eventually appear on a future *Homebrew*, as the words actually mean a lot to me. It might seem strange that I should say that, since I haven't released them but sometimes lyrics can be quite personal and I get a little secretive – perhaps, some say, too much so.

'The Longing' has guitar synths galore but I seriously don't know what kind they are. They remind me of the sound of ARP synths and I'd very much like to find them again – they might have come from a Stepp DG-1, but I might never know. The virtual guitars mentioned on the sleeve are from Roland's VG-88 system and feature only on 'Bee Sting' and 'Smoke Silver'.

Producing my own music is very important to me. I know what I like and what I don't like. My ears can't be deceived. I'm constantly evaluating tuning, timing and tone when I'm listening: if there is room for improvement, let's improve; if it feels good, let it play, it must be right. In 1955, my favourite blues musician, Big Bill Broonzy, put it like this: 'If you believe in it and it's right, then you're happy, and that's me.' All songs have unique stories – there's no one way to produce music and your mind can be at its most open when less is more. Just a simple pulse or rhythm can allow an instrument to go into unforeseen directions.

For 'Westwinds', for example, I set up a good Fender Twin reverb amp in our control room and an AKG C 414 EB mic, plugged in my 175 and, while listening on headphones to a drum pattern that was also being recorded, I improvised for quite a while. I did this again, changing the bpm (beats per minute) and the feel of the drum and off I went again for quite a while. To both 'Westwinds' and 'Pacific Haze' I added a bass guitar and a rhythm guitar, plotting out the chord movements that the first guitar implied. I had a drum part, an electric guitar, a bass guitar and acoustic rhythm guitar all playing something that hadn't previously existed. I then sight-edited at various points, experimenting by tightening up these points and removing any dead spots.

On 'Westwinds' I went fairly crazy and impersonated a brass section on keyboards with ideas that complemented the top line and the structure. These were written out by Andrew for the band to play. On 'Pacific Haze', I had only the guide drums, electric, bass and acoustic rhythm guitars, giving Andrew full rein for the brass arrangements. These tracks were both recorded at the Snake Ranch Studios on 8 May, engineered by Cameron McBride. I mixed *Elements* with Curtis and it was released on 7 September in the US and on 29 September in Europe.

Meantime, the touring machine of Yes was in motion again. On 3 June, we met in Dublin to rehearse in the venue of our first show, which was not an ideal space for preparations. It was a big old void of a venue, where our crew feverishly set up a new European PA system with all the plugs in the right holes, XLRs into female XLRs, with the setup eating into rehearsal time. Each of us had to get our own rig into shape after the equipment had been shipped halfway round the world. Some

}might be dealing with a new monitor engineer or lighting designer, attempting to learn cues. We had to finalise intro tapes, running order, arrangements, and lighting, while cries of 'When's dinner?' and 'Where's so-and-so?' echoed around the stage and the rest of us were always waiting for someone or other. Then it was, 'When do we have to stop tonight?'

Looking back, Yes were undisciplined and disorganised, at least in comparison with the way we run things now. Hours would be lost fixing some ancient piece of supposedly vital equipment which didn't have a backup. The crew, who were often at the gig from 8 a.m., were stretched to the limit and the tour hadn't even begun. We rarely managed to play the whole set through at rehearsal, and, although the last day was called a 'production run-through', we often gave up waiting around. And as soon as one person left, the whole thing came to an end.

The Full Circle tour zipped about the UK, Europe, back to the UK and back to Europe, taking in Glastonbury Festival on 29 June and the Montreux Festival on 14 July and finishing a week later in the Portuguese capital of Lisbon.

Unfortunately, an element of sloppiness had entered the camp on this tour. Hard drinking and indulgence in certain substances dangerously influenced the late-night activities of the band. When I was going to bed, others were going out to bars and clubs – like in them olden days past. Volume levels were exceeded on stage and mistakes in arrangements riddled the set: not so clever. Some suggested that the audience hardly noticed or – a more extreme view – that rough edges added to the live feel. I wasn't so sure, and it certainly wouldn't be the case if it had become so bad that we fell apart. We'd had stricter rules in place since 2001 about no drinking until the show was over. However, the rules would only be followed for a few days, and, without firm policing, enforcement was more or less impossible.

A secretive element prevailed. Before one show I was in Chris's dressing room, asking him about some musical point, and I could seriously smell the brandy. He simply denied drinking. Ha-ha, yeah... sure. Chris could still play very well but our communication would be interrupted in the excitement, once everything ignited on stage: the super-troopers, the party in the front row with adoring superfans – fuel for some, but just showbusiness fodder for others. Chris later admitted the drinking, but he could never change. Look, a drink's OK, but a *bottle*? Perhaps not. Beer was decanted and smuggled in everywhere we went. Yet performing on stage was our actual work – people paid money to see us and we really ought to turn up ready, clear-headed and up. Don't tell me again you're suffering and aren't feeling great. Get ready, be ready. We always got through the tours – but sometimes only by the skin of our teeth.

We continued, heading to the Pacific Rim and opening in Japan on 12 September in Osaka, followed by two nights in Tokyo before flying overnight to Australia – Melbourne and Sydney, where I got to see my brother Philip and his wife Sarah. It was good to catch up in person. Perth was next before Singapore – the only time we would ever perform there – then Honolulu to finish and back to Irvine, California.

Rhino Records contacted me about a planned thirty-fifth-anniversary boxset. I'd been uncredited as a resource for the previous compilation, *Yesyears*, in the nineties and, as I'd always kept the quarter-inch tapes from our studio sessions, I remained a good archive of rarities and master mixes for these repackaging projects. Later, with Yes's *In A Word* boxset, Rhino would again draw heavily from my tape store. For this thirty-fifth anniversary, they included a bonus CD (sadly, only in the US, for what was a triple boxset, but not in Europe), on which new grooves had been found for the acoustic 'Roundabout' and 'South Side Of The Sky', recorded by the classic line-up assembled in LA on 28 September. Jon added a new song, I arranged my 1975 song 'Australia' for solo acoustic guitar and Chris recorded an excerpt from Dvořák's No. 9 Symphony, *From The New World*, a challenging prospect – brave but weird. Using fuzz bass and bass pedals was surely an arrangement first for this famous piece of Dvořák's music. This material later formed part of a DVD release, *Yes Acoustic*, taken from a January 2004 satellite broadcast. This sewed up things for Yes this year, and now was a time to reflect back.

Christmas 2003 was great. Jan, Dylan, Virgil, Georgia, Steph and I had a wonderful time together in Devon. This was before they'd settled down with wives and husbands of their own, just us and them – simple heaven.

CHAPTER 18

Remedy Plus

My own band, Remedy, was making plans for its first ever tour in January 2004 but I was interrupted when I had to fly to LA to appear with Yes on various TV slots, such as the *Kilburn Show*, and an in-store signing in Sherman Oaks.

By the end of the month I was back, preparing for Remedy's tour. I'd bitten off a lot with my selection of highly arranged tunes for the setlist. I had much to learn for each title, each of which required detailing time. 'So Bad' was in the minority, with opportunities for stretching out and jamming, and the likes of this song provided balance for the more arranged pieces. None of the tunes had ever been played on stage before. 'Diary Of A Man Who Vanished' was played with the band as it is on my second album. It really was a case of calling up an entirely new repertoire that had only existed in the recording studio. My memory needed a to grow a new layer to deal with all the lines, chords, words and guitar switches – several between guitar and steel. Some of these tunes had waited almost thirty years for their stage debut. It certainly was a nice musical challenge. I was also going to play a solo acoustic set to introduce the second half of the show.

Fundamentally, it worked. We rehearsed for four days, which gave us enough time to have it pretty well down, and the first show was on 2 March at the Warwick Centre, Coventry. We played six more shows in the UK, including the Queen Elizabeth Hall, London, finishing in Glasgow at the Renfrew Ferry. We went on to Belgium, Holland, Italy and Spain, which is where the tour bus broke down. We had the lot on this tour – breakdowns, no A/C, fires, and I felt the strain of taking on all the band responsibilities for the first time.

Touring solo was different to being with Yes, while Remedy was about communication, learning about each other and feeling ideas out, quickly settling into a routine. Ric French did a great job mixing the shows, tour managing and driving us about in a rented Sprinter van. He also took care of running the day-to-day finances. Behind the scenes, we had expenses to watch, bills to pay, wages going out, fees coming in: we needed to keep within budget all the while.

Remedy Live came out later in the year, filmed at Newcastle Opera House on 8 March. It had been a gentle show where everybody held their position, very orderly and dear to my heart. Ray Fenwick, Derrick Taylor, Dylan and Virgil all played their part in what was a beautiful experience. This DVD is now owned by our company.

The dust had hardly settled when, on 3 April, I was in Seattle rehearsing once again with Yes. I'd been lucky on the Remedy tour to have Hugh Manson as my guitar technician and he continued on Yes's touring legs. The job requires dedication and timing and my set contained many changes, switching of guitars and different amp setups, stereo at times and the two acoustics on stands. It really was quite intricate but we got it down quickly. When he had some time off, Tim Stark took over. Tim is still part of the Manson guitar shop and Manson

Guitars business, building guitars for the stars and anyone else who wants them.

The tour kicked off in Seattle at the Key Arena on 15 April, then on to LA, Las Vegas, Atlanta, back to Florida then Chicago, Toronto, Philadelphia, New York and ending at the Tsongas Center in Lowell, Massachusetts, on 15 May, a show that was filmed for the DVD *Songs From Tsongas*. The outstanding track is 'The Rhythm Of Love', particularly the guitar solo. The Stratocaster sounds good and I climb about the neck comfortably with my workmanlike facial expression. When the music deepens, I frown a bit, looking slightly in pain but I'm not, I'm just into it. Sometimes other people's material is easier to work up something different in.

I stayed in the US, driving down to Lititz where I had dinner with Mickey Tait and Roy Clair, then visited the Twentieth Century Guitar Show on 22 May before performing on guitar at downtown Farmington, New York. This was a fairly impromptu affair, but a breath of fresh air again, the solo performance reinvigorating and loose.

On 26 May, I returned to London for a five-day turnaround before flying to Helsinki, Finland, to warm up before the first European show there on 2 June. We visited most cities, returning to the UK for Wembley Arena, before heading to Paris and, after Italy, we returned for three odd UK gigs – Exeter, Kettering and, on 12 July, the final show in Braintree. Our show at Lugano in Italy was broadcast and released as a DVD. Like *Yes In Montreux*, it was loose and off the cuff; perhaps not that well balanced in the audio department but compensated for by us being unaware of the filming. I was in Montreux again in early July, teaming up with Steve Morse for a few hours before he played the Montreux Jazz Festival with Deep Purple. We were summoned to Claude Nobs' house

1980: On a shoot with Yes. Alan, Geoff, Chris, Trevor and me. *Michael Putland/Getty*

1980: The Newsman and me, after being invited to watch a filming of *The Muppets*.

1982: On stage with Asia at the Palladium in New York City. John, Carl, Geoff and me. *Ebet Roberts/Getty*

1985: A break from recording *GTR*, our self-titled debut album at the Townhouse in London. Jonathan Mover, me, Max Baco, Steve Hackett and Phil Spalding.

1986: Putting the Stepp DG1 Guitar Synth through its paces. *Steve Back/ANL/Shutterstock*

1986: Jamming with Steve Hackett at the National Association of Music Manufacturers Convention in Chicago. *Paul Natkin/Getty*

1986: At Hank Marvin's Fender presentation with Hal Lindes, Dan Smith, Bill Schultz, Jeff Beck, David Gilmour, Stuart Adamson, Eric Clapton, Hank Marvin, yours truly and Richard Thompson.

1989: Promo shot for Anderson Bruford Wakeman Howe. *Michael Putland/Getty*

1991: The Yes men. Chris, Tony, Rick, Alan, Jon, Trevor, Bill and me backstage at Wembley Arena on the *Union* tour. *Ian Dickson/Redferns*

1991: The *Union* tour at Shoreline Amphitheatre in Mountain View, California. *Tim Mosenfelder/Getty*

1994: Me, Martin Taylor and the Batmobile.

1996: With jazz legend Tal Farlow.

2000: Bigger is better in Argentina. *Dave Wilkerson*

2002: A jam with Elvis Presley's guitarist Scotty Moore.

2012: When two guitars are better than one on the *Fly From Here* tour.

2017: On stage with Yes and Rush's Geddy Lee on bass at the 32nd Annual Rock & Roll Hall Of Fame Induction Ceremony at Barclays Center in New York City. *Jamie McCarthy/WireImage*

2019: Live at the Jazz Cafe. *Colin Hart*

2020: Three generations of the Howe family. Dylan, Georgia, Cal, me, Jan, Zuni, Steph and Diego.

on the mountainside looking over Lake Geneva. He showed us a guitar with curved frets, a bit like a sitar, given to him by John McLaughlin. Everyone was in a nice mood and the air smelt clean.

This year had been unbelievably busy and now I had a break. I drove to Marsellan in the south of France, settled in and two days later collected Georgia and a friend at Nîmes airport. We hung around the small town and wandered down to the beach for a few days before we headed off together to Schönried, Switzerland, for a few more days. After a forgettable night in a hotel at Calais we got back the next day in time for Jan's birthday and a small celebration.

In early August I spent a week in southern Ireland, writing lyrics and resting up. I write more words than I could ever use in songs and a lot of my ramblings get discarded. Every so often I review what I've been writing, looking for the strength of a line, a twist of phrase, the odd rhyme and something that sings well. I might get a few lines of words while strumming some chords but mostly the words and music come separately. I enjoy putting them together, seeing how they might shape up and drive my tune along. There are often several layers to lyrics: a story may have come from different ideas that are not always obviously connected, but to me they become one.

After two days at home in London, I left for Quebec where Yes were touring with an amazing stage set by Roger Dean. Huge blow-up shapes hung around us, some parts looking slightly like cow skins – wonderful. Amazing designs and colours illuminated by the lights painted a changing set of patterns that dramatically altered the impression of space. This seemed the appropriate time to elevate the production side and put on a show-show. The latest extensive tour of North America ended in Monterrey, Mexico, on 22 September, the last time that the classic line-up – Jon, Chris, Rick, Alan and me – would play together (all but Jon and Rick played on 11 November 2004, at the Produced By Trevor Horn concert in front of the Prince of Wales at Wembley Arena).

Following all the work and touring, Jon made the not unreasonable request: 'Let's take a year off.' After the supposed clean-up attempted back in 2001, certain members were gradually becoming more and more difficult to tour with. Jon felt this most keenly and it was agreed that a break would give everyone a chance to re-evaluate their position and we could pick things up again in the future. Unfortunately, Jon fell off a ladder at his home while hanging Christmas decorations. This led to some physical complications that required a considerable recuperation period and the break was extended over the next three years. Vain attempts would be made to tour together once again in 2008, but more on that later.

I was back in London on 24 September 2004, taking two weeks off before I got stuck in with Paul Sutin in Gland, just outside Geneva, where he had relocated to build a small studio complex. For just over four weeks I wrote and recorded various tunes, of which two tracks were included in my album *Time* in 2011. Back in Schönried, the isolation was conducive to producing several simple demos that became useful later. At Paul's chalet I had some powered speakers, a drum machine, a mic and one electric and one acoustic guitar. I ran the drum box, played over it and recorded on the mic to MiniDisc, before editing.

By 8 November, I'd driven back to the UK for that Trevor Horn show, which included a rehearsal the day before. This was frantic and hard to keep together, given the characters involved. Someone drank half a bottle of whisky before going on, but it wasn't Chris. He was nevertheless on a roll and walked on stage before Trevor had finished announcing us to get a cheer for Trevor. This was all good fun and before playing 'Owner', I played with Frankie Goes To Hollywood.

On 15 November, I returned to Gland for three and a half weeks, then it was back to the UK for three days' recording Dylan on my next solo album and back to Gland until 22 December, before Christmas in London with the family. I left my car in Geneva, trusting to luck that it would be there when I got back in the new year, which it was, once I remembered where I'd left it. I'd mistakenly left a small window open – perhaps I knocked the button in a rush to catch the plane home. I returned to work on four different musical projects, each requiring a different balance of the skills of my trade.

I had brought fifteen instrumental tracks on ADAT tapes with Dylan playing drums, Virgil and Oliver Wakeman on keyboards and Tony Levin on stick and bass guitar on seven of the tracks (I played the other bass guitar parts). It was time to do the final guitars, percussion and prepare them for mixing. This was to become *Spectrum*. Similar in a way to *Turbulence*, it features more of my prog-rock guitar approach. All tracks emanated from our Devon studio and, as digital files could easily be sent around the world, Tony and Oliver had stayed at home to record, before sending the files to me. This made many things fairly easy. I could check, edit, equalise and balance the parts, as I had when making *Portraits Of Bob Dylan*. Purists may endorse all players being in the same room at the same time as a whole song is recorded. Yeah, this can be done – it's beautiful when it works and when it's humanly possible to do it. But recording separately saves a lot of time and money and expands the possibilities so much, especially for me, with the geography involved. This debate has been going on since my earliest days in the studio. Playing together is, of course, a tried and tested method and has produced some of the greatest recordings – but it's definitely not how most records are made.

Yes's method was to have two or three weeks of rehearsing, record a guitar or keyboard guide part with the bass and drums – maybe a guide vocal too, to get a decent backing track – repair or replace the bass and, eventually, all the other instruments except the odd rhythm guitar part, in a focused and individualistic way. The drums could be fixed but only by editing between different takes of us playing together.

My earliest solo albums, *Beginnings* and *The Steve Howe Album*, were begun in a slightly similar way. I played a rhythm guitar with Alan and Bill on their drums right through each song, both of us referencing a click, locking the drums to the arrangement. Then I'd stack the rest of the parts, getting a bass next and whatever followed, building it up gradually. This retained a little of the live feel of a rhythm guitar and drums playing together.

From *Turbulence* onwards, I adopted the method of recording most of my guitars and bass to a drum machine or programmed drums, before adding real drums in overdub mode. Much more detail can be achieved recording just one instrument at a time. Some 99 per cent of popular recordings are made like this. Just as films are not just theatre with a camera in front of the cast, recording is not just the document of a performance.

Recording expanded enormously once people didn't just try to replicate reality, and instead developed into producing something that was satisfying whether real or not, fiction or non-fiction. The *Guinness Book Of Recording History* is worth a read in this respect. Although little is ever played at the same time, the art is to create that illusion and at the same time expand the possibilities of what can be achieved in the recording studio, with tasteful music at the heart of it.

As I now had most of what I needed for *Spectrum*, I cracked on with Greg Epps, engineering for a solid ten days. I'd been in touch with a company called Line 6 and had one of their Vetta II amps that I directly injected into Pro Tools and, armed with a stack of good travelling guitars, I was off and running, adding the final details, as some areas still needed a little attention.

It would always be disappointing not to thoroughly check everything when I was finishing an album, especially where parts of music link. Introductions and endings can make or break a piece but what happens in between also has to make sense: it needs development and moments of hold and release. I do like a tune myself, and the tune is pivotal, but improvisation adds something less predictable – a little wildness and abandonment can intensify the sound. I often set up interplay in my recordings between, say, steel and guitar, as spring boarding between different textures gets me thinking. Of course, the structure sets up the whole scene – that's actual writing to me – but often the top lines come because they have to.

'Labyrinth', 'Ultra Definition' and 'Raga Of Our Times' demonstrate lots of different time signatures. On 'Ebb And Flow' I rotate from the clean chordal part to move around the more mobile and tougher-sounding melodic stream of my consciousness. 'Highly Strung', sometimes in 7/8 time, gets a load of wah-wah guitars and a walking bass section from me, while elsewhere pedal steel gently slips in. 'Hour Of Need' is the *Spectrum* version of the Yes song of the same name, but here my words have been allied to a completely different melody and chords (the Yes track was supposed to be called 'In The Hour Of Need'). This tune is fairly haunting for me, with Tony's bass assuring and deep. From around two minutes ten seconds in on 'Where Words Fail' I am accompanied by a Spanish guitar, my Gibson Chet Atkins, which I think is most effective, as is the end, from three minutes twenty-six seconds on, with volume pedal swells.

The sleeve incorporated more of my photographs and a Mark Hadley photo of me. *Spectrum* was mixed later at Curtis's on my return to the UK, which was still another month away. I returned to Dinemec Studios in Gland, Switzerland, where I was compiling *Homebrew 3*.

I had the usual batch of ADATs, DATs, MiniDiscs, quarter-inch tapes and cassettes, the contents of much of which was in the process of being written while it was being recorded. Greg Epps helped with the compilation. The material starts with *Turbulence* and *Grand Scheme*, continuing across other solo albums before I touch on *Magnification*, *Union* and GTR tracks. It's a very different 'Turbulence' on *Homebrew*, with something that never translated before, an atmosphere that prevails today. The tracks were like models that became something beyond their humblest of beginnings. 'Pyramidology' and 'In The Course Of The Day' are totally different texturally from their *Natural Timbre* arrangements, yet it is mostly the same material.

The sleeve notes tell some of the stories behind the music. 'It's Too Late' contains much I enjoy; from one minute thirty-five seconds the Rockman unit allowed me to blister up some guitar breaks. It was fun to include photos on the Gottlieb Bros. sleeve. The inner slip had Montecito, California, then Barbados and then the UK coastline. As usual, we included an equipment shot, and this time it's my stereo/mono board with three volume pedals for stereo guitar and steel, Big Muff and a Danelectro Daddy-O distortion box – limited, but sufficient for what I needed, even with Yes. Also, the guitar went through delay units, of course.

I spent some time on post-GTR tracks that would be released on *Anthology 2*, CD three in 2017. With Max Bacon and Phil

Spalding I gave all the collaborations a shot in the arm with fresh guitars and vocals.

Paul Sutin had some synthesised orchestral recordings on which I had recorded guitar – one at Dinemec, the other earlier at Langley, my own studio in Devon – which I brought over on ADAT tapes. We transferred them to Paul's DASH 48-track digital machine by Studer, an amazing piece of equipment, along with his AMS desk. These two tracks became part of my *Time* album with Paul K. Joyce, but were utterly changed, apart from my guitars. PKJ made some wonderful interventions right across the *Time* album.

Paul Sutin had all sorts of crazy productions going on – people, bands, classical musicians, engineers, all gyrating about the studio complex. He also held events and for a few years Ferrari had their very latest car unveiled in the big studio. The car park looked like a Ferrari dealership. I had to park my Mercedes-Benz CL500 around the corner, out of the way. Paul was helping Phil Collins run the Little Dreams Foundation for younger talent and has considerable involvement with the Yehudi Menuhin Foundation. He has very diverse interests – he used to teach once a week and when we met he was a financial trader.

We also had some tunes developing, and we even videoed one of them. We hope to write together more soon. Paul introduced me to Philippe Nicolas, a film-maker with whom we documented all sorts of sessions and walks in the park. The footage got lost with the passing of years. He was experimenting in 3D but this still hasn't been defined beyond 5.1 (its audio cousin), 3D glasses or VR. It gives me a headache after a few minutes.

After spending so much time in Gland and Schönried I decided to rent an apartment for two weeks in Clarens, on Lake

Geneva and within walking distance from Montreux. It was fairly complicated getting in and out of this property, requiring special codes and keys. Finally, I spent four days at the Majestic Hotel in Montreux. Although not as comfortable as the famous Palace hotel, it was as relaxing as it was intended to be. I finally got back to the UK on 25 February after a stay of nine weeks. This time my car stayed at Dinemec.

Early in March, Curtis and I mixed *Spectrum* at his studio. On 14 March I flew back to Schönried to make a start on writing this book, working there until 3 April and moving to Gland for ten days before driving home to London. This was one of my fastest ever return journeys, travelling 700 miles in just a day. Well, the Chunnel crossing was fast, which helped. Two weeks later, we celebrated Georgia's 23rd birthday.

On 18 May, I left for New York for another of Larry's guitar shows, rehearsing with Larry on bass, his brother Jim on drums and Ray Matusa on guitar for the usual Saturday-night show the following day in Patchogue at a very nice theatre. I played an acoustic solo spot and then a short band set with the lads. It went over pretty well. I was back in the UK for a few days before heading to Weert, the Netherlands, to give a guitar workshop and a mini-concert. Then I drove to Scotland to play at Martin Taylor's fifth Guitar Festival in Kirkmichael, Ayrshire. After my acoustic solo spot, Albert Lee played with Hogan's Heroes – and, as usual, his playing was a joy to hear. Later, I had a pretty wild jam with Tommy Emmanuel, Albert and Martin Taylor. I brought my Steinberger six-string and a Tube Screamer, which gave me a strong rocking sound amid these towering improvisers.

Tribute bands are now a genre of their own but they don't often feature a member of the subject band, the exception being Yes covers band Fragile. We got on well – well enough to do some shows together while Yes were inactive. We did a little rehearsing then played at the Robin, a club in Wolverhampton. One-off shows and mini-tours were set up. It was kind of weird but doable, because we all got something out of it. They would open, after the interval I'd play some solos and then we closed with Fragile playing Yes songs with me as special guest.

I also sometimes made appearances for the Steve Howe Appreciation Society, run by Pam Bay, and did one on 18 June in High Wycombe. I played a solo set, with extra chatting and discussion that always went down well.

I was in London doing a video interview for a Yes documentary the day before the London bombings of 7/7 in 2005. This attack was similar to IRA bombings – innocent people killed or injured for some abstract cause. I wondered, 'Why can't we all be pacifists?'

August and September drifted by with a few Yes calls and an increasing background hum but no plans were made beyond attempts to clarify business and company issues. We still had monthly expenses and were running up bills. The only thing I could do was keep on keeping on.

On 18 September, Jan and I went to the Hammersmith Apollo to watch Alison Krauss and Union Station, featuring Jerry Douglas. We went early to get the chance to meet them before the show and, as it happened, we spent far more time with them than we'd imagined. There was a power failure, knocking out all but emergency lighting. After we'd said hello to everyone, we wandered on stage, pre-show, and Ron Block offered me their guitars to check out. They were both beautiful post-war Martin D-28s. We met Alison's son and the whole experience couldn't have been nicer. The show was really great although the band all said afterwards that they couldn't get a decent sound on the stage. We said our farewells and left, delighted. This band says it all without trying to say anything. The sound they have together is the finest in the land, any land, every land. Jerry's Dobro work is beyond superlatives. As Brad Paisley said, 'If I get to heaven and the angels don't sing as well as Alison, I'm coming back!'

Compared to recent years, October to December were quiet months, so I just fiddled about in my own fashion, saving up energy for next year's onslaught of work.

CHAPTER 19

Finding My Feet

Early in 2006 I was called by manager Martin Darvill about reforming the original Asia. Oh wow: I felt like doing this, if it was really possible.

We met on 5 January at a hotel near Paddington Station. 'Hello', 'Hello', and 'Hello' echoed around the room as Geoff Downes, Carl Palmer and, of course, John Wetton and I sat down together. Some straight talking went down. The general consensus was that the past was over and by putting that behind us perhaps we could move forward together. There would be enthusiasm from Japan, the US and UK and Europe for tour dates. We could record anew and see what's what. Yes were on holiday and while the cat's away, the mice will play. If Asia could once again demonstrate the great teamwork we had twenty-three years ago, we just might have something good here. John and I had started the band and if we were now in harmony it would make it easier for Geoff and Carl.

By 1 April, I was working up my solo setlist by practising every day, as I do for a week before the first show. On 4 April, I departed to Lititz to reset my gear and meet up with Dave Wilkerson who was mixing FOH and driving me on my In The Groove tour. We're a good team when we're working and just travelling about. Pete Pappalardo at API booked the tour and all the shows were within drivable distances. The second show was at the TLA in Philadelphia on 8 April, my 59th birthday. Other dates included B. B. King's in New York and the Cubby Bear Club in Chicago with a guest choir, the Lincolnwood Chorale, who sung on my medley of Yes songs – 'Hour Of Need', 'Nine Voices', 'Wonderous Stories' and 'Your Move' from 'I've Seen All Good People' – that I play on my Portuguese guitar. We finished the tour in Milwaukee on 1 May.

Playing mainly club gigs, our expectations of the facilities available to us, especially backstage, weren't high. At B. B. King's, the shoebox-size dressing room was only mine for a limited period, just before the show and just after. It was pandemonium back there the whole time. Trays of food and trays of drinks hurtled round the corner. They say, 'You gotta love it all,' but I'm not so sure.

Performing my own set was and is still the most pleasurable kind of playing, the independence focusing my attention on my inner goals as a musician. Since writing 'Clap' in 1969 I knew this style of playing optimises what I really want to see myself doing. Fortunately, almost everywhere I play usually involves some kind of solo moment, which keeps the flame burning. As this was the first of my solo tours in 2006, I knew I had to pace myself as best I could.

A week after getting home, Asia and Martin met to update the ongoing plans. US and UK tours had been booked to start in late August, billed as The Original Asia, lest there be any doubt about it.

A week later I left with Ric French, who'd be mixing FOH, driving and tour managing my solo shows in Italy, visiting Salina, Sarzana and Seriate. These were festival-type shows, on a bill mostly consisting of other guitar players and bands. After two days off, or travelling, whichever you want to call it, I played in Zoetermeer, the Netherlands, followed by Spirit Of 66 in Verviers, Belgium, before getting home just before the May bank holiday weekend. Open-air festival shows are slightly testing due to the weather – be it the sun in your face or rain pouring down on the stage, or temperature and humidity leading to tuning problems, let alone the distraction caused by people coming and going with drinks in hand. It's so very far removed from the concert hall or even a theatre, where everyone can just focus on the music.

On 14 June, I gave a workshop and short performance in Birmingham at PMT, a music trade show, and then a couple of days later I did a spot at a small parish hall in Sandford, Devon. This was near where Hugh Manson lived and when I heard the village needed to raise money to keep their post office, I played a concert to raise the cash.

Next up were more shows with Fragile, starting on 27 June in caves at Liskeard, Cornwall – actual, natural wet caves! Water dripped onto the stage at times, which looked a bit dangerous for the performers. It was a bit like The Cavern in Liverpool, but the real deal was far less accommodating. We followed this date with a round of venues known and unknown, ending at the Brook in Southampton.

The first Asia reunion rehearsals were scheduled for August at Liscombe Park, Buckinghamshire, Martin's base at the time, where there was a studio with a small live space. Somehow, we all squeezed in and worked for a week before the equipment was shipped to the US. We played a warm-up show in Rochester, New York, on 29 August, before starting for real in Atlantic City at the Trump Marina casino – hardly my kind of place! Nevertheless, we played well. The first album was thoroughly explored and we went down terrifically well every night. It was a true coming-together, filled with renewed excitement for our music.

Meet-and-greets after the show had become the norm, as I refused to do it at any other time. It's always good to hear what people have to say after they've had a photo opportunity and it's become part of the routine of the show, although it never seems to be enough. More autograph hunters could usually be found, both waiting outside the gig and, less acceptably, even back at the hotel. I do have to ask – please don't follow artists back to their hotel; that absolutely crosses the line. It feels spooky and if we see someone coming after us we attempt to confuse them or lose them, as safely as possible.

Two more casinos followed, then it was on to Boston, New York, Philadelphia, Cleveland and Chicago, with fill-in dates too, before a two-day hop to play Long Beach, California, on 20 September, finishing in Palm Desert four days later. Here we parted company for a while. I had shows in eastern Canada, both solo and with Martin Taylor, and I had to organise the guitars and equipment.

It was great meeting with Martin at our nice Montreal hotel the day before our first show. This was our first tour together in Canada, starting around Montreal – playing in L'Assomption, Sainte-Thérèse and Beloeil. Our shows were diverse and relaxing: Martin plays with such ease, it's really astonishing. It's always a thrill to play together; he commands my full respect. I then totally enjoyed going to play solo at the Jane Mallett theatre, Toronto. The acoustics were fabulous for a solo guitarist and an attentive audience drove me towards the highest levels of performance. After Ottawa, Kingston and Rochester I could go home. Thanks, Randy!

Dylan married the writer Zoë Street on 5 November. The small church was full of family and friends and at the couple's request I attempted to play 'Mood For A Day' in the coolish chapel. The reception afterwards was held at Kenwood in London and The Blockheads played (with the occasional jamming guitarist dad).

Fragile and I played at a party in Lausanne in Switzerland on 11 November before Asia opened later the same month in Liverpool. We played Newcastle, Glasgow, Wolverhampton and Shepherd's Bush. We liked being back and judging by the audience reaction, it seemed they liked us being back too.

To wrap up the year, Martin Taylor and I played two concerts near Paris, in Cléon and Lillebonne. I spent January and February 2007 preparing for several ventures that would involve me later in the year. There were songs for Asia, plans to work with Dylan, meetings with Paul K. Joyce, trying to start a project with Yumi Cawkwell, solo guitar recordings and plans for *Homebrew 4*.

My relationship with Line 6, now owned by Yamaha, had become even more healthy since I got one of their Variax modelling guitars in my hands. By endorsing the programming technology of Line 6's Vetta II amplifiers, I ended my forty-five-year run playing through Fender amps. I couldn't and still don't program this kind of equipment myself. Steve Burnett, an ex-Manson guitar shop tech, who had also worked at Apple before he became a freelancer, programmed each song on the setlist with its own four settings. I could simply call up the right tones, delays, distortion and other effects suitable for the textures I needed. This is still how I set up on all my Asia and Yes tours. The equipment has vastly improved since Line 6 developed the HD500 and its current Helix system, the ultimate guitar effects processor and amp modeller. By the way, I always tour with a minimum of two identical amps – you never know when you might need backup.

Asia were to appear in Japan, starting in Nagoya on 4 March. We rehearsed before our equipment was shipped out there, where there was quite a buzz and a big buildup. Apparently, they were itching to have us play there – so much so that we played five nights in Tokyo, after Osaka. Wherever we went it felt like the old days of Asia. By this time, we had a setlist comprising not just Asia songs, but so-called 'career songs' representing the four of us: 'Roundabout' for me, 'Video...' for Geoff, 'Fanfare...' for Carl and 'Crimson King' for John. We needed to work at bringing them all together, the songs certainly demonstrating our heritage and opening up a new side of our show. They allowed the audience to reminisce about five different bands as we ploughed through our set. I also got my solo acoustic guitar spot, playing 'Intersection Blues'. Each night, I'd also pick one or two different solo tunes to play. Many in the audience came up to me afterwards. They'd really noticed my choices – 'Steve, it was nice that you played such-and-such tonight.' Playing many different solos added excitement for me. Even our crew would comment. That soloist in me was still trying to escape but I was content with the amount of freedom I had, at least for now.

Loads of fans – showing heartfelt admiration and love of the band – suddenly came out of nowhere, having lain dormant for the past twenty-three years. The *Fantasia* DVD was filmed during this tour, released in 2009 (one of three DVDs that came out over the next six years). The concert that was recorded wasn't the hottest we'd played, with the atmosphere in the concert hall dead and studio-like, the bold lighting a constant reminder to us of the presence of cameras. This showed we had some flaws and that we needed to tighten up.

Asia clocked up some serious miles in the course of the tour. On 14 March we played in Mexico for the first time. This is where Dave Wilkerson started mixing FOH, much to my delight. The audience were considerably wilder here than in Japan, running about taking photos or trying to record the whole show on their phones. We travelled on to Chile, playing Santiago, then Buenos Aires, Argentina, followed by Rio de Janeiro and São Paulo. There's always something touch-and-go about flying in South America. Would there be a strike? Would there be a delay? Would our luggage arrive? No one knew for sure, although we survived. One Boeing 727 appeared to have gaps around the door that caused a swishing noise. The pilots flew these planes like racing cars, blaring up into the sky.

In the middle of all of this, the Steve Howe Trio came about. Dylan and I loved the Jimmy Smith and Kenny Burrell collaborations on albums like 1963's *Blue Bash!* Dylan introduced me to Ross Stanley, who played sensational organ. He could play the bass parts with his left hand, instead of his feet, and had enormous chops and an ear that could pick out chords and harmonies instantly. We rehearsed some of the Smith and Burrell tunes, like 'Kenny's Sound', 'Travelin'' and 'Blue Bash'. One day Dylan suggested we add my 'Mood For A Day' from *Fragile*, somewhat to my surprise – they would play it in their style and we'd see if I could pick it up. I did, and realised that music can go through remarkable changes, allowing it to grow and expand. I was delighted so we tried a few other tunes I'd written and they seemed to fit perfectly with the other, jazzier pieces. We played some other Yes songs and had a riot choosing the appropriate sections. We had come up with a strange but quite wonderful repertoire, completely reliant on the three of us.

Ric French came on board to mix, drive and tour manage. We did our final rehearsals in May, in Devon. It was going to be a thrill playing with a new band on stage featuring my

Gibson 175 – it needed a good airing since I hadn't been using it overseas for too long. I'd be playing exclusively in clean mode, besides 'Laughing With Larry' on a Martin MC-28 acoustic.

On 13 May, we started a short tour of the UK in Cardiff, at the Glee Club, taking in London's Bloomsbury Theatre, where Chris Squire came to see us – which was incredibly nice of him – then Milton Keynes Stables, the Platform, Morecambe (a converted railway station where Adrian Payne, my sister's younger son, came to watch us). We finished on 20 May in Birmingham at the Arcadian. The music was fun, lots of soloing, and it swung like mad. This was the test bed for many more tours and recordings to come.

Asia would fully occupy June and July with tour dates starting in Sarasota, Florida, with three further shows in the state before we went north to New York, Albany, Philadelphia and a return visit to that casino in Atlantic City before Toronto, Chicago and, lastly, Detroit. Then it was back to Europe for dates in Germany and Italy. I remember finishing on 26 July in Naples where the rubbish hadn't been collected for months and the hotel stank really badly. I flipped out at the squalor. 'This really doesn't make it as a hotel – a prison, more like!' I shouted down the staircase to the receptionist.

After the tour, Asia started preparing to write and record our first reunion studio CD, to be called *Phoenix*, which would come out in 2008. This gave me some decent opportunities to play guitar: after the difficulties we had working together in the eighties, John Wetton and I felt healed and fixed as collaborators throughout this period. Hearing him singing my songs so comfortably is still heartwarming. Steve Rispin, who'd been doing FOH in Europe for us, engineered the project, getting some great sounds. Four tracks which everyone liked immensely

– 'Alibis', 'Parallel Worlds', 'Wish I'd Known All Along' and 'Over And Over' – were mixed by Curtis Schwartz. Roger Dean presented Asia visually.

I was also preparing *Motif*, my only strictly solo guitar CD to date. I recorded all twenty solos myself, including four new unreleased tunes, at Langley. This is the first of two volumes to encompass my entire solo repertoire, including tunes that I didn't write, 'Trambone' by Chet Atkins and Vivaldi's Concerto for Lute in D, second movement. *Motif* was to be the first release on our own label, HoweSound. I'm now preparing and writing volume two.

On 8 and 9 September, the Steve Howe Trio and engineer Will Worsley, with his mobile recording setup, met at Langley to record all of *The Haunted Melody* CD. I recorded my acoustic solo, 'Laughing With Larry', an extremely challenging composition, and added it to the group tracks that were mixed later by Curtis at his London apartment.

In September, I was back on stage with Fragile for a short run of shows, returning to Wolverhampton, Southampton and Dartford before two European shows in Verviers, Belgium, and Tilburg, the Netherlands.

I spent January 2008 overdubbing *Phoenix* at Liscombe and tidying up *The Haunted Melody*. On 16 February, I did another Steve Howe Appreciation Society show at Beaconsfield and at the end of February I rehearsed with Asia for a UK tour that opened on 1 March in Falmouth, Cornwall. For a change this time we often travelled by train – from London to Liverpool, Newcastle and Glasgow, finishing at Perth in Scotland on 20 March, the last of our dozen shows. *Motif* was released during this period.

An enormous background hum was coming from the Yes camp. Somewhat surprisingly, Trudy Green, who looked after

Aerosmith, offered to manage Yes and put us back on the road with a tour paying $250,000 a night during the summer. It would feature Jon Anderson – who had recovered his health – Chris Squire, Alan White and me. Since Rick wasn't going to be part of it, I suggested Oliver Wakeman play keyboards.

Dates and rehearsal periods were scheduled while negotiations took place between management and members about how proceeds would be shared. Although we'd all come up together, so to speak, to our utter horror Jon now believed he was worth more and demanded a greater percentage. Chris was beside himself and I had to calm him down. As it happened, Jon developed further health issues and his family were called to his hospital bedside. The whole tour was called off: it vanished completely from our schedules. We'd been quick to try and resurrect Yes in a blaze of glory and, after waiting three years to reassemble, we weren't going to let it all simply fall apart again. Unwisely, we briefly considered getting a guest singer but it was better to plan for getting everyone together for the future. Chris and Alan wanted to tour again only if we had each member we needed.

Asia kicked off a three-legged tour starting in Wilkes Barre, Pennsylvania, on 4 April, playing just two songs from the *Phoenix* album. We did an extensive US tour, all the usual cities from east to west and in the middle, including Texas. We finished in San Francisco's Grand Ballroom. The very next day we flew to Japan once again: Fukuoka, Osaka and Nagoya, and Tokyo for two nights, finishing 13 May. The third leg began immediately. We flew via Amsterdam to Bilbao, Spain, opening there on 17 May. After Madrid, we continued to France, Holland, the Czech Republic and Budapest, finishing in Bratislava on 31 May.

Looking back, it's hard for me to believe that, just five days later, the Steve Howe Trio did the rounds in the UK with twelve shows. We had our new CD, *The Haunted Melody*, on sale, the second HoweSound release.

I then left for Switzerland for a break in Schönried, before it was back to work with Paul Sutin in Gland. I met up again with Philippe to work on the documentary and, on 4 August, I moved to his lakeside apartment on Lake Geneva. Jan and Georgia came for a weekend at this beautiful location, the mountains behind and a subsidiary of the big lake out front. Évian, France, was ten minutes one way, Montreux ten minutes the other way. I continued working across the tracks that evolved to form parts of *Anthology 2*, CD three, with Paul's music and my own compositions. There were always things going on around Dinemec Studios, people dropping by to work and socialise.

The possibility of a new Yes era was growing and developing, even against the background noise of uncertainty. We'd spotted a Canadian singer called Benoît David singing Yes songs in a tribute band called Close To The Edge and he was good. It was clear that Jon Anderson was going to be recuperating from his illness for a while, so Chris, Alan and I took the bull by the horns and booked Oliver Wakeman to play keyboards for our planned resurrection. It was now mid-2008 and the last Yes show had taken place four years earlier. We couldn't wait any longer. We committed to a tour that November. There was enough time to pull all the ingredients together and go for it. It was now or never.

Meantime, I had a tour booked in Canada that was part solo, part Trio, an usual idea but productive in every respect. I opened in Montreal on 27 September, then went on to Quebec and Toronto, before switching to the Trio the next day for a show in Hamilton, Ontario. We went back to a different venue in Toronto, Kingston and Montreal, finishing back in Toronto. I stayed on to give a workshop, which actually led straight away to new Yes rehearsals in Hamilton. I'd met Benoît at the end of September and we ran through some songs on my guitar at the Montreal hotel. We had two weeks and two days to play through a demanding setlist as many times as possible.

It was cold in late October but, fortunately, the hotel was directly opposite the rehearsal room that was itself part of the venue for our first show. Preparation was the key to things flowing well. We had all committed to being ready but Chris didn't do much in practice. He compensated by at least not forgetting many of his parts, though there were often smaller details he'd have to refresh, usually using my CD desk hooked to the monitoring system in the rehearsal room. Oliver stepped up nicely, playing all his dad's parts on his keyboards and Benoît knew the song list pretty well. Most of all, there was a feeling of excitement about the challenge ahead. As in the *Drama* era, Chris, Alan and I were once again holding the baby. There was also a learning curve the new guys had to bridge with the rest of us, in and out of work. Fortunately, we had picked two reliable, professional and likeable musicians who could hold their own on stage while endearing themselves to the whole team – us, the crew, our agent and the manager too.

I can recall the first night of this phase of Yes's career quite well, its mood, feeling and atmospherics all coming back to me now. There was a buzz going on between us, the anticipation before the show that ran right through to the final chords: yes, we got through the show quite cleanly. After that show, Chris was most kind and flattering, saying he was impressed with how I'd played and the energy I put into the performance. He noted that, having toured recently with Asia, I was well warmed up, as he and Alan had mostly been off the road for three years. I was, after all, firing on all cylinders, in a solo capacity, with the Trio, with Asia and now with Yes. Had I ever been this busy? No, I don't think so. I was in demand and fulfilling that dream from way back when.

From 4 November, we toured around Canada and America for six weeks, finishing up in Hollywood, Florida. The audiences seemed to delight in the reinvention of Yes. We'd returned in a different, but clearly acceptable, format. Oliver was instantly liked by the crowds, and he delivered all the stylish embellishments he'd crafted through studying the original recordings. Benoît pulled it off well, taking this huge task under his belt. Like the previous line-ups of Yes which had also had to withstand big changes, we pushed the show forwards each night.

Perhaps now we could put to bed the ill-fated More Drama tour, planned a year earlier, in which I was going to play solo, and Alan and Chris were going to play with The Syn. This idea had fallen apart when Chris changed his line-up and a red flag went up at immigration when the whole party applied for work permits. It was a nightmare for me as, for the next three years, each time I entered the US I was sent back for further immigration checks. It required an enormous effort on my part to resolve. Letters and emails were sent but bemused immigration officials couldn't seem to square what had happened with my previously unquestionable compliance with the rules. Eventually it was straightened out and I was a good guy, again.

After Christmas with Jan and our family, I spent a few days in the new year of 2009 in Devon before leaving for Switzerland, working at Dinemec in Gland until 4 February, when I flew to Mexico City via Paris for two Yes shows. There were supposed to be further US shows to follow, but as we assembled at the Hard Rock in Houston on 9 February, Chris called in sick. He ended up spending time in hospital and then needed recuperation. We pulled the plug, going our different ways, claiming on our insurance cover and rescheduling the remaining dates.

I flew back to Switzerland and continued working on recordings, both solo and Paul's projects. I returned to Le Bouveret on the Petit Lac, Lake Geneva, and back in Gland compiled *Travelling* for the Trio's live release, mastered with Reda Kazoun. After three days in London, in March I was off to Russia, where Asia played Moscow, and we then went around Europe, playing in the UK in late April, where we finished at the Forum in London on 24 April. We had a gap around my 62nd birthday for some family time together in Devon across the Easter weekend. In June I compiled *Homebrew 4* with Will Worsley. Asia released that live DVD recorded in 2007 of the Japanese tour, *Fantasia* (note the play on words).

At the end of the month I shipped my guitars for an unusual tour schedule. We had given some thought to the all-important summer US season and decided that, since Asia was doing quite well at the time, why not combine them with Yes? It took some organising but I was prepared and happy to do double duties – although Chris wasn't too pleased when he realised I would get more pay. But that's how it was – Asia would open for a fee, Yes would close for a bigger fee and, indeed, I would get my share of both. That was one good return for me, but an even more delightful twist was getting the chance to play two guitar styles – a pretty central part of each band's sound – on the same night. Could I do this? I didn't know, but why not try?

I needed to get into the right headspace for negotiating before we achieved a balance between both camps. I was caught between the two factions at certain points – what was better for Asia or better for Yes, and where would my loyalty prevail? I ducked and dived a little but I couldn't really lose either way. Anyway, it was nice presenting the two styles together and it wasn't too burdensome for me to do this each night. From 26 June until 2 August we toured together with no major glitches, despite a bit of infighting, mainly between the managers, as Trudy Green at HK (Yes) and Martin Darvill (Asia) banged heads a few times. I kept quiet and stuck to my plan: get through this, whatever it takes. This tour could have been billed as 'Asia versus Yes' in a showdown battle-of-the-bands-style competition. Vote for your favourite group! Thank goodness it didn't turn out like that, as most of the fans liked both bands.

I toured with more than a dozen instruments, including two Variax guitars. One of them had to be tuned a semitone below concert pitch for Asia and the other at concert pitch for Yes. Asia played the most popular four songs from our first album, and the career songs, excluding 'Roundabout', obviously, as Yes would play that, which left 'Fanfare...', 'Video...' and 'Crimson King'. I played Dobro on 'The Smile' and mandolin on 'Don't Cry'. Yes played a broad selection from the seventies era plus 'Owner...' 'Machine Messiah' had a good run as the last song of the set, alternating with 'Heart Of The Sunrise', always Chris's favourite. He often referred to it as his solo. The tour ended in Bethlehem, Pennsylvania, after a fairly short run of fourteen concerts.

On 4 August, Dylan celebrated his 40th birthday and we all got together for dinner in London. Asia then played the Cambridge Festival, filmed for DVD release, and Hamm Festival in Dortmund, Germany. September was fairly quiet with some interviews and some work with Paul K. Joyce on the music that would be released in 2011 as *Time* on the WB Classics label.

From 29 October through 12 December, Yes toured across Europe, then the UK and back to close in Gothenburg, Sweden, and this seems an appropriate place for me to pay tribute to the army of technicians that work diligently with us, some of whom have come and gone, others who have stayed with Yes and Asia through several eras and a few who are still with us today. I work closely with Steve Burnett, who programs the Line 6 pedalboards and Tim Stark, who prepares and adjusts all the touring guitars, simultaneously keeping an eye on my whole guitar collection. The tour manager back then, Paul Silveira, had a long relationship with all of us and for a while also managed Yes. On tour, Andre Cholmondeley has been looking after the guitar rig, guitars and all the restringing, but back in 2009 Joe Comeau was doing my equipment and now he tour manages Yes.

Richard Davis not only worked on Chris Squire's equipment from the mid-seventies onwards but also took care of Billy Sherwood's bass, working for us throughout his career. Andy Clark creates our projection, often with Roger Dean content, while Don Weeks was lighting director until 2019. Dean Mattson has been our FOH for nearly a decade, although Jeff Gex mixed the Yes/Asia tour. Simone Angelini was and has continued doing the on-stage monitor mixing for us. Wade Ellis has been production assistant for many years, taking care of the backstage, the dressing rooms, guests and security.

Rick Coberly has driven me safely about for years. We've done thousands of miles together, mostly in a Mercedes rental car. He often drives it back after a tour ends, sometimes right across the country, returning it to where it came from. We've discussed things in so many different realms, shared music, eaten hundreds of lunches, checked into endless hotels while helping to keep each other sane. He was a Clair Brothers monitor engineer for many artists, including Michael Jackson, but since coming off the road he's settled into repairing guitar amps and most things electrical.

CHAPTER 20

Forty Years On

In January 2010 Asia put the finishing touches to *Omega*, produced by Mike Paxman with Steve Rispin engineering again. They were a good team, although the arrival of snow slowed everything down.

I went to the studio in Liscombe by train one day, to maintain progress. As usual there was a deadline. 'Through My Veins' and 'Light The Way' were co-writes with John Wetton, but the first song was noticeably over-compressed at mastering – as were most of the tracks, actually.

At the end of the month I left for Poughkeepsie, New York, to rehearse for Yes's In The Present tour, finishing on 28 February in Boca Raton, Florida. Both Oliver and Benoît held up but the wilder side of Chris's and Alan's rock'n'roll lifestyles caused the problems that overindulgence invariably creates. It was a contrast to the three of us who had fairly clean-living routines that included going to sleep at night and conserving our energy for the shows. They often paid the full price. Alan started getting sick or Chris would leap on to the stage and play at full volume, fuelled by a unwise mix of chemicals that weren't prescribed by his doctor. He was getting more out of control, still performing brilliantly but definitely in a world of his own.

I attempted to bring back Yes's three-hour rule, requiring that no alcoholic beverages or other substances would be consumed before or during the show. This was so we could all go on straight, in touch with each other and clear about what was happening on stage. After the show, everyone could do what they wanted but before, we each needed to get ready to entertain the paying audience. This had last been tried back in 2001 and – as happened then, too – the rules were first bent and then totally forgotten by both of our wilder members. The shows always went on, but in what fashion? I would say on the edge of greatness but in danger of falling apart, kind of like The Libertines.

I wrote so many emails to the band members pointing out the delicacy of Yes music and the level of perfectionism expected of us at all times. Sometimes someone would start to play in a section in which they weren't at any point to make a contribution and I'd announce, 'That's no mistake, you shouldn't really be playing then!' By the time we made it to Boca Raton everyone's patience had been fully tested. Fortunately, Yes had a gap of a few months to recover and lick our wounds.

I had only three days off back in London before starting rehearsals for my next Trio UK tour, starting on 7 March in Birkenhead, taking in shows at the Sage, Gateshead (one of our favourite gigs) and finishing with two nights at the Pizza on the Park, London. Some of the material we played was pretty tough and good communication was vital. Ross and Dylan were both very consistent and invented new things literally every night. Ric French utilised the soundcheck to get the balance together while fixing any gremlins in the PA or in the room. We discussed arrangement changes in the dressing room before going out to implement our ideas. These shows certainly kept me on my toes but then again I could stretch out as much as I wanted on my 175. I played my best 175 on all these UK Trio tours, as it definitely has a unique something. If only airlines weren't so messed up about carrying guitars and, indeed, all instruments, I could take it everywhere.

Asia rehearsed for three days at the end of the month before I left for a one-off Yes show at an open-air festival, in Zacatecas, Mexico, on 5 April. Crazy! The planning turned out OK, as we stayed in the US, spending ten days or so writing material for a new Yes album in Phoenix, Arizona. The location was chosen because Chris lived in Phoenix and, also, why not? We rented a house with five bedrooms and a pool and positioned Oliver's laptop in the centre of the lounge table, sharing the different tracks he and I had prepared and exploring whatever Chris and Alan had. This started as a bit of a laugh, grown men in an expensive commune trying to be musically creative. Chris put in more appearances towards the end of the period and we ended up with about six demos of songs. We'd come back to these later in the year, as I needed to leave by 17 April as Asia were booked to start a tour in Helsinki, Iceland, on the 21st.

I should have had a small breathing space, but a volcano erupted in Iceland, right at that same time, the massive clouds of dust and debris causing travel chaos for us (and a good deal of the rest of the world). It wasn't until the fifth morning that a car arrived to take us to the airport after many days of rumours about flights leaving. This meant we lived, waiting, day to day, while Asia lost the first two shows, in Helsinki and Moscow. I finally got to Rome, we rehearsed and opened there three days later. This Asia leg also took in a Japanese tour, finishing in Nagoya on 18 May.

With less than three weeks off, touring madness resumed in West Palm Beach, Florida, on 8 June, when Yes opened a five-week leg with Peter Frampton co-headlining on all but two shows. Just as when we played in the seventies, this was a good billing that also attracted a considerable audience for this second time around. Peter had matured gracefully, as I've hoped to do, and is now a great guitarist/singer/all-rounder. Dean Mattson started doing our FOH sound and the final date was 15 July, Snoqualmie, Washington.

When I returned to the UK, my wife Jan and our daughter Steph took off for New York to visit Georgia, who was living there. Jan and Steph stayed in an apartment near Georgia for nearly two weeks.

I got home in time for Asia to play in London to promote the release of *Omega*. Unfortunately, the day after Jan and Steph returned, I had to fly out to play three Asia shows in Germany, followed by a US tour that closed in Seattle on 9 September after nearly thirty shows.

Throughout the previous decade I'd often enjoyed playing different guitar solos other than 'Mood For A Day' or 'Clap', both of which I love. I also liked to explore other tunes from my solo work, 'Sketches In The Sun' or 'Cactus Boogie', for example, bringing variety to my spot. I'd also been enjoying the luxury of my own dressing room as I prepared to go on stage. In my own space I can get ready properly for the show. In the hour before Asia or Yes would begin, I'd spend fifteen minutes organising my clothes and bits and pieces, half an hour in meditation and then I would do a few exercises, leaving fifteen minutes to put on my stage clothes and leave for the stage. I do this whatever the show. On the rare occasions I arrive late for a concert, I'll relax in the car as we drive the last half-hour of the journey and simply get dressed straight away.

In early October, Yes assembled in LA to start recording *Fly From Here*. We stayed at the Oakwood apartment block in Woodland Hills. We met at Trevor Horn's Linda Flora Drive property to listen to demos and decide how we would record the title track, which, at the time, was about five minutes long. We spent days working on the arrangements before starting to record it properly at a secret location – Neptune Studios, owned by Paul Allen, also in Beverly Hills, with Tim Weidner engineering. We had recorded around six songs with Tim by mid-November and we would work on them again in the new year.

Two days later, Yes departed LA for a quick South American tour, beginning in Caracas on 17 November. It felt a bit like the Amazon rainforest, a jungle of sorts, but so alive with musical appreciation. We then went to Buenos Aires, Córdoba, Santiago, Florianópolis, São Paulo, Asunción and Mendoza. We got strong vibrations from the audiences, all of them passionate, responsive and excitable. Political instability means we don't often get down there. On this tour there was a military presence in most cities, demonstrations and many examples of extreme poverty. We stayed at the best hotels and yet, looking out from the windows, we couldn't escape the images of disorder.

There were problems developing within Yes as we toured. I, for one, thought Chris was driving me and everyone else totally crazy. By the time we got to Paraguay I needed to have a long and desperate conversation with tour manager Paul Silveira about whether I could go on working with him. The level of his bass guitar on stage had been a bone of contention for as long as I could remember but in his excitement he was now completely blasting us off the stage. His performance antics also became more pronounced. At the same time, the sound coming from the large PA behind the drums was also becoming impossible to work with. The bass level particularly affected the FOH, as did all the other instruments going into the drum microphones from this PA. Audio heaven? No, it was audio chaos.

Off stage, things had got rather icy too, in particular when we finished in Mendoza. My hotel room was (unfortunately) next to Chris's, and the walls were paper-thin. I could hear him speak *very* loudly on the phone when he was talking about me – in a most uncomplimentary way – to Trevor Horn. 'Oh dear,' I thought. 'This is going to be a badass situation.' I immediately went next door to his room and took issue, letting him know how disappointed I was. I don't often get really mad, but I was furious. The next day we all left to go home, my ears still ringing, as they usually did after a tour. It invariably took about a week to heal after the barrage of sound.

Geoff Downes and I flew straight to St Petersburg in Russia for a one-off Asia show in December. What could be finer? Well, being back in London on 8 December was certainly finer. We had the following day off in London to collect our thoughts before Asia played just two of our booked UK dates because I'd come down with a bad cold. We managed to conclude things in London on 14 December at the Shepherd's Bush Empire.

After Christmas 2010 and New Year at home, I headed to Vancouver to write and prepare for *Fly From Here* in LA, getting back in the studio on 24 January after rehearsals with Trevor and Geoff Downes to finally sort out the arrangement for the title track. We set about recording parts two to five of the track 'Fly From Here' over the next month, although it was a bit stop start, as Trevor and Tim had a few other commitments. Originally, Trevor was only going to produce the original version of 'Fly From Here' but Chris felt he should produce the whole album. This was a complicated transition. I won't go into it all but things started to unravel when 'Fly From Here' went from being a five-minute song to becoming a twenty-six-minute suite due to the inclusion of other songs written by Trevor and Geoff, as well as my 'Bumpy Ride'.

Some of our other material got put aside, partly because Trevor had struggled to get what he was looking for from Oliver's keyboard. This led to Geoff coming to rehearsals and into the studio, bringing his familiar sound and approach. Without formalising what this implied, things drifted on without clarity or agreement with Geoff, until it was decided that he should join and Oliver should leave. It was a painful transition and a huge disappointment for Oliver, a strange and gradual breakdown. Chaos was prevailing. Benoît hung in there and was guided by Trevor to deliver great vocals. He'd told me before that recording might be a distraction to our touring plans. How right he was. He didn't need to be in Yes; he knew it might get complicated and he'd found other things as or more enjoyable to do in his life. I think he has a good personal philosophy that meant he was not unhappy about the outcome.

Oliver suffered more from the throes of Yes's determination to keep changing members and he bowed out gracefully from the recording sessions, although he does appear in an additional keyboard capacity on parts one and five of 'Fly From Here' and 'Hour Of Need'. The other songs we recorded together would be found on the re-release of *Live From Lyon – From A Page*.

During this mad time I was delighted that Jan and Georgia joined me in Woodland Hills. We visited some familiar local places like Malibu and took a longer trip to Huntingdon. A week after Jan left for London, Yes were back on stage at

Houston's House of Blues, on 6 March with Oliver Wakeman, who was happy to continue playing with us for this tour.

We played five different House of Blues locations in total, going on to Dallas, New Orleans, Chicago and Cleveland. They all had the coldest dressing rooms known to man, requiring that Wade Ellis block the stream of freezing air into my room. These gigs were also notorious for rowdy crowds with spontaneous parties erupting in the front row, too often right in front of me. Our songs often have quiet and sensitive moments but, sadly, this was when the noisy folk started to make their presence felt – shouting out dumb things, calling out other song titles and being overly ecstatic, obviously due to their indulgent, party-animal intake of alcohol. They disrupted the performance for everyone. They always said there was one in every crowd – one at least. I learned to ignore the squalor backstage and move on rapidly. Good planning meant we could move swiftly on to another town, ensuring that we stayed in a hotel away from fans – anywhere else, in fact, to stay intact but at the same time no further than an hour's drive from the venue. We did run the risk of occasionally checking into a hotel at 1 a.m., perhaps a golfing hotel where we needed a golf cart to get to the room. Near the end of the tour we played a familiar casino gig in Hampton Beach, as we had before and often still do. The accommodation was dreadful, the noise from the room was loud and it smelled. I won't go on. I guess after a lifetime of this I'm qualified to be a hotel inspector.

Washington followed on 4 April to close out the tour. Georgia and her now-husband Drew had come to see the show at the Tropicana in Atlantic City and Drew's parents, John and Claudine Norton, came to see the final Washington show. The next day I gave a workshop for the School of Rock in Philadelphia, then went back to Washington to leave for recording a synth orchestra. Andrew sadly passed away and I didn't know anyone who orchestrated like him until I started collaborating with Paul. He really liked the banjo guitar tune 'Orange', and in the end he arranged everything for a twelve-piece orchestra. Small but effective because of that size. HoweSound plan to re-release the album in the future.

October was a quiet month until the 28th, when Yes travelled to Portugal for rehearsals prior to the first show in Lisbon the following week. During the course of this tour we went around the UK and Europe several times, back and forwards – no sooner were we in one place than we were back over in that other place again. Besides being fed up with the volume on stage, which compromised his ability to sing as strongly as he knew he could, Benoît David gradually got sick towards the end of the tour. Nevertheless, when we arrived in Oslo on 7 December, we didn't know it was going to be our last show together. We were due to go on to Sweden, Finland, Estonia and Russia, but on a day off before Stockholm we held a group meeting in the busy hotel lobby. We all thought that Benoît might get better but he told us he wasn't able to continue. He was struggling with the show and felt extremely unwell.

Cancellations are always bad news. We'd have to recover our reputation on our next European tour. The 'we're out of here' feeling came over us and we quickly disappeared to our various home destinations for Christmas.

There's so much you can do in January: it's usually a fairly light work month, and nicely so, and 2012 was no exception. I like to write and demo in the hush of winter, but February was very busy as Asia began work on what was to be the group's final reunion album. It was called *XXX* and I fought that title pretty hard but John Wetton wouldn't give in. He had come up with the name of the previous two albums and as he was our main lyricist he wanted to do the same with this one. I pointed out the hazards but still it was a no: '*XXX*' was it. Fortunately, Roger Dean delivered a really spacious sleeve design and painting. The three fishes representing the three 'X's were vague, but I've always like vague.

It's strange how Asia music works. John and Geoff's writing is always central, but there's usually room for some of my writing too. My role is often more structural on tunes of mine and Geoff gets a chance to play more single-line ideas. The songs by the main writing team have always embodied what John felt his direction should be after leaving King Crimson. Back in 1982 he had wanted to connect with our listeners through his mix of rock and pop, hoping to achieve a high level of success, something that he'd worked at since the seventies. There were two Howe/Wetton/Downes songs on *XXX*, but 'Reno' – a bonus track on the special edition of the CD – has the true flavour of Howe/Wetton. It's lighter and floats through the story of a desert casino city, always the poor man's Vegas.

Producer Mike Paxman returned – he had a nice way of recording and was a good laugh. You can't have too much of that serious endeavour stuff, it's got to be fun. Yet I do believe that only the first Asia album fulfilled in full, 100 per cent, the blueprint of what the band could be. Mike Stone balanced the album right, bringing that little bit extra in the way of production ideas that made it so cohesive. By 2012, everything had really changed beyond recognition. We'd each been through the mill – fighting, winning and losing battles. We had learned to keep our distance from possible confrontations and maintain the utmost respect for one another.

Yes had found a vocalist, Jon Davison, who could sing the band's songs to the level we needed. He went on to successfully establish himself with us and our audience. He isn't a copyist. He sings in his own fashion and has found a style which he's at home with in our music. Beginning in late March, the band was to go on a very adventurous outing, right around the Pacific's Ring of Fire to places we'd never been to before. Trepidation would ensue.

We had met in LA on 22 March to rehearse before starting this new phase of Yes in Christchurch, New Zealand, on 1 April, rashly ignoring that this was April Fool's Day. Perth, Byron Bay and Melbourne were followed by Sydney where I met up again with my dear brother Philip and his wife Sarah. The *Fly From Here* tour then ventured on to Japan by way of a 3.30 a.m. wake-up call to catch a plane on 15 April. We played three nights in their capital followed by another in Osaka. The very next day we flew to Jakarta, Indonesia. It felt pretty scary there, some bad stuff had gone down in recent years in terms of terrorism, both internally and against tourists, and now we were there. Our vehicle had to be scanned in a vehicle scanner. Then the luggage was checked.

The journey to Honolulu was interrupted by a stopover of several hours in Seoul, the capital of South Korea. Honolulu, of course, is part of the US, and feels like it. We next flew to Kahului for our final show on 29 April, followed by an inadvisable red-eye flight to LA. My advice is to avoid these overnights at all costs – on our flight the bathroom door squeaked open and was bashed closed all night long, the lights were on and there was turbulence. A twelve-hour flight to London followed, arriving the next afternoon.

I took May as a recovery period. I'd missed Jan and the family so much, as I always do, and I wanted to enjoy these valuable weeks off. It was Steph's 26th birthday, and Georgia and Drew came over from New York, making it a lovely family get-together.

A week before the start of the next Yes tour on 10 July, the band arrived in Toronto to rehearse another setlist. The area around the city centre hotel in which we stayed seemed to reflect the very worst of this otherwise fair city. I like Canada a lot but the people in this area were out of their crazy minds. Apparently, many such sad folk had recently been discharged from an institution, while others were from the local homeless community. This pattern is evident in every city in the world and is not particularly worse in Toronto, not by any means, but I can't help empathising and feeling touched by their predicament. The circumstances they find themselves in are tragic; perhaps it's only hope that can keep them going.

Toronto is actually a really nice place. It's where I run into friends like Alan, Jean, Joey, Max and Benny Burke, and Dimo Safari and his good friend Paul, who's now greatly missed. I had a steel guitar lesson with a friend of Joey's and I often see Dave Barrett and Tony McManus, both extremely fine guitarists. I've often found nice clothes and gifts there, too. Le Commensal had a couple of vegetarian buffets that I used to eat at regularly during my visits.

The tour featured openers Procol Harum, which felt real good. Gary Brooker and the band swung in a way only an English band can, with heft and swagger. They joined us in Atlantic City for the full six weeks of US dates, until 19 August, and then we went off to Mexico City for a one-off show to round things off. I needed special food in Mexico as the local fare didn't seem to agree with me – it never has. Joe Comeau's dear friend, Wendy Daly, a qualified chef, prepared macrobiotic-style food, often visiting markets to buy the best produce. It was a luxury, yes – but also a necessity.

September was spectacular, as the arrival of our first grandchild brought Jan and I much joy. Jen and Virgil had been married a year or two earlier and Zuni was born on 23 September (actually on her dad's birthday). She's a treasure to us all.

Next, it was Asia's turn to play Japan. Across the last week of September we played two nights in Tokyo and then shows in Osaka and Nagoya. It hardly needed a tour book of its own, but we still had one. Asia had been back together for six years now, since 2006, but ever since Yes also got together again – two years after that – my time and energy had been increasingly sapped. Sooner or later, I knew, I would have to leave Asia and just focus on Yes, the Trio and my solo work.

In October I flew to LA, spent four days off before cutting back to Cleveland for a Yes Rock and Roll Hall of Fame press event, after which we jetted up to Quebec to begin another tour there on 11 October – just another six-week tour! This is roughly the maximum I like, or can do – a timeframe that allows for a complete round trip of the main big cities of the USA and Canada (although we could probably criss-cross the country endlessly if we wanted). We closed with a perfect example of bad routing. Awkward journeys can't be totally eliminated, but try this for size. It was Wednesday and we played the penultimate gig in Orlando, central Florida. The next day should have been a rest but the wake-up call was 7 a.m., to fly 1,236 miles to Grand Rapids, Michigan, then drive 120 miles to a place called Manistee for a show at the Little River Casino Resort on Thanksgiving Day. The shows ended on 23 November. This meant I had to take three flights in order to get home to the UK. I proposed a new and very sensible rule for future tours – always finish in a major city offering direct flights to the UK.

When I eventually made it back, Dylan came by the studio and we recorded a small koto part for his *Subterranean* project, featuring arrangements of David Bowie's instrumental music. Georgia and Drew came back from New York for Christmas with us in London. Phew, what a schedule it had been.

CHAPTER 21

Merry-Go-Round

My departure from Asia was announced in early in 2013. We had been due to tour the UK in December, but Carl got an *E. coli* infection and the dates were cancelled. It had been good fun up to then, but now I needed to consolidate my time.

For the first few months of 2013, I was moving about between London and Devon. I was casually building a list for a compilation of the best tracks from my solo albums, with Virgil making a big contribution. Over many hours we sat and listened to my twelve albums, sharing and noting our feedback on each track, in order to tie together the sequencing for my double CD *Anthology*. We generally chose two or three tracks from each album in chronological order. These selections worked like snapshots of each album. Tim Fraser-Harding and his team at Rhino were great to work with. Gottlieb Bros. worked up the sleeve design, including artwork by Roger Dean.

After yet another week's rehearsal, Yes opened in West Wendover, Nevada, on 1 March. What a place to be for a whole week: a desert on the border of Nevada and Arizona, indoors intensely air-conditioned while the sun beat down outside. It's a complete intellectual void where there's nothing to do but gamble. Unfortunately, we often stay at these casinos to rehearse. It's not all bad: the rooms can be OK, it's cheap, but the food can be lacking in anything with wholewheat and the general environment is totally naff. Nonetheless, I guess it's fortunate for Yes that they put on live shows: the casinos keep us gainfully employed, certainly providing fillers between major cities. Speaking of which, in the next six weeks we covered the West, Midwest and Texas.

Next up was our first Cruise To The Edge, floating festival of prog and rock, departing from Fort Lauderdale, Florida, calling at George Town, the Cayman Islands and Ocho Rios before heading back to Fort Lauderdale. Following my own experience in 2000, I hadn't planned to do a cruise again, but I gave it a try, Yes-style, and we've gone on to do a total of six. The ships can vary in size but they usually hold about two thousand fans. We always play two nights and sometimes do a Q&A. We have done meet-and-greets but they get silly, with drunk folk trying to hug band members and the like. Steve Hackett has been involved in several different cruises that often feature more than twenty bands playing in different venues on board, including on the deck.

After the cruise, we carried on touring the US. Some venues were quite nice – the Ruth Eckerd Hall in Clearwater, Florida, was pleasant enough and was followed by Jackson, then we went to Connecticut, New Hampshire, Pennsylvania, New York's Beacon Theatre, Toronto and finished in Detroit on 12 April. Another six-week US tour, under our belt.

In early May I attended the mastering session for *Homebrew 5* at Super Audio Mastering with Simon Heyworth at the controls. He'd done a nice job with the *Anthology* double CD and I wanted all my projects to finish with a similar level of attention. The inter-track levels had to be consistent and the final call had to be made on adjusting the frequencies so that the tracks matched up nicely together. *Anthology*, like *Homebrew*, was made up of tracks that came from different recording periods, and that meant a bit of work was required to get them all sounding together. Since I enjoy each stage of releasing music, not just the writing and recording, I like to see it all the way so that it's 'music to my ears' all the way until the final product is complete. After release I may find some tiny faults that I somehow missed but I'm sure few listeners would ever hear them. Perfection is my goal, but it is rarely achievable. Solo performance greatly simplifies things – perhaps that's why I like it so much. One can get close to an idea playing just one instrument. Think of Bach's great organ works or solo cello: they are intimate and singular and the air around the music breathes, making the notes enter our ears in a perfect manner.

By mid-May, the Yes party was touring South America. We opened in Peru, followed by a string of shows in Brazil, then on to Chile and finished in Argentina. Things hadn't changed much. There were still demonstrations and military vehicles in the streets and at the hotels, some shaky flights in old planes, a constant search for vegetarian food, strikes at airports, hassle and bustle the whole time but the South Americans make great audiences. They are passionate and responsive, often taking the music to higher levels through their devotion.

For a couple of days in early June I recorded Dylan and his drums on tracks for my next solo release, which would comprise an equal number of vocal and instrumental pieces. I've been working on these with Curtis Schwartz through a slow and gradual process ever since.

A week later I started the first of a series of UK solo tours that I'd perform over the next four years. I felt it was right to play at home, around the people and places I knew and loved best, especially since so much energy seemed to go into playing everywhere else. Each tour allowed me to vary and explore what I've learned to play as a solo guitarist. I began trying different formulas, settings and titles to wrap each show around. Ric French did all the sound mixing and tour managing and driving, so he was kept busy, too.

The sound I make encircles the audience, making it extremely special for me. I want to play at my very best level for them and that makes it a fascinating challenge for mind and body. If the guitar I'm playing sounds extremely good then I'm able to play smoothly and spontaneously. The way the guitar feels to play is almost as important. I prepare my guitars myself each day during solo tours, checking that the string quality is good enough for another night of playing. I'll check my – minimal – equipment rigs and then listen through the PA. I haven't been using onstage monitoring of my guitar. I hear the room I'm playing in and judge it from there. I might return to onstage guitar monitoring so that I hear the same sound every night – that is more conventional.

Ric and I collaborate as adjustments are made to suit my guitar and voice. We've done a considerable mileage together around the UK and Europe, mostly in rental cars. What became annual solo tours across the next four years would be made up of fairly short runs of two or three weeks to avoid them becoming a slog of travelling and hotels. I like the independence and while playing my solo tunes I can lose myself, so to speak, providing I'm sufficiently well prepared.

The ensuing summer would require loads of guitar-playing, starting with Yes at Paso Robles, California, on 6 July. Over the years, I had suggested we performed entire studio albums live, but management weren't content with just one or two full albums and suggested three complete works. The first Album Series tour saw us playing – in their entirety – *Going For The*

One, *The Yes Album* and *Close To The Edge*. I had wanted to play them chronologically to demonstrate the development of our music but this wasn't practical. Other forces were at work: every combination of the possible ordering of the three albums was tried out but they never settled completely.

The tour did make sense. What was Yes, if not an album band? Starting at the first track somehow added to the excitement, when there were forty minutes or more in which to fully explore the mood of a particular album. I was thankful that our singles were few and far between. Of course, this type of setlist required plenty of homework and careful equipment preparation. Multiple styles and textures were required to achieve a version of each album that correctly reflected its contours and dynamics. Then there were all the vocal parts and, since I mostly sang only the low parts, I had to combine providing lyrics and harmonies with playing the guitar. Thank goodness I know the verses of 'Siberian Khatru'. I'd hate to have to learn to combine those elements but, since it comes to me on autopilot now, I could sing and play it in the bath. We ended in Indianapolis on 12 August.

I didn't leave for the UK as usual as I was due at a guitar camp at the Full Moon Resort in Big Indian, New York, a week later. Instead, I went to Lititz where I recorded some guitar for a Doors tribute album with Dave Wilkerson at Right Coast Recording. I chose to play on 'Light My Fire'. Dave then drove us to the resort where the camp was held and mixed the sound from the 19th until the 23rd. I had my own cabin in the woods. I'd invited Ray Matuza and Flavio Sala to provide workshops for the guests in various styles of guitar, Ray with some insights into my playing and Flavio classical and flamenco. It was all good fun and it was especially nice that Dick Boak from the Martin guitar company came and told the story of their great guitars with help from myself. This was entitled 'The Evolution of the American Guitar' and I demonstrated the sound of about five rare, old models with some short solo pieces. I gave afternoon talks on different aspects of my musical work, one on the Line 6 Variax, another focusing on my influences and I touched on some health issues and also threw in some business advice along the way. Much of what I did was videoed for the archive. Then I went back home.

September was mostly taken up with a Steve Howe Trio tour. After rehearsing with Dylan and Ross for three days we started in Wimborne, continuing with another ten shows with the Pizza Express in Soho as our London venue. The following day was Zuni's 1st birthday. Virgil was 38 the same day. He and I did some further work on the *Anthology* project. During November the Trio got stuck in, recording at Dylan's studio for our second studio album, entitled *New Frontier,* eventually released in 2019 on Cherry Red Records. Jon Davison then came to our studio to write and demo ideas for some of what would become Yes's *Heaven & Earth*. Jon made a determined effort to involve all members by visiting each of us in different parts of the world to collaborate. This left December free to nicely wind down for Christmas.

Now we come to a classic malfunction in the long and complex saga of Yes. Oh dear, how much do you really need to know? Are we so stupid or what? Planning on shaky ground leaves everything at risk if things don't go well, and they didn't go well this time around. Many mistakes were made, classic blunders of judgement were had and there was an utter lack of insight. Sit tight, dear reader, and enjoy the ride.

The making of *Heaven & Earth* continued on 14 January in the new year of 2014, when we met in LA with producer Roy Thomas Baker. Recalling Paris in 1979, we were not all convinced about the prospect of him coming on board again to produce us. He acted quite strangely, offering little enthusiasm for the tapes we'd prepared, and he didn't even notice when we reworked one of the songs while he kept visiting the bathroom. Even so, some thought we should still give him a try and then, if it wasn't working, abort.

There followed another week of rehearsals at Neptune Studios in LA, where we'd often worked in the past. We had about two months to finish recording this new album before our next touring commitments kicked in. We flapped about doing backing tracks while trying to get used to Roy's strange ways. He wasn't taking any decisive, producer-style decisions, he was vague about everything and he seemed unable to prevent either Chris or myself from dominating the backing track sessions. Twice he left the studio in a rage: the first time because the engineer replaced one microphone without informing him; the second for an even more ridiculous reason, too trivial to mention.

Roy had a pile of outboard effects units through which everything overdubbed had to go – compressors, limiters, parametric equalisers, old equalisers… you name it, all in a huge chain. He'd fiddle with the settings on this infernal tower of stuff for his own amusement, and to our horror. Then he treated Jon appallingly, driving him on to make endless vocal takes until he was just mildly satisfied with Jon's performance. Never did he display any enthusiasm after one of us performed on the recordings. Even when I was overdubbing, he hardly mustered a response along the lines of 'That was a great take.' It always came out more like, 'Just good enough.' There was also much flapping about the methodology. We were (predictably) recording on Pro Tools, which makes so many things possible. Roy wanted the multi-tracked harmonies to be autotuned even if they sounded fine. How fine was fine? Fine to the ear. Each voice had been properly checked, but he still insisted on every vocal track going through an autotuner called Melodyne, which was considered sophisticated. Loads of time was wasted, leading to unnecessary pressure. In a nutshell, we had to drive it through, regardless of Roy's lack of direction. Geoff and Alan then went off to the NAMM Show, the music industry trade event, at the end of the month, after we'd recorded the backing tracks.

To prevent me from going completely bonkers, Jan, Steph and Adam came to my rescue for a break in LA for ten days in late February. They visited to the studio a couple of times but were pretty much unaware that things were going awry. We were supposed to have finished at the studio three days later but we were starting to realise that we wouldn't. I was even supposed to have a nice week back home between these recording sessions and the next gigs but there was obviously no time.

I wanted to finish off the album properly later in the year but – bad decision number two – we stayed to work furiously to finish it off in a rush. Billy Sherwood was brought in to double up on the production side, recording Chris's and my vocals upstairs in one of the smaller studios. There was no attempt to mix at this time – it wasn't even contemplated. Instead, an ill-conceived plan was hatched whereby, to maintain momentum, Roy would mix the tracks at his own studio in Nevada after we left for the tour. This turned out to be bad decision number three.

We had gigs to play, starting in Victoria Island, Canada, on 19 March. Then we headed roughly east across snowy terrain, arriving in Hamilton, Ontario, on 2 April. Rick Coberly and I drove the whole way for two casino shows that followed in the US before Cruise To The Edge 2 set sail from Miami on

7 April. The cruise was scheduled to stop in Honduras but, due to bad weather, this was cancelled and extra time was spent in Cozumel, Mexico.

With just a week off after the cruise, Yes then went to the UK for a tour, meeting up in Oxford and beginning there on 29 April, followed by Europe, finishing in Oslo on 5 June. We were delighted to play the Royal Albert Hall on 8 May, always a special occasion. Chris smoked a pure grass joint in the dressing room which caused me to go just a little crazy. 'Step outside if you must, Chris!' I said, as I had so often before.

We had three days off in Tilburg and attempted to focus on the mixes of *Heaven & Earth* coming from Billy Sherwood. When we heard Roy's mixes, we told him immediately, 'Stop' and 'No more, thank you.' It hadn't been such a bad idea asking Billy to mix but it was a bad idea (number four) to mix via Skype. Audio levels are a delicate matter – a little higher or lower can be misinterpreted 1,000 miles away. Some parts were literally lost within the files and the overall result lacked any real cohesion. 'Subway Walls' was slightly spared the generally befuddling sound. The saving grace was that Roger Dean did the most fantastic painting for the CD sleeve. It was I who suggested to Roger the use of some sort of black-and-white, zigzag logo treatment, which he made work really well.

One likes to close the book on recording a new album with a sense of achievement and satisfaction, but that rarely happens these days with Yes albums. We had achieved a great deal of exactly that in our seventies period and to have more than one well-received album would seem to have been a terrific result. It's hard to imagine Yes making an album as good as *Close To The Edge* again: too much has changed; we've moved on and altered our approach. We don't generally have the hunger to challenge musical genres today – that's for others to do. We have done our bit to establish and now perform these works from our greatest period. I'm happy with that. I still love writing new music and will continue to do so while Yes create new work, but it'll be very much in our own time and only when we're ready will we commit to the next instalment.

By the middle of June I was programming my pedalboard for the next phase of the Album Series tour with Steve Burnett, this time building *Fragile* programs and creating a complete list for the set. I then got back working on guitar parts for the Steve Howe Trio's *New Frontier* album. Recordings take time but they are worth it, providing you see them right through to their logical conclusion.

At the end of the month, I flew to New York to rehearse *Fragile* with Yes before the tour kicked off in Nichols, New York, on 5 July. We had seven weeks of shows with Syd Arthur opening, except at our first show which was in the round at the Westbury, Long Island, on 12 July. We then went all over the US, finishing at the Greek Theatre, LA, on 24 August, the shows featuring *Close To The Edge* and *Fragile*. The order of these two albums had also proved to be quite controversial. Chris and I would endlessly discuss the merits of which should come first. Starting with *Fragile* was the toughest way to perform them. More often than not, we started with *Close To The Edge* and then played *Fragile*, with its final track – 'Heart Of The Sunrise' – forming a consistently great end for the set. Its sudden ending cued a blackout of all projection and lighting, the perfect climax.

Our family was further enhanced by the arrival of Georgia's first baby, Diego Berry Norton, on 5 August, one day after Dylan's birthday. I was then in Houston, playing at the Bayou (now Revention) Music Center. Drew and Georgia were, of course, delighted and he's now grown into a great young boy, full of imagination and energy. He loves nature, science fiction and music. He plays his own ukulele, aided by Drew, who also plays guitar – Diego will never escape the influence of the guitar.

After catching my breath, I played my next solo UK tour, starting in Wimborne in Dorset on 11 September and finishing in Exeter on the 28th. Dylan, Ross and I then recorded some more tunes for the Trio's album during the second week of October. After that Simon Heyworth mastered my solo *Anthology* CDs.

In November, Yes set off on yet another tour, this time starting in Auckland, New Zealand, on the 10th. Two days later we were in Perth, Australia, before going to the Gold Coast, Sydney, and we finished in Australia by playing Melbourne on the 18th. There were four days to get to Japan, where we played three nights in Tokyo, Osaka and Nagoya before returning to Tokyo for one more show.

This second Album Series was received extremely well. We were getting more and more into performing complete albums, realising that playing individual songs was never as deep or immersive. 'Five Per Cent For Nothing' by Bill Bruford was the most challenging piece to play. There didn't seem to be a groove that Alan could adapt from Bill's original part. Only three minutes and thirty-two seconds long, it fortunately repeats halfway through but it took a lot of rehearsing for us to end on the same beat. Separately our parts are quite easy – we only play on beats from one of the drums in the drum part. For instance, the bass is on the off-beat with the bass drum. I knew exactly where the last beat was so I would often swing my guitar headstock down in time. Sometimes someone would play another beat after that, which was not so clever. The next day, in the late afternoon, you might have heard us struggling with this oddball musical animal that had never before been played on stage by us or, presumably, anybody else. That was forty-two years of *not* being played on stage. There may be other songs that didn't get much live time, but 'Five Per Cent For Nothing' was particularly tricky and totally unlike anything else in our entire songbook, I guess it never fitted in until we played the whole of the *Fragile* album.

Why 5 per cent? It was a percentage lost to a manager, I believe, gone in a handshake, though the affair did later get sorted out. This business is messy but there are also benefits. For example, we play more seasonally now, like sportspeople, often having whole months off, and that's something to celebrate.

In my calendar for December 2014 there is the underlined word 'OFF' followed by a large exclamation mark, signifying the enormous relief I must have felt.

CHAPTER 22

Chris Leaves The Stage

For the first three months of 2015 I moved between finalising the many details of the *Anthology* sleeve, recording more parts for *Resonance* and writing this book. I've come to accept how long it takes doing several things at once. Yet I like building several projects, leaving and then returning to them with fresh ears or eyes, eventually picking the one that's nearest to completion and finishing it.

Through April, I played my third UK solo tour, calling it the *Anthology* tour, starting in Buxton with gaps along the way, finishing on the 28th in Basingstoke. I once again enjoyed changing my setlist around, with the first part of the show a mixture of country-picking tunes like 'In The Course Of The Day' and 'Trambone' with classical guitar tunes like 'Corkscrew' and 'Mood For A Day'. After the interval, I split the second set with more folk-country-picking, also electric guitar – tunes like 'Dorothy' and 'Catnapping'. I ended the set with four excerpts from Yes songs, 'Hour Of Need', 'Wonderous Stories', 'Nine Voice' and 'Your Move', featuring my Portuguese guitar. I simply played the intros, a verse or two and the chorus. I then encored with Bob Dylan's song 'Buckets Of Rain' and 'Clap'.

May, June and even July continued to be free of work so I could make hay while the sun shone.

Chris Squire had not been well, on and off for some time now. On 7 May, he wrote to the rest of Yes that he couldn't work this whole year. He needed some special treatment that required a lengthy period of convalescence. Knowing the summer tour was already booked, Chris, Alan, Geoff, Jon and I eventually agreed to invite Billy Sherwood to stand in for Chris through the period of his absence.

Chris's health continued to deteriorate. He was confined to a sealed room in a clinic in Phoenix, Arizona, his adopted hometown, and was unable to receive visitors besides his wife Scotland and youngest daughter, Xilan. Then, on 27 June 2015, Chris sadly passed away from acute erythroid leukaemia. He'd lived his life to the fullest extent and was a superb musician of the highest possible calibre. For Yes, this was the end of an era. Tributes were paid from around the world and several events were held in LA and London in his memory. Chris was a loveable, larger than life character whose impact on all of us will never be forgotten.

We needed to strengthen our internal structure to find an answer to the unfathomable question: could Yes continue without Chris Squire? This was the biggest issue we'd ever faced but, as Billy was already preparing, we held firm. After all, this was Chris's legacy and what better way to remember his sheer determination to keep Yes going, whatever the cost and no matter what, than to continue playing the music to which he devoted his life?

We did our best to resolve our doubts and bridge this sad crossroads in the ongoing story of Yes. We announced we'd be playing all of *Close To The Edge*, and also some of *Tales From Topographic Oceans*, specifically 'The Revealing Science Of God' and 'Ritual', as well as an excerpt from side three, the guitar cadenza and 'The Leaves Of Green' song. At the beginning of the shows for the next year we ran a tribute to Chris, using our recording of his song 'Onward' with selected photos of the great man himself.

For this upcoming tour, Dylan was officially asked to be on standby as backup drummer. He was ready, willing and able, with charts of the setlist, but due to visa problems he missed the opportunity he'd always dreamed of – being there to stand in for Alan White. Well, Alan did indeed get sick just before the tour and Jay Schellen rushed in to fill in for what we thought would be only a few weeks, but which turned out to be the whole tour. Alan didn't get well enough to join us at all. Jay had worked with Billy before and they were well locked in, as bass and drums need to be. Some very serious work had to be done at rehearsals in Lititz for the band's next phase, a US tour co-headlining with Toto that started on 7 August in Mashantucket, Connecticut. Steve Lukather was extremely kind and appreciative of my work, as I am with his. He covers so many bases on the guitar exceedingly well, a natural talent. All of Toto are world-class musicians, and they put on a great show that included their fantastic stage arrangement of 'Africa'.

Travelling around by car allowed me to eat at restaurants of my choice. Whole Foods is a good stopgap. There are lots of them in different cities and you know what you'll get there – a buffet, supplies, organic bananas, jam and marmalade, etc. Unfortunately, since they were taken over by Amazon, they stopped having English breakfast tea in their cafes. Assam or Darjeeling? No, English breakfast, please. I have to buy a packet in the store and get them to brew it for my lunch stop.

The Yes and Toto tour travelled extensively up and down the north-east corridor, over to Chicago, Iowa, down to Biloxi,

Florida then to Texas, where El Paso smelled really bad, and finishing up in Calgary, Alberta, on 14 September. Here I met an old guitar hero of mine, Brian Griffiths from the sixties band The Big Three. We had a nice chat. He used to play a Hofner guitar through a Fender amp and was way ahead of his time. His guitar break on The Big Three's 'Some Other Guy' is historic, classy, classic rock.

October was free and open, and in its last few days I got around to compiling *Homebrew 6* with Paul K. Joyce at his studio in Cornwall. This volume has been the most successful in the series so far. The hidden, tongue-in-cheek factor through the *Homebrew* series is my slight send-up of groupings of my recordings, taking them in a similar order to their versions by Yes, Asia or GTR. *Homebrew 6* references Yes's *Heaven & Earth* and my solo album *The Grand Scheme Of Things*.

After some preparation, Yes played three shows in Florida, starting on 11 November with Sarasota, Melbourne and Fort Lauderdale before boarding our third Cruise To The Edge, with Jay and Alan playing drums at different times in the set. By the time of this cruise I had become used to playing my guitars while rocking left then right on the water. Sometimes my steel guitar would shift position when not required. I can still be surprised by the wobbling to and fro over the waves, especially when the ship was powering up the knots. As before, the ship was supposed to go to Key West and the Bahamas but ended up in Nassau instead, due to bad weather. It sailed back to Miami on the 19th and after that we had the rest of the year off.

In the last two weeks of February 2016, Georgia, Drew, Diego, Steph, Adam, Jan and I went to Palm Springs for a holiday. We rented a house in the same area we had stayed when Georgia and Drew were married. A picture taken of Jan and me at this time appears on the inside back page of

Anthology 2. Back home, Easter with Jan in the beautiful English countryside was equally enjoyable.

After all this uncharacteristic leisure time I worked for three days with Paul K. Joyce, compiling all three CDs of *Anthology 2: Groups and Collaborations*. There were fifty-six tracks, making this my biggest project ever. Later, Simon Heyworth mastered the albums, taking them to the final stage with the inter-track balances and individual track equalisation. The first two CDs covered all the bands I've been in and the third took in the collaborations, some previously unreleased. It tells a story about me and the strength of the bands and musicians I've worked with over the years.

On 18 April, Yes assembled in Monnow Studios in Monmouth, Wales, to rehearse the whole of the *Drama* album and brush up on *Fragile*. We knew 'Machine Messiah' and 'Tempus Fugit' very well but the other tracks hadn't been played live since 1980. Geoff, Alan and I are in both line-ups and we enjoyed this process immensely, although it was fairly hard getting 'Does It Really Happen?', 'Into The Lens' and 'Run To The Light' up and running properly. Alan took on the whole performance and Jay stayed away, but Billy became really exhausted at rehearsals as he had to home in on the drum parts while playing the bass guitar, bass pedals and singing backing harmonies. Having to talk loudly to Alan during most of the day made him hoarse.

This UK and European tour started in Glasgow on 27 April. We then travelled round the usual cities, finishing in London at the Royal Albert Hall on 10 May. I always adore it when Jan comes to Yes, Trio or solo concerts, and Steph and Adam came that night too. Trevor Horn joined us on the last two nights in the UK, singing 'Tempus Fugit'. There were two days off before Paris, followed by many other major European cities –

seven in Germany alone. Zurich was an opportunity to get together with Paul Sutin. The tour concluded in Rome on 1 June and I was back in time to celebrate Steph's 30th birthday the following day.

Three weeks later, the UK voted in the referendum on whether to leave the EU. We and the rest of the 48 per cent wanted to remain. What a mess and a tremendous loss. It was far too important a decision to throw out to the general public, but Government, Parliament and the House of Commons couldn't make up their minds or agree on anything. There wasn't much hope that this would turn out well.

The Album Series tour, featuring *Drama* and *Topographic Oceans*, continued, with a week's rehearsal to sort out how we would play the albums. Jay and Alan joined at 'Ritual' and then the encores. We opened close to Lititz in Lancaster, Pennsylvania, and then toured extensively up and down the north-east corridor through the usual cities. From Washington, we went to Chicago, Denver and LA and then casinos in Nevada, ending at Humphrey's Half Moon in San Diego on 4 September. When we played Washington I met up with Flavio Sala. When we met he'd usually bring a guitar, made by Camillo Perrella in Flavio's Italian hometown of Bojano. These are wonderful instruments, and I keep thinking how I'm unable to do without one myself! Flavio and I get on really great together and I admire his dedication to the classical and flamenco guitar repertoire and its rich history. He also steps right out of those areas with other music and his own compositions.

It was now the turn of my solo music and a fourth UK tour in consecutive years. My plan was to play close to home to ensure minimal travel and all by road, with low-pressure, intimate gigs that suited my performance style. If I've learned om this kind of touring it's that it's as much about ... as it is about the music of others. My appearance at Montreux Jazz in 1979 was really the first time I attempted this kind of setlist and, with Ric French's help, I took the stage at the Landmark Arts Centre on 6 October. The Jazz Cafe was my London gig on the 12th with an old favourite, the Queen's Hall, Edinburgh, on the 15th, finishing after fourteen shows in Trowbridge on the 23rd. *Homebrew 6* was released at this time and I used the same name for the tour. Peter Conway was running HoweSound and organised this and earlier solo tours – he has since semi-retired and I'd like to thank him for all his efforts and encouragement over the years.

There was one more show that was not so publicly announced, in a village in north Devon near our studio. This was the village with the very old church that we've helped out with over the years. It's always nice to give back something to this community as it's one we've known since 1971. These were salt-of-the-earth people from a farming community who help each other whenever they can. I do relish being in the countryside – when you travel there, it lets you breathe.

Enough is surely enough, you might think, but Yes were once again off touring. You might be forgiven for thinking that Japan would have seen enough of us but, oh, no, we did four shows in Tokyo plus Osaka and Nagoya from 21 to 29 November. We liked Mr Udo, the boss of the Japanese promotion company, very much and his team was superb in every way. *Topographic…* was played but *Drama* was replaced with a more general bunch of songs. It was always a delight to be in Japan as we were so well looked after by warm, friendly, efficient and considerate people. I recently told my friends, Hide and Kana Hayashi, that Japan is unique in the way it works and hangs together. I'm impressed by the mindset of the Japanese people, along with their technology and infrastructure, their standards of food, their service and the quality of their hotels. What's also remarkable is the calm behaviour of their children and young adults. They seem to have a wonderful sensitivity and clarity of mind.

In 2017, I was 70 years old, so I grew a beard to celebrate. It was something I'd never had before – nor ever again. But, combined with my long ponytail, it suited my take on things at this time. At the end of January, Yes rehearsed and on 3 February we opened another tour in Cherokee in North Carolina.

After a travel day and a further few days off, our next Cruise To The Edge departed from Tampa on 7 February. Roger Dean's Gallery had become a regular feature of the cruise, displaying his Yes and related sleeves, alongside various other paintings. He's still highly productive, I'm pleased to say, and it's really nice to see so much of his work in one place. Many regular fans took the ship year after year, bringing their enjoyment and appreciation for all things Yes. This time the cruise travelled to Cozumel, Mexico, and then back to Tampa on the 11th, when we dashed to St Petersburg for a show that same night, followed by gigs in Pompano Beach, Atlanta, Jacksonville, Biloxi, Shreveport and Dallas, before finishing in Midland, Texas, on the 20th. Jay Schellen had to step up to the plate on this leg as Alan missed a few nights due to being unwell. The rest of February and March were fluid and that meant I could get back to recording and mixing other projects.

In April 2017, various past and present members of Yes spoke and performed at our induction into the Rock and Roll Hall of Fame, New York. I need hardly say that it was an episode as daunting as any in the long and winding road on which the group and I have travelled since I jumped on this slightly surreal roundabout almost fifty years ago.

At the end of April our eldest daughter Georgia turned 35. Then, in late May, Virgil brought a friend to the Langley studio to take a break from London. This was a very lovely time. We'd been recording our album *Nexus*, an instrumental freedom-of-expression album with a spacey, world theme featuring Virgil's writing, keyboard-playing and drums. I found it easy to add a guitar to each of the tracks he'd let me select from his own recordings for this special collaboration. He told me when it was finished that he was really super-proud of it. The sleeve featured a picture drawn by his daughter Zuni and the audio was mastered by Simon for Inside Out Music.

Jon Barry, who had been helping with the studio property in so many ways, got married to Steph in mid-June, and Jan and I attended the happy couple's ceremony in Devon. It was a lovely afternoon that Jan and I followed by taking a break at our old Devon cottage.

Well, it seems to me that it's getting close to the time when I must wrap up my story. You've been with me through seventy years of my life and times, the ups, the downs and a few of my thoughts along the way. Life's become a much more private matter recently.

Yes continue to keep me busy, while I'm also able to produce my own music and release it to the outside world, which I so enjoy. Tours and cruises continue, while all things guitaristic still interest me. When I enter the room where my guitars live, I think to myself, 'Oh, I have a little time to play any of these instruments,' I choose one or two and get them out of their cases and tune them and see what happens. Often an idea will come, which I capture with my digital recorder. I can later return to the idea to discover it fits perfectly with another short piece I recorded on another occasion. Music in the making is so much about the journey: it really is exciting to find ideas forming on the journey to making music beautiful.

CODA

Time Is When

Having more or less discussed all of my professional life as a guitarist, I ought to add that there is a bit more to me that hasn't been covered between these pages. I made personal choices along the way that empowered my appreciation of nature and beauty, helped me focus my concentration, increased my determination to be productive, provided me with the energy to be resilient and steered me with what I hoped were degrees of faithfulness and honour.

Taking an interest in developing my five senses encouraged my natural instinct to become free. It taught me about restraint and self-control. I like to think of these issues as a convergence of Zen, macrobiotics, vegetarianism, meditation, hypnotherapy, psychosynthesis, naturopathic therapies and medications, yoga, shiatsu, homeopathic remedies, Tao and more Tao. Eating organic and wholefoods with absolutely no GM ingredients and minimal pharmaceutical drugs came to make sense to me. At the start of this journey I had no idea I would ever be interested in such things, but as it is said, 'Seek and you shall find.'

Books have only become part of my life during the last twenty years and I had some catching up to do. I couldn't attempt to read all the essential masterpieces of the literary world, although I do consider some of the books I've read to be just that. As a boy I really only read *Sherlock Holmes* by Arthur Conan Doyle and the much-anticipated weekly *Eagle* comic. Music papers and regular newspapers fed my teens, and I succumbed to a fad for movie and horror film magazines featuring *Frankenstein*, *The Mummy*, etc., leading on to science fiction comics. In my hippy days I read a couple of Hermann Hesse's books, of course, and in the interim magazines filled a gap when there was no time to read books.

In the seventies I subscribed to *Interavia*, an international aeroplane publication – bi-monthly, I think. Besides showcasing great photos and reporting news it also covered aircraft design, with all the facts and figures, reports and evaluations of everything aeronautical. At the time I thought business jets, like Concorde, were out of this world but recently I've changed my mind. They are the most wasteful, uneconomical method of moving a small group of people between two places known to man. Peculiarly, the safety figures for private flying aren't good either, this partly being due to single-engine propeller plane incidents.

Country Life is a terribly British read. It begins with ads for houses – or should I say mansions, estates, islands and penthouses? Then there's the coverage of art, art for sale, art at exhibitions and museums, artefacts old and new described, photographed and valued. Articles about the countryside can be illuminating – nothing beats nature in bloom, even in the winter months. Farmers are the very backbone of society: their food is our most important but greatly misunderstood produce. The magazine goes to great lengths to feature, say, arts and craft houses or wonderful castles. I like castles. I used to want to own one. It's also about interesting people in all sorts of areas who design things for our lives now and those who did so in the past and have become guiding lights.

Private Eye is funny, satirical and has absolutely no regard for good taste, yet at the same time it carries reports about truly awesome things I don't know about, or that perhaps I wasn't supposed to know about – like who took what from a company coffers when they merged, offshore banking scandals, insights into ministers' consultancy fees and even music-related funding crises, as our great orchestras struggle financially. There are also lots of cartoons, sometimes as twisted as hell. Never underestimate the whole back story, like the investment blunders of city and rural councils, or millions wasted on inadvisable but costly schemes. *Private Eye* digs up the real dirt and, because of it, gets sued a lot. I much enjoyed their cartoon series '101 ways to cross Trump's wall'. It was hilarious but strangely important at the same time. I have recently rather tended to ignore the political intrigues that have been so present since 2016, in favour of the brighter side of life.

Auto Design is a bi-monthly Italian and English car magazine that specialises in showing how models evolve from the drawing boards and computers, and how technology designs the shapes that appeal to those who buy and drive cars. It explores what happens when students collaborate with professionals, and carries reports on car shows around the world. It covers the advancements in materials used in the manufacturing process, paving the future for electric and automated vehicles. Although it ingratiates itself with the car industry, it does so with plenty of excitement and optimism.

Resolution is produced for the those in the world of recording studios and audio and visual production. A solid read: I particularly like articles by guest audio engineers and producers or those written by the in-house team who illuminate ideas with their own experience. The equipment reviews are a big part of its function but, as I'm fairly low-tech, I rely on those I work with in this world to have this sort of knowledge. The plug-in prevails today, often recreating something old that we used to like. The advancements are truly astonishing. Pro Tools and systems like it bear no resemblance to recording in the seventies, other than the need for musicians to have dreamed a little, learned an instrument, found a voice in music and been able to convey their ideas to other people. *Resolution* gives a voice to those who create, develop and actually finish what they are supposed to. You can sit at home on a computer but there's so much more to recording. Audio engineers rarely get a chance to explain their work and it provides a sense of community. Studios and bits of equipment look good to us and they do remarkable things. They merge their design with functionality, to a pleasing end. Surely, we work better when the eye isn't offended by junk.

We British care about sound excellence: if it doesn't sound excellent, we'll damn well make it sound excellent. Hugh Padgham was recently given recognition with the Music Producers Guild Award for his outstanding contributions to UK music. I worked with Hugh on Yes's *Drama* album in 1980 and I'm sure he continues to be recognised for his engineering and production skills, and for the originality he brings to the party. *Resolution* also discusses business ideas, sales of recordings and live concerts. It avoids celebrity as the entry ticket here is talent, through experience and sharing.

Returning to books, here's a few quite different books I found interesting over the years:

The Science And Art Of Healing by Ralph Twentyman was the book that started me off reading non-fiction with an ever-increasing interest. Its three main themes are compared across the centuries for their relevance to our interconnecting world of mind and body.

The Fabric Of The Universe by Brian Greene is a huge statement of all things universal. The scale ratio of quantum in an expanding solar system where things get seriously small highlights the minutest changes that only mathematics can accurately describe. Stop and think how amazing the world is. The sheer multitude of astounding systems running simultaneously inside and outside of us and across the entire cosmos is just mind-boggling.

Reinventing Bach by Paul Elie is fascinating, because it charts the role of the performer in keeping music alive by reinterpretation and re-recording. Before recording was invented there was, of course, only live music to experience and, once Bach and other composers' music was carried by notation, it then relied on different performers to bring work to the public's attention. Once recording existed, musicians returned to the great scores and, with their reinterpretations, revitalised interest in particular composers. Down the ages and through the recording mediums music has been reinterpreted and spread across the world.

Transform Stress Into Vitality by Mantak Chia is a total package of Taoism. Seemingly little of what's contained in this book is known in the West. It's based on ancient traditions and naturopathic principles through the inner harmony of the altered state of mind. Much of it to is do with the body's energy points and using one own internal energy to invigorate yourself, as the title suggests. The Chinese have been aware about the road map of the human body for thousands of years.

The Collector's Guide To Paperweights by Sara Rossi and *Glass As Contemporary Art* by Dan Klein nicely cover the world of glass design in these two aspects: small paperweights by Baccarat, Clichy, Whitefriars and Sandwich, while Klein's book has the international and more European-influenced artists like Newell, Woodruff and Chihuly. I also like Kosta Boda and Cathy who, although more commercial, still retain very high standards. My collection started in the late sixties with a Victorian spinning wheel in pale green glass. Through my travels my collection grew larger with pieces from San Francisco, Milan and Sweden. A work by Mary Kay Simoni called 'Counterpoint' from 1993 is a small but beautiful piece that is central to one of my displays. Marie-Louise Rennicks, who is from Switzerland but lives in Toronto, gave me two delightful Yes logos: one a piece of stained glass, while the other bubbles up from a large square piece of glass, I also like Murano and Lalique glass.

Metronomes And Musical Time is by Tony Bingham and Anthony Turner. Tony got me started in antique guitars and many of my much-loved lyre guitars came from his shop, originally in Poland Street in London's West End before he moved to Pond Street, Hampstead. Tony has a great knowledge of most musical instruments, particularly of old and antique museum pieces. It's a good idea to save historic instruments as they are made with such skill and care. I have several metronomes, mostly bought from Tony's shop, and I was delighted when he released this book of his collection. Nobody thinks much about these intriguing objects but Tony has built up an amazing array of examples, some very old, others more recent.

Homo Deus and *Sapiens* by Yuval Noah Harari were both in the book charts for a long time. Many of you must have read one or both of them and I'm sure you've been equally astounded at his writing. The stories we believe – well, they're all stories, of course. We like a good story but what's the next good story we need to lock into now, I wonder? These books are certainly revelations in their own way.

Seven Brief Lessons On Physics and *The Order Of Time* by Carlo Rovelli and *Being Ecological* by Timothy Morton are examples of broad topics covered in small books that convey information in a digestible form. Physics is complicated, but it's within our grasp to absorb at least an impression of what holds us and everything else together. *Being Ecological* draws a surprisingly unconventional conclusion – in essence, that it's of prime importance to engage and respect the species closest to us, the rest of the animal kingdom on this planet. If they're all right, we're all right – which, sadly, isn't the case. Morton explains the scale of the problem, as it runs much deeper than is revealed by mere public debate, with its errors and misunderstandings. Will anything effective be done in time? Surely, 'Where there's a will, there's a way'? It's taken a Swedish schoolgirl to raise the global awareness – well done, Greta Thunberg. Wake up people, the time is now.

Art can be more or less anything today but fifty years ago it was mainly paintings that occupied the public's attention. I saw the strange paintings of Hieronymus Bosch, like *The Garden Of Earthly Delights*, and became quite intrigued. The dark ages were represented in such gory detail that my fascination with them wore thin after a while. Then came Salvador Dalí; no less strange or unconventional, but focused and brilliant in his deception and relationship with scale. Besides having a few of his signed lithographs, I also have number 371 of 1,500 of *The Surrealistic Angel*, a bronze sculpture of the feminine shape with an open triangular space where the heart should be. His style is so distinct and recognisable, with a personality that shines through in all his work. I've seen much of his work at galleries in Florida, exhibitions in Germany, in the UK and other places around the world. As always, the original is best and Dalí's works are awesome to view, whether for scale, colours or shapes. Funny as it seems, I wrote to Dalí in the seventies asking him if he'd do an album sleeve. I later found out that he'd already dabbled in this medium with an album called *Lonesome Echo* by Jackie Gleason on Capitol Records, released in 1955. Dalí and Gleason are pictured on the rear cover shaking hands. The image on the front comprises a mandolin, a butterfly that casts its shadow onto a towering rock in a desert-like scene, a small figure of a woman and a shell.

It'll be no surprise that Roger Dean is a favourite artist of mine. Despite a couple of rather embarrassing gaps along the way, he's made a huge contribution to the Yes imagery from the *Fragile* sleeve onwards, right up to *Yes 50 Live*. Roger's landscapes and figures convey such architectural power and he continues to paint fresh and vital images. His choice of colours pinpoint his precision in perspective and proportion.

David Hockney is a highly sensitive artist, creating much ebb and flow that really draws you into his work, so wistful and dreamlike that he always leaves an indelible impression on me. His travels brought new ideas to his paintings before he returned to the UK to concentrate on the places he knew best and could readily interpret.

Clothes, especially stage attire, have always been important, as a good outfit instils confidence around a performance. I have to thank Chrissie Walsh in the UK for making my custom stage clothes from around the end of the seventies into the eighties. She made me some wonderful outfits to wear in Asia, one of which had a First Nation American influence. By the *Union* tour I was wearing Versace, then Agnès B, Alexander McQueen and Vivienne Westwood. Recently, Paul Smith and Ted Baker have been designing great clothes. Whether I'm playing to 200 or 20,000 people, I need to feel good. Etienne Aigner from Germany is another design house from whom I've bought many clothes, though they're often made in Italy. They don't have so many men's options but every now and again something appeals to me. I always liked their old horseshoe logo, the symbol of good luck.

Snooker is my favourite sport and Ronnie O'Sullivan is surely the most outstanding and watchable snooker player. Though Judd Trump has recently won three titles, there's Mark Selby, Neil Robertson, Ali Carter and Luca Brecel, who all play with such unbelievable accuracy, but Ronnie shows them how it's done under the most intense pressure. His character reflects his total command of the game and he's a genius for precise ball control. Even when it seems there are no balls to pot he'll find one to set up another huge break. Besides all his championship wins, I'd like to add a 'Well done, Ronnie' on the thousandth century of his career – and, as of March 2019, still counting!

Tennis came to me through my amazing wife Jan, who is a big Rafael Nadal fan, although it's Federer who really caught my imagination. With his calm consistency and smooth determination he's never seemingly hurried or flustered. I can enjoy and connect better with a performance if the skills of a player (or musician) are naturally expressed in their body language and particularly their facial expressions. Federer's demeanour often seems to imply, 'That was water off a duck's back.' He appears to be someone whose terrific personal regime will hopefully enable him to continue playing for many years yet. Having won twenty Grand Slams at the time of writing, he is right up there, thanks to his incredible footwork, total use of the court and those long winning rallies. I might not know exactly what a single-handed backhand is, but I know he delivers it.

Formula 1 motor racing hotted up when Lewis Hamilton rose to dominance with McLaren. Then Mercedes really got behind him: they needed him and he needed their reliability and power to rival McLaren. What a serious competitor he is – he's great to watch and great to hear talking about what he does. Not all famous people have anything much to say, it has to be said. McLaren cars have amazing shapes but I do also like their collaboration with MB: the Mercedes-Benz SLR McLaren is a real supercar. A few of my old favourite coupés might be the Ferrari 456M, Maserati Khamsin, a Studebaker Commander from the fifties or a new Mercedes-Benz S 500 Coupé 4Matic. As a boy, I made a point of knowing all the model numbers or names of cars I liked. I still enjoy driving but I wouldn't necessarily attempt London to Geneva in a day like I used to. Am I a *Top Gear* fan? No way – seeing someone drive like a lunatic doesn't entertain me. And their stunts, trips and silly banter just don't add up to a good show for me. On the other hand, Jay Leno brings much more to his TV show and his magazine articles in *Octane* magazine.

Archery was a sport in which I took part during the late seventies. I joined a Hampstead club and stayed for a couple of years, learning how it was supposed to be done. The club met outdoors in a field opposite Kenwood to shoot arrows at a target about 60 feet away. I didn't get many bullseyes but most of my arrows landed somewhere on the target. The club rules were mostly about how to discharge the arrow and about safety. It would be pretty dangerous walking about not knowing the rules of the field. When an arrow is set to go, I await an inner signal to release it. In *Kyudo: The Art of Zen in Archery*, H. J. Stein considers deeper aspects of practice and preparations with five checks before releasing an arrow, all deeply rooted in Eastern philosophy. I thought students were taught to shut their eyes, merely sensing the target's exact position but I can't seem to verify that now. My own problems were caused by the tension in the bowstring. I think it was 36 pounds for men and 28 pounds for ladies. This created a strain on my quite delicate wrists and I quit. I could have switched to a recoil-assisted bow but it didn't seem right. Nevertheless, it was good to learn a little about the form and style that makes for better shots, for there lies the methodology of good practice.

Films play an influential role in my work too, although for the last twenty years I haven't watched very many new films, as I can't watch violence at all. I don't believe that the mainstream's preoccupation with violence is good for anyone. Sadly, this decision excludes thousands of films which, although made with apparent good intent, only seem pointless and disgusting. Fellini had other things on his mind, as his films were more like surrealistic adventures. Jan and I would relish the idea of seeing his latest movie – you really didn't know what to expect. The audio dubbing was always taken to extremes, recreating his reality through intense visual and audio manipulation. This was taken to the point of abstraction during such highly acclaimed films as *Roma*, *8 ½*, *Amarcord* and his earlier *La Dolce Vita*.

On the other hand, John Cassavetes brought something much closer to actual reality with films like *Gloria*, *Opening Night*, *A Woman Under The Influence* and *Faces*, which starred Gena Rowlands in the main role. He started with a script, got the actors to learn it, but then he'd throw it out and start again with them ad-libbing dialogue. His fees from his big acting roles merely subsidised his own films, helping to make him America's first truly independent film-maker. I think *Shadows* was the first of his films I saw. He had a preoccupation with his homeland that seemed to have steered me towards our own UK humour for much-needed light relief. The Monty Python team brought a wave of crazy, funny sketches to their TV series and with their films *The Holy Grail*, *The Meaning Of Life* and *The Life Of Brian*. Their talents stretched over many different mediums – for instance, Eric Idle's song 'Always Look On The Bright Side Of Life', *Fawlty Towers* and Beatles-spoof *The Rutles* showed off their individual talents so well. But surely no one could fail to laugh at the US comedy classics like *Blazing Saddles*, *Naked Gun* or *The King of Comedy*. I certainly did.

So, again, it's been an enormous journey through these seventy years, full of joy, happiness, difficulties, sadness, love, loss, ups, downs, creation and destruction, some memories in full colour, others in black and white. I guess I shouldn't have expected anything else.

Discography

Titles and performers listed for each record. Live albums, compilations and *Homebrew* series are not included.

THE SYNDICATS

'Maybellene' (1964)
'True To Me' (1964)
(SH guitar, Tom Ladd vocals, Kevin Driscoll bass, Johnny Melton drums)

'Howlin' For My Baby' (1964)
(SH guitar, Kevin Driscoll vocals & bass, Johnny Melton drums)

'On The Horizon' (1965)
(SH guitar, John Lamb vocals; Kevin Driscoll bass, Jeff Williams piano, S. Truelove drums)

THE IN CROWD

'Stop! Wait A Minute' (1965)
'Why Must They Criticise' (1965)
'You're On Your Own' (1965)
(SH guitar, Keith West vocals, Junior Wood rhythm guitar, Simon 'Boots' Alcott bass guitar, Ken Lawrence drums)

'Blow Up' (1966)
'Am I Glad To See You' (1966)
(SH guitar, Keith West vocals, Junior Wood bass, John 'Twink' Adler drums)

TOMORROW

'My White Bicycle' (1967)
'Revolution' (1968)
TOMORROW (1968)
(SH guitar, Keith West vocals, Junior Wood bass, John 'Twink' Adler drums)

CANTO

'The Spanish Song'
'The Power Of Music'
'Come Over Stranger'
(SH guitar, Dave Curtis vocals & bass guitar, Bobby Woodman drums)

BODAST

THE BODAST TAPES (1981)
Re-released as *TOWARDS UTOPIA* (2017)
(SH guitar, Clive Skinner vocals, Dave Curtis bass & vocals, Bobby Woodman drums)

YES

THE YES ALBUM (1971)
(SH guitar & vocals, Jon Anderson vocals, Tony Kaye keyboards, Chris Squire bass, Bill Bruford drums)

FRAGILE (1971)
CLOSE TO THE EDGE (1972)
(SH guitar & vocals, Jon Anderson vocals, Rick Wakeman keyboards, Chris Squire bass, Bill Bruford drums)

TALES FROM TOPOGRAPHIC OCEANS (1973)
(SH guitar & vocals, Jon Anderson vocals, Rick Wakeman keyboards, Chris Squire bass, Alan White drums)

RELAYER (1974)
(SH guitar & vocals, Jon Anderson vocals, Patrick Moraz keyboards, Chris Squire bass, Alan White drums)

GOING FOR THE ONE (1977)
TORMATO (1978)
(SH guitar & vocals, Jon Anderson vocals, Rick Wakeman keyboards, Chris Squire bass, Alan White drums)

DRAMA (1980)
(SH guitar & vocals, Chris Squire bass, Alan White drums, Geoff Downes, keyboards, Trevor Horn vocals)

UNION (1991)
(SH guitar & vocals, Jon Anderson vocals, Rick Wakeman & Tony Kay keyboards, Bill Bruford & Alan White drums, Chris Squire bass, Trevor Rabin guitars)

KEYS TO ASCENSION (1996)
KEYS TO ASCENSION 2 (1997)
KEYS STUDIO CD (1997)
(SH guitar & vocals, Jon Anderson vocals, Chris Squire bass, Rick Wakeman keyboards, Alan White drums)

Discography

OPEN YOUR EYES (1997)
(SH guitar & vocals, Jon Anderson vocals, Chris Squire bass, Rick Wakeman keyboards, Alan White drums, Billy Sherwood guitar)

THE LADDER (1999)
(SH guitar & vocals, Jon Anderson vocals, Chris Squire bass, Igor Khoroshev keyboards, Alan White drums, Billy Sherwood guitar)

MAGNIFICATION (2001)
(SH guitar & vocals, Jon Anderson vocals, Chris Squire bass, Alan White drums, plus orchestra)

FLY FROM HERE (2011)
(SH guitar & vocals, Chris Squire bass, Geoff Downes keyboards, Alan White drums, Benoît David vocals)

HEAVEN & EARTH (2014)
(SH guitar & vocals, Chris Squire bass, Geoff Downes keyboards, Alan White drums, Jon Davison vocals)

FLY FROM HERE – RETURN TICKET (2018)
(SH guitar & vocals, Chris Squire bass, Geoff Downes keyboards, Alan White drums, Trevor Horn vocals)

FROM A PAGE (2019)
(Benoît David lead vocals, SH guitars & vocals, Chris Squire bass & vocals, Oliver Wakeman keyboard, Alan White drums)

ABWH

ABWH (1989)
(SH guitar & vocals, Jon Anderson vocals, Rick Wakeman keyboards, Tony Levin bass, Bill Bruford drums)

ASIA

ASIA (1982)
ALPHA (1983)
(SH guitar, John Wetton vocals & bass guitar, Geoff Downes keyboards & vocals, Carl Palmer drums)

AQUA (1992)
(SH guitar, Geoff Downes keyboards, John Payne bass guitar & vocals, Carl Palmer drums)

PHOENIX (2008)
OMEGA (2010)
XXX (2012)
(SH guitar, John Wetton vocals & bass guitar, Geoff Downes keyboards & vocals, Carl Palmer drums)

GTR

GTR (1986)
(SH guitar, Steve Hackett guitar, Max Bacon vocals, Phil Spalding bass, Jonathan Mover drums)

STEVE HOWE TRIO

THE HAUNTED MELODY (2008)
TRAVELIN' (2009)
NEW FRONTIER (2019)
(SH guitar, Dylan Howe drums, Ross Stanley organ)

SOLO

BEGININNGS (1975)
(SH vocals, guitar, steel & bass, Patrick Moraz keyboards, title track arranger & conductor, Alan White & Bill Bruford drums)

Discography

THE STEVE HOWE ALBUM (1979)
(SH guitars, steel, vocals & bass, Claire Hamill vocals, Ronnie Leahy & Patrick Moraz keyboards, Graham Presket violin, Alan White & Bill Bruford drums, Andrew Jackman orchestrations)

TURBULENCE (1991)
(SH guitars, Billy Currie keyboards, Nick Beggs bass, Bill Bruford & Alan White drums)

THE GRAND SCHEME OF THINGS (1993)
(SH guitars & vocals, Dylan Howe drums, Keith West harmonies)

QUANTUM GUITAR (1998)
(SH guitars, Dylan Howe drums)

PORTRAITS OF BOB DYLAN (1999)
(SH guitar & vocals, Dylan Howe drums, guest vocalists)

NATURAL TIMBRE (2001)
(SH acoustic guitars & bass, Dylan Howe drums)

SKYLINE (2002)
(SH guitars & bass, Paul Sutin keyboards, Dylan Howe drums)

ELEMENTS (2003)
(SH guitars & vocals, Virgil Howe keyboards, Dylan Howe drums, Derrick Taylor bass, Gilad Atzman saxophones & additional further brass)

SPECTRUM (2005)
(SH guitars, Virgil Howe & Oliver Wakeman keyboards, Dylan Howe drums)

MOTIF (2008)
(SH guitars)

TIME (2011)
(SH guitars, Paul K. Joyce arrangements)

ANTHOLOGY – A SOLO CAREER RETROSPECTIVE (2015)

ANTHOLOGY 2 – GROUPS AND COLLABORATIONS (2017)

LOVE IS (2020)
(SH lead vocals, guitars, keyboards & bass, Jon Davison harmony vocals & bass on songs, Dylan Howe drums)

Acknowledgements

Following all that was said at the Rock and Roll Hall of Fame ceremony, here are many of the talented people who so deserved a mention on that night:

TONY KAYE for his organ and piano work on *Yes*, *Time And A Word* and *The Yes Album*.

PETER BANKS (1947–2013) for his guitar work on *Yes* and *Time And A Word*.

PATRICK MORAZ for his amazing keyboards on *Relayer*.

TREVOR HORN for his vocal, lyrical and production ideas on *Drama* and *Fly From Here* (and *90125*).

BENOÎT DAVID for his singing on *Fly From Here*.

OLIVER WAKEMAN for his touring work from 2008 to 2010.

ROGER DEAN for his sleeve designs from *Fragile* to *Heaven & Earth* and for the many great stage designs done with Martyn Dean.

MICKEY TAIT, who, before and when I first joined Yes, was our all-round tour tech and lighting designer, and who designed the round stage, and for all the great assistance his company Tait Towers has given over the years.

ROY CLAIR, who has given the band consistent assistance and provided excellent sound systems to us since our early tours.

RICHARD DAVIS, who has recently retired from being our resident bass tech, originally for Chris Squire and then for Billy Sherwood. Well done, Richard!

DEAN, DON & ANDY, our sound, light and projection specialists across our tours since 2008.

ANDRE, WILL and JOHN, our top guitar, keyboard and drum techs.

SIMONE, WADE and RICK, our monitor engineer, production assistant and my personal assistant/driver.

MARTIN and JOE, our manager and tour manager.

A further mention is due to the members of Yes's current line-up, who were not listed by the Rock and Roll Hall of Fame: GEOFF DOWNES, JON DAVISON and BILLY SHERWOOD. Thank you for the talents you brought to Yes.

This book is all my own work, written on my Macbook Pro from various resources I have, from my diaries and my tour books and from the inside of my head where memories of historic events are often as clear to me now as the day they occurred. Nevertheless, it has occasionally felt like being in the mid-Atlantic, alone in a sailing boat as it cuts through the waves.

That said, the support and encouragement I have received from my wife Jan and our immediate family, Dylan, Georgia and Steph, has been wondrous. Virgil was also enthused about the project, bless him. Dylan's wife, Zoë, an author in her own right, helped things along very nicely. Chris Charlesworth brought his expertise to the editing table and further guidance came from David Barraclough at Omnibus Press.

The thought that anyone might want to read my autobiography is, in itself, profoundly encouraging. I must have written this for you, my audience, who for many years now has

Acknowledgements

listened to my ramblings, my performances and my recordings and felt something... or other. That connection is my acknowledgement here: it's always been an honour to play for you.

Steve Howe, October 2019.